The Authors

W Norton Grubb is Professor and the David Garner Chair in Higher Education at the University of California at Berkeley. He holds a PhD in Economics from Harvard University. As a specialist in the fields of labour economics and the economics of education, he has authored many books, monographs and technical reports as well as a prodigious number of articles and book chapters.

Paul Ryan is a Fellow and Director of Studies in Economics at King's College, University of Cambridge. He was awarded a PhD in Economics from Harvard University and has held the post of visiting professor at several universities in the USA, France and Austria. His work has also appeared in numerous articles and several books and monographs.

The Roles of Evaluation for

VOCATIONAL EDUCATION *and* TRAINING

W NORTON GRUBB   PAUL RYAN

The Roles of Evaluation for

VOCATIONAL EDUCATION and TRAINING

Plain Talk *on the Field of Dreams*

KOGAN
PAGE

© International Labour Office, 1999

Hardback edition first published in 1999 by Kogan Page, 120 Pentonville Road, London N1 9JN and distributed in the US by Stylus Publishing Inc., 22883 Quicksilver Drive Sterling, VA 20166, USA

International Labour Office
Rights and Permissions
Publications Bureau
CH-1211 Geneva 22

British Library Cataloguing in Publication Data

A CIP record for this book is available from the British Library

ISBN 0 7494 3070 2

Typeset by Kogan Page Limited
Printed and bound by Biddles Ltd, Guildford and King's Lynn

Preface

For various reasons, countries around the globe are increasingly concerned – or so it appears – about skills development beyond the regular school system. Training for employment, as distinct from education, features prominently on many a national policy agenda and has become a fashionable topic in international economic fora. Examples of training objectives currently pursued by governments include enhancing national competitiveness in the light of globalization, or improving the labour market chances of either first-time jobseekers or older workers made redundant in the wake of economic crisis. Training systems are being reformed so as to respond better to rapidly changing demands and opportunities. New clients are being targeted for new types of training activities. New actors are given new roles on the training scene, and new formulas are applied to make sure that the necessary financial resources will be available and distributed in a manner which is both efficient and equitable.

Although meaningful financial statistics are hard to obtain – if they exist at all – it should be obvious, even to the casual observer, that overall levels of investment in training or skills development, or the same by another name, must be enormous. Indeed, training is a major industry in most countries, and there are no signs suggesting that spending, by whoever pays for training, is (or soon will be) on the decline.

One might expect it to be of considerable interest to those who invest in training and skills development, be they governments, private enterprises, individuals or others, to know with some degree of certainty about the returns to their investment, that is, about the impact of training. In theory, people expect the benefits of training, however defined, to exceed the costs; otherwise they would not invest. Or would they? In practice, it appears that few questions are asked. Impact assessments or serious evaluations at the system – or even at the programme – level are relatively rare and, where efforts of the kind have been undertaken, results have often met with reservations. In any event, decisions on devoting public resources to training hardly ever seem to be based on solid evidence of past performance. More often than not, the benefits of training are, literally, taken for granted.

It is against this background that the Training Policies and Systems Branch of the International Labour Office invited W. Norton Grubb of the University of California, Berkeley, and Paul Ryan of the University of Cambridge, to reflect on the matter and prepare the present publication. The ILO's interest in furthering the debate about the merits of training for employment, and in ways and means of demonstrating or (as necessary) questioning such merits, derives directly from the Organization's long-standing commitment to social progress and economic development worldwide.

Aimed at training policy analysts and the evaluation community at large, this book presents issues and case material that, it is hoped, may also be of interest to a wider audience of professionals and academics concerned with public policy, as well as representatives of the world of work and the world of training.

Following a discussion on concepts of training, the authors essentially focus on the 'why' and 'how' of evaluation, before presenting and commenting on the results of a number of evaluation exercises. Two concluding chapters treat the use (and abuse) of evaluation results in policy making and the implications for evaluation of recent trends in vocational education and training, such as decentralization, the declining role of the State, a shift towards work-based learning and a continued concern for meeting equity objectives through training.

I wish to thank W. Norton Grubb and Paul Ryan for their valuable contributions to this publication, and also Fred Fluitman of the ILO's Training Policies and Systems Branch for directing the project.

Werner Sengenberger
Director, Employment and Training Department
International Labour Office

Contents

Lists of tables and boxes

List of tables

List of boxes

Acknowledgements

We gratefully acknowledge financial support for this research by the International Labour Office (ILO). This report represents the personal views of the authors, and not necessarily the views of the ILO.

The authors would like to thank Joe Colombano for being a diligent research assistant; Jane Auvré and Jenny Sang for all-purpose support; Fred Fluitman, Maria Ducci, Neil O'Higgins, Pierre Martin, and Jacques Gaude for suggestions, direction and help with sources; Enrique Bru, Carlos Maldonado, and Jon McLin for other source material. Paul Ryan thanks also for related research support and assistance, and advice concerning national issues and evidence: Clair Brown, Michael Reich, David Stern, Lloyd Ulman and colleagues at the Institute of Industrial Relations, Berkeley, California; Günther Schmid and colleagues at WZB, Berlin; and Eric Verdier and colleagues at LEST, Aix-en-Provence.

The title is borrowed (with permission) from Marvin Lazerson's paper in progress about higher education in the United States.

Introduction

The need for plain talk

Many countries are yearning to improve their education and training. For developed countries, greater investment in human resources promises to give them a 'workforce for the 21st century', highly skilled, productive, and capable of restoring competitiveness, growth, and equity. For developing countries, more basic levels of education and training hold out hopes of modernizing their traditional sectors, facilitating the growth of more modern sectors, and stabilizing political conditions. For some transitional countries (like China), where skill shortages are sometimes the most obvious, more and higher-quality education and training often seem all that is necessary for an enormous boost to their economies and their roles in the world community. Report after report, plan after plan has embodied these hopes – and warned about the dreadful consequences, in an increasingly competitive world, for any country that fails to follow this path.

These are wonderful dreams, grand dreams. They are also dreams that have some basis in reality, since many countries have already gone down this path with some success – and, for most individuals in countries relying on market systems, education is now the principal route to their own well-being. But the dreams of success through education and training are not simple to realize, both because of the resources involved and because the design of education and training programmes that contribute to economic progress proves difficult. And so, in the national debates over education and training – the field of dreams on which virtually every country now plays – some plain talk is necessary, some careful understanding of when education and training can work and when it cannot, some honest discussion of what is necessary to achieve these dreams.

1

There is another ubiquitous problem with dreams for education and training. In the movie version of *Field of Dreams* (1989), the protagonist builds a baseball field in the midst of the American Midwest, with the conviction that the great baseball players of previous years will somehow show up if only he provides them with a suitable place to play. The movie and its central motif – 'If you build it, they will come' – are an extended metaphor about faith in dreams and an approach that can be characterized as a supply-side belief. And so the movie is, unwittingly, a good metaphor for much of the faith about education and training, which often assumes that building schools and training the unskilled will lead to employment and economic progress. But this approach tends to neglect the demand side: education without suitable employment and specific skill training without jobs requiring such skills may be valuable in their own right, but they cannot enhance economic conditions. And so the other conditions necessary for education and training to be effective – the employment necessary, the capital required, the institutions that can give these arrangements some permanence – also need to be carefully understood, and the most successful programmes carefully consider the nature of local employment (King *et al.*, 1999). Building baseball diamonds or soccer fields does not itself create great teams, and plain talk about the limits of supply-side views is necessary.

We admit to some ambivalence about plain talk. Sometimes this amounts to getting it straight – getting at the truth of what an education or training programme does – and this is a necessary and a noble enterprise. Sometimes this provides information that its advocates need, for example, by providing support for a particular type of education. But plain talk also has to indicate the limits of what is possible, to be modest about what education and training can do, and in the process to moderate the dreams that lie at the root of the current enthusiasm. Sometimes the deflation becomes extreme, as in the cynical notion that 'nothing works'. We do not believe this, and we will provide many examples of education and training programmes that have been quite effective for their students. But our general point is that generating new and more reliable information can lead to many different conclusions, some of which support education and training and some of which do not.

Now sometimes plain talk is the role of the political process, in countries where it is more capable of discussion free of overt bias, or debate without covert threats behind it. But more often this role falls to social science, and to evaluation research specifically, as methods of providing information that can, sometimes and under the right circumstances, avoid the traps of politics as usual. In this monograph, therefore, we examine the role of evaluation in providing new and more trustworthy information – plain talk – about the vexing issues of education and training. Evaluation operates under different rules from politics, in order to generate information that is as reliable and valid as possible. These rules are themselves controversial in their own way, and there are many approaches that call themselves evaluation to sort through.

And so some plain talk is necessary about evaluation itself. At one end of the spectrum, some methods of doubtful value – for example, asking the opinions of individuals who run programmes, or asking participants whether they liked their experiences – have been used without any other evidence to claim success for a programme, sometimes without finding out anything about what they have accomplished. At the other end, an orthodoxy has developed in some places (particularly the United States) that only the most sophisticated experimental methods can generate any valid information at all. Both these extremes may be uninformative, particularly depending on the use for which evaluation is intended. We will argue instead for a broader and more eclectic approach to evaluation, one that tries to collect information in a variety of ways about different aspects of education and training programmes.

Throughout, we argue that it is crucial to understand what evaluation can and cannot do. Most methods of evaluation are best suited to assessing the effectiveness of individual projects or programmes. But this tends to reinforce an approach, common in education and training policy, of generating specific programmes (often in response to particular problems) that are not linked to one another, that provide services for a restricted subset of the population, and that therefore cannot do much for a country's growth and development. There is a different view, which we call a 'systems' perspective, that emphasizes instead the development of programmes that could become more universal and linked to one another – this could comprise a more coherent vocational education and training (VET) system. Just as a systems perspective takes a different view of what VET policy should do, we can articulate a systems approach to evaluation as well, one that stresses the ways individual programmes relate to one another in addition to their individual effectiveness.[1]

Plain talk is useless without a forum in which to speak, and so we are concerned throughout with the use made of evaluation evidence. Research in general, and evaluation evidence in particular, are often ignored in the political process, or abused or twisted to serve predetermined conceptions of how the world works. Under these conditions, evaluation cannot fulfil its role of improving the quality of discussion on education and training, and so it is important to clarify what might enhance the role. This is, then, plain talk about the policy process and the use (and abuse) it makes of evaluation. Policy-makers may call for 'hard data', and think they want evidence of success and failure to make decisions; but if they and others fail to acknowledge the political use they make of evidence, then the entire evaluation enterprise may be worthless.

Throughout this monograph, we rely heavily on evidence and examples of evaluation from developed countries particularly the United States (the leader in evaluation research) and the United Kingdom, the two countries with which we are the most familiar, as well as other European countries. But we hope that our examination of evaluation applies to transitional and developing countries as well because most of them have the same dreams for education and training as do developed countries, most of them are considering different approaches and need ways to think carefully about the alternatives, and each of them needs plain talk about what can help that specific country, with its particular conditions and institutions. Many of the issues in education and training are quite common across countries, as we point out in Chapter 7, making it somewhat easier to draw implications for transitional and developing countries. And developing countries, new to evaluation, cannot possibly use the expensive and difficult methods of orthodox approaches to evaluation, so our eclectic approach is much more appropriate for them.

There are, of course, many forms of education and training. Because of the pervasive concern with economic effects, we concentrate on vocational education and training, or VET, though arguing consistently that broader forms of VET, closer to 'education' than to 'training', may be the most valuable. In Chapter 1 we outline the different conceptions of VET. Various forms of education and training and different sponsors of VET generate different evaluation problems, and so it becomes crucial to understand what kind of training is being considered before deciding on the form of evaluation.

We also emphasize in this chapter the causal mechanisms usually assumed when policy-makers and advocates call for VET as a solution to economic problems. The process of human capital development, which we break into four related stages, also implies different types of evaluation; some of these are routinely ignored, even though an improved understanding of VET requires knowledge of all four stages. More to the point, evaluation should not be viewed simply as a process of collecting more and better data, as some have argued;[2] while good data are important, the central issue is understanding why a programme might work or not, and so this causal process is critical to evaluation.

In Chapter 2, we clarify that evaluation may be used for many distinct purposes. Again, different purposes lead to different forms of evaluation, and the methods appropriate for one may not generate the information necessary for another. Therefore, a clear sense of purpose is necessary before deciding on any evaluation method, and the mixture of purposes common in public debates implies once again that several different approaches to evaluation may be necessary.

In Chapter 3 we present a number of methods, including some that are not frequently included among conventional evaluation techniques, partly because the causal mechanism we outline in Chapter 1 suggests that some stages (like the teaching/learning process) are more important than most evaluations have recognized, and also because some information gathered in ways not normally considered to be part of evaluation is better than no information at all. We would emphasize that different approaches to evaluation have their own technical requirements – these are, after all, what enables them under the right conditions to generate plain talk, free of the biases of the political process – and vary in the validity of their conclusions, but all of them can be useful in some contexts.

In Chapter 4 we present some of the leading findings from the evaluation of VET in developed countries. We concentrate on three areas where there has been the most research, and where generalizations are possible: remedial training programmes for the unemployed and those on public assistance; firm-sponsored training, including apprenticeship; and certain forms of VET sought by individuals themselves.

Chapter 5 evaluates the evaluation enterprise itself, providing plain talk about the methods themselves. Of course, individual evaluations can come up with the 'wrong' answers, particularly if they ignore the technical issues discussed in Chapter 3. But the larger question is whether evaluation as it is normally practised might lead to misleading or incorrect results. Frank recognition of these biases may not by itself eliminate them; for example, it is easy to say that short-run results may misstate long-run outcomes, while collecting long-run information may be technically or fiscally impossible. However, if evaluation is to provide useful information for public debate, then all possible biases must be clearly in view.

Then Chapter 6 takes up the question of how evaluation evidence is used in the political process. Like Chapters 4 and 5, the experiences reviewed in this chapter are drawn largely from developed countries, particularly Germany, the United States, and the United Kingdom. But they are sufficiently similar, across a number of countries and over at least 30 years, that some generalizations are possible, and also some recommendations about when evaluation might be made most useful.

Chapter 7 addresses a number of developments common to many countries, developed, transitional, and developing alike. Some of these generate special problems for evaluation, and others threaten to limit funding and political support for evaluation, so policy-makers considering the role that evaluation can play need to consider these trends. While most of this discussion is applicable to a variety of countries, the end of Chapter 7 focuses specifically on implications for developing and transitional countries. Much of the discussion around these countries has concentrated on six issues, most of which are surprisingly similar to debates in developed countries, despite the differences among them in economic development, labour markets and institutional structure. Our purpose in this chapter is not, of course, to provide any resolution of these issues, but instead to clarify what kind of evaluation evidence is

necessary to come to some resolution and to indicate how previous evaluations have sometimes failed to collect the most relevant information.

Finally, Chapter 8 presents a series of recommendations, drawing on earlier
sections. We think that these recommendations flow naturally from the limitations of current practices in evaluation education and training. But, in addition, they are quite consistent with positions and interests that have already
been articulated by the International Labour Office (ILO). They constitute,
then, not an ILO orthodoxy – since our eclectic approach to evaluation argues
against the orthodoxy that now exists, and precludes replacing one orthodoxy
with another – but, rather, a distinctive perspective on how evaluation might
take place, given the particular values and concerns of the ILO.

We have intended this volume for policy-makers, administrators of VET
programmes and others interested in the role VET can play in a country's
growth and development. This is not a 'how to' manual for evaluators themselves, although our analysis of the limits of much evaluation – and our call for
multiple methods of evaluating programmes – should be useful to those
designing evaluations.[3] Nor are we particularly concerned with the technical
issues, which we often relegate to notes. Instead, we concentrate on conveying
an understanding of what VET programmes and evaluation can accomplish,
so that those individuals who need to think about the effectiveness of VET
programmes and systems can understand what evaluation can accomplish.

In the end, the role of evaluation in providing plain talk about an area as difficult and contentious as education and training requires some judgement,
rather than a formulaic approach. A cookbook approach to evaluation does
exist, after all – select a programme, define the outcomes, assign eligible individuals to an experimental group and a control group, collect the data, etc –
and it is certainly valuable in its own right. But at other times this conventional
form is quite useless, or generates information that is neglected in the political
process. Providing information that improves understanding often requires
some judgement about which aspects of a programme are most difficult, about
the purposes of evaluation, about the limits of political discussion. Only with
these many factors in mind can useful evaluations be formulated, and only
then will it be possible for countries to advance the dreams they have for education and training.

Notes

1. Our interest in a system-oriented approach to evaluation parallels that of Schmid,
    O'Reilly and Schömann (1996) in 'target-oriented' evaluation.
2. For example, a common statement is that any evaluation problem can be resolved
    by collecting more and better data; see, for example, Dolton (1993) and Heckman
    and Smith (1996). While this is in theory true, in practice a hypothesis about how a

programme might or might not work is necessary to suggest which of the impossibly large amount of information to collect. Since the range of such hypotheses is vast, in practice some understanding about how a programme works – a 'theory' of the programme – is necessary to direct what kind of data are collected.

3. For a review of basic evaluation techniques, see, eg Hunting, Zymelman and Godfrey (1986).

1

Conceptions of vocational education and training

Variety, causality and implications for evaluation

A great many efforts march under the banner of vocational education and training (VET). The differences are not always clear; in fact, evaluations of VET programmes often fail to describe with any precision what particular programmes do; what a programme is, and why it should have any positive effects at all, are too often assumed rather than clarified. But as we shall argue throughout this chapter, the type and purpose of a particular VET programme may influence the kind of evaluation that should be undertaken. We therefore clarify several different conceptions of VET in this chapter, since programmes can vary according to their sponsorship, their target groups, and their specificity or generality. We then examine the basic conception of why any VET programme should work, since this process of human capital development proves to be important in understanding the limits of evaluation.

Sponsorship of education and training

VET can be sponsored by various parties. We interpret sponsorship as the primary responsibility for organizing and financing training, but not necessarily for providing training directly. For example, firms often sponsor training while contracting with external providers to provide the training itself.

We adopt three categories of training sponsorship: employer, individual and government. *Employer sponsorship* covers all the training that employers organize for their employees, including on-the-job training, apprenticeship, and off-the-job training courses. *Individual sponsorship* refers to the training that workers, both prospective and current, organize for themselves, typically with a view to improving their employment prospects, and typically in relation to the wider labour market rather than to any one employer. Examples include the post-secondary vocational courses taken by Americans at community colleges and proprietary schools, whether before or after starting employment, by the British at Further Education Colleges, and by the Japanese at *senshu-gakko* (Special Training Schools). *Government sponsorship* includes VET organized by public agencies both for young people in secondary education and for workers other than their own employees. The category includes vocational secondary education, and training programmes for the unemployed – such as Job Corps courses for deprived inner city youth in the United States and work-based insertion programmes for unemployed young workers in France, Italy, Sweden and the United Kingdom.

The three categories of sponsorship prove useful in discussing evaluation findings, where different methods and conclusions emerge for each category (see Chapter 4). In practice, however, the distinction between the three categories of sponsorship is sometimes unclear. For example, public insertion programmes for unemployed youth, such as the British Youth Training Scheme, have relied heavily on employers to provide job training and work experience, thereby eliding the distinction between government and employer sponsorship. Similarly, the employer/individual distinction is softened when employees contribute to the finance of employer-sponsored training by accepting lower pay while in training. Such arrangements characterize apprenticeship training for young Germans. Indeed, German apprenticeship could be said to involve four major sponsoring parties – the employer, the public authority, the trainee and the trade union (Streeck *et al.*, 1987). Finally, the government/individual boundary is widely blurred by the various public subsidies, including scholarships, loans and subsidized tuition fees, that are extensively provided to individuals who purchase training from community colleges in the United States.

Even in these cases, however, sponsorship can usually be assigned unambiguously to the party *primarily* responsible for organizing, and usually financing, the training. For apprenticeship, this is typically the employer; for remedial training and insertion schemes, government; and for full-time courses at community colleges (and their counterparts in other countries), the individual.

Targets of education and training

A basic and critical distinction is that between the different targets of VET programmes. There have been several categorizations of these programmes,[1] but for our purposes four will suffice:

1. *Pre-employment VET* prepares individuals for initial entry into employment. These are the 'traditional' programmes of vocational education, based in schools in most countries, and in both schools and workplaces in dual systems, and often operated by national ministries of education.
2. *Upgrade training* provides additional training for individuals who are already employed, as their jobs change, technology and work organization become more complex, or as they advance within a firm or occupation.
3. *Retraining* provides training so that individuals who have lost their jobs can find new ones, or so that individuals who seek new careers can develop the competencies necessary for other employment. The individuals in retraining programmes have by definition already been employed, and so have some labour market experience – though it may or may not be related to the occupation they want to enter.
4. *Remedial VET* provides education and training for individuals who are in some way marginal or out of the mainstream labour force – typically those who have been unemployed for long periods of time, those who are underemployed and therefore in poverty despite employment, or those who depend on public income support (welfare recipients). In contrast to individuals in upgrade training or retraining, individuals in remedial training are likely to have little or no labour market experience, may have low levels of basic skills, and may have other problems (like inability to speak a country's language, alcohol or drug abuse problems, or health problems, whether physical or mental) that generate other barriers to employment.

These different types of training generate several difficulties for evaluation. The most obvious is simply that these conceptually distinct types of VET are all called 'training', and results from one kind of programme may be mistakenly applied to other types. The technical problems of evaluation vary between different forms of VET. For example, those receiving upgrade training are already employed, so the problem of finding employment is not an issue (unlike remedial training, where finding employment is a potential benefit of training). Instead, the important question is whether training changes productivity, earnings, employment stability, or upward mobility. The problems of *negative selection* – of enrolling in a programme individuals who face special barriers to employment, including inadequate skills and motivation – are quite different for remedial training than they are for upgrade training, where *positive selection* may occur as employers select their best and most able employees for training. Retraining may have both positive and negative selection effects, because individuals in need of retraining have been employed, which suggests favourable attributes; but they may also have been the least able employees and therefore the first to be laid off, which suggests negative attributes. Therefore the design of evaluations must be sensitive to the purposes of training, and to the particular problems they create.

Conceptions of education and training: from specific to general

A perennial problem in examining VET programmes is the boundary between VET programmes and general (or academic) education, and between *education* and *training*. Commonly, these are distinguished on the basis of the competencies taught, and how general or specific they are. Programmes that aim to enhance competencies (like literacy) that are useful in all occupations, or that are not particularly focused on occupational effects, are considered academic or general; those that convey competencies useful only within a single firm, or within a narrowly defined occupation, are denoted training; and programmes with mixtures of general education and occupationally specific training may be considered forms of vocational education.[2] Another criterion is the programme's intention: general education does not typically intend to prepare individuals for particular occupations, while vocational education and job training clearly do. In practice, these conceptions mean that education and training exist along a continuum, with training more specific and more vocationally focused than education, with no sharp delineation between education and training. Indeed, with increased interest in many countries in broader forms of vocational education, which integrate more academic competencies, some forms of vocational education have moved closer to academic or general education, and education and training may have started to converge (de Moura Castro, Alfthan and Oliveira, 1990; Grubb 1996a).

But a *conceptual* distinction between education and job training ignores the *institutional* distinctions that have developed in many countries. In the United States, for example, education tends to last much longer than training; it is generally open to all, rather than restricted to specific groups like the unemployed or welfare recipients; it provides a relatively standardized form of classroom-based teaching, while training offers a greater variety of services including job search assistance, counselling and job referral; it tends to take place within well-developed institutions (secondary schools, community colleges, and the like), while job training is provided in a variety of non-governmental organizations (NGOs), unions, firms and educational institutions; education is funded by state and local taxes, while remedial training and some retraining are funded by the federal government and upgrade training is usually funded by firms themselves. Finally, a great deal of remedial training is viewed as a second-chance system for individuals who have failed in the first-chance educational system – and the stigma attached to being part of the second-chance system creates its own barriers to employment (Grubb, 1996a). In most countries, 'education' is administered by ministries of education concerned with learning outcomes, pedagogical improvement, the preparation of regulations, and children and youth whose employment is in the future; 'training' programmes are more likely to be supervised by labour or employment ministries, more concerned with labour markets, employers, adults already in the labour force, and unemployment levels. In practice, therefore, education and training are often sharply divided by the public institutions that support them.[3]

Another problem about the distinction between education and training involves the purposes of any VET programme. It has become common, certainly in developed countries but also in many developing countries, to call for expanding and improving education and training as a way to prepare a highly skilled labour force, the workers required in high-performance firms who have mastered certain core or key skills including problem-solving, communications skills, judgement and other higher-order skills. But these kinds of higher-order skills, no matter how they are defined, are quite complex, and require both lengthy periods of instruction and (in most cases) new methods of teaching quite different from the prevalent didactic methods. They certainly cannot be taught in short-term job training programmes, particularly to individuals whose formal schooling is limited and whose basic academic competencies are lacking. It is a serious mistake, therefore, to call for 'skills for the 21st century' and then to introduce short-term, job-specific and low-level job training. The ambitions of preparing a highly skilled workforce require programmes that are much closer to what most countries have called education – and a broader and less routinized form of education at that.

For evaluation, the institutional differences between education (or vocational education) and training mean that the conditions of programmes that might influence the outcomes – the details of programme design and learning processes – vary substantially among different types of education and training. For certain purposes of evaluation, it may be sufficient to know simply whether a programme has the desired effects, for example, increased amounts of employment and earnings, – or not – and this is the way many of the most sophisticated outcome evaluations have been framed. For other purposes, however – especially understanding why programmes have failed, and trying to improve the quality of VET – the causal links leading to outcomes must be known with greater precision, and for this reason the institutional details surrounding conceptions of education and training are much more important.

Why should VET work? The stages of human capital development and the alternatives

The most basic question of any kind of education or training programme is why it should have any effect at all. A particular conception underlies most VET programmes, often assumed but less often articulated – what we will call the 'amplified' conception of human capital development. In it, there are at least four different stages or outcomes, each linked to its predecessor through a particular process. These four stages are causal and sequential, so that if any one of them is missing, the subsequent stages are aborted. Our conception of human capital development is more elaborated than the human capital theory, often used by economists to explain the relationship between VET and earnings; conventionally, human capital theory pays little attention to several stages that are important, either ignoring them or making restrictive assumptions about the way they operate. Our conception of human capital development is therefore more precise about the changes that must take place before a VET programme has any meaningful effect. As we will use them, the four stages of human capital development are the following.

Stage 1: implementation

The resources allocated for a particular VET programme generate a programme with particular characteristics, for example, a 15-week retraining effort for dislocated workers, teaching them certain computer applications. The implementation stage is critical because there are many ways in which resources intended for training may fail to result in a programme being established: the funds may be misspent, or may be spent on initial planning and administrative costs without hiring the instructors who are the heart of the programme, or a programme may start but fail to attract any students or trainees. Alternatively, a programme may be initiated, but its characteristics may be different from those intended; for example, a programme intended to provide computer training may be forced to redirect its attention to basic literacy or mathematics.

Because the existence of a programme with specific characteristics is so important – after all, there can be no effects on employment, earnings, or any other outcomes if the programme does not exist, or does not function as intended – the first stage of any evaluation is often a 'process evaluation' or implementation study, designed to see whether the programme was established as intended. Because the characteristics of a programme can be quite complex, many implementation studies try to determine whether the programme is consistent with the initial design or legislative intention (when it is a governmental programme) or whether the original plans have been changed or undermined in some way.[4]

Stage 2: the learning process

Once a programme is established, it presumably increases the skills or competencies of the individuals enrolled. These competencies may be cognitive, like literacy or mathematical skills; or, particularly in vocational education and training, non-cognitive skills and abilities may be particularly important, including manual or kinaesthetic skills (like the ability to weld, or to insert an intravenous needle), spatial or visual skills (necessary for reading blueprints, or building three-dimensional objects like houses). Interpersonal skills, for example, the ability to work in teams, or to behave appropriately with supervisors, co-workers, or customers, are valuable outcomes of many programmes, and certain personal traits – independence, persistence, motivation – are necessary in virtually all kinds of employment.[5]

Recently, individuals and government commissions writing about changes in work have articulated yet other competencies necessary for high-performance workplaces, sometimes labelled 'higher-order skills' or 'core' or 'key' skills, and encompassing such capacities as problem-solving, communications skills and judgement; many governments have included such abilities in the 'core' or 'key' skills required of VET programmes. Finally, particular occupations usually require particular *combinations* of skills, and the particular combination varies not only among occupations but even among similar jobs within different firms. The competencies enhanced by a VET programme can vary substantially, then, but the amplified version of human capital development generally assumes that a programme operates by enhancing one or more of this vast array of competencies.

The processes generating increases in competencies are, of course, those involving teaching and learning, and enhancing these competencies therefore requires an understanding of teaching and learning. In general, these processes have been extensively investigated within general education, but badly ignored in VET.[6] Even for those programmes that depend on effective approaches to teaching, for example, remedial literacy programmes for adults whose reading and writing abilities are inadequate, the existing evaluation literature fails to describe how this process takes place.[7] When we examine possible improvements in the quality of programmes, the neglect of teaching and learning will be a central concern.

In some programmes, there is even a serious question whether any teaching and learning at all take place. For example, remedial programmes in the United States often use on-the-job training, where individuals are placed in employment and presumably learn the skills required for keeping their jobs and finding promotion, but a large proportion of these placements simply require the trainees to perform routine work, and little enhancement of skills can be observed (Kogan *et al.*, 1989). Similarly, traditional apprenticeship programmes in the United Kingdom were often ways for employers to get routinized work performed at low cost, at the expense of actually training young people in the technical and interpersonal skills required in advanced work (Ryan, 1999). Even in the widely praised German dual system, the school-based component of the training is carried out independently of the work-based component, and, in large firms, the work-based component takes place not on the job but in special training centres set apart from work; thus both components can become disconnected from production as well as independent of one another (Heidigger and Rauner, 1996). In all cases, therefore, the question of what learning takes place, and what learning is related to future employment, needs to be examined carefully, rather than just assumed.

Stage 3: changing economic behaviour, in the labour market and on the job

The enhanced competencies learned within a VET programme then change the economic behaviour of workers, for example, by allowing them to work more quickly, more effectively, more intensively, or with less waste or wasted time. Sometimes, VET programmes stress services – like job search assistance, or information about labour market conditions that improves their job-seeking behaviour – that enable individuals to find their way in the labour market, without necessarily giving them the skills necessary for particular jobs. In other cases, programmes stress job-keeping behaviour, for example, the flexibility necessary to respond as the job changes, the interpersonal skills necessary to cope with supervisors and co-workers, and the persistence and discipline necessary in most jobs, so that the individuals trained do not find themselves unemployed because of their inability to keep jobs.

This stage assumes that the individuals trained in a VET programme either have jobs – in the case of upgrade training – or find jobs where they might use their newly acquired competencies, for pre-employment training, retraining, or remedial training. This assumption, while not troublesome for upgrade training, is critical for other forms of VET because of the emphasis on paid employment: individuals without jobs cannot possibly use the learning achieved in a programme (except those devoted entirely to job search). Presumably, for those who do not have jobs, the programme changes the *potential* productivity on the job so that an employer hires them. Thus many VET programmes end up using measures of employment as evidence of success. Furthermore, successful programmes are often concerned with choosing occupations where high growth rates or unfilled employment opportunities make high placement rates more likely, or the programmes provide services like placement services to enhance placement rates.

The effect of a VET programme on job-related behaviour assumes that the job requires those competencies enhanced by the programme – rather than the programme teaching competencies that are not required on the job an individual has or finds. In evaluating VET programmes, the concern with placement in jobs related to the area of training reflects the concern that – particularly for relatively job-specific forms of training – the benefits emerge only for some occupations where competencies are required, and not in others.

The amplified version of human capital development often appears to assume that individuals participate in smoothly functioning labour markets with well-defined jobs that trainees either obtain or fail to obtain. However, this conception can be applied to the informal sectors of developing countries, as well as to entrepreneurs in developed and transitional countries, because the process of getting a job may involve *creating* a job by identifying potential opportunities, obtaining the necessary capital, and otherwise creating a position as a small-scale entrepreneur. If the skills acquired in training enhance these entrepreneurial abilities – and many training programmes in developing countries emphasize basic business practices, precisely to enhance success in creating opportunities in the informal sector – then their design is consistent with this stage of human capital development.

Stage 4: creating long-run employment and non-employment outcomes

The changes in economic behaviour then lead to outcomes that are more readily measurable, for example, to higher productivity for individual workers that in turn increases their wages and earnings, or the firm's overall productivity and profit, or the productivity and wages of other workers. Particularly where training concentrates on middle-skilled positions as helpers to professional and managerial employees (for example, technicians who help engineers, or clerical workers who help managers, or health technicians like nurse assistants and physician assistants), the effect of a training programme may show up in forms other than the individual's wage.

Of course, training programmes (particularly remedial programmes aimed at youth) may have non-economic goals as well, for example, reducing criminal activity, or alcohol and drug abuse, or sexual behaviour including unwanted pregnancies, or health-related measures. This process assumes that, at least in societies where employment is critical in defining a person's identity and generating income, a variety of non-economic benefits flow from employment. In some cases the causal relationship between employment and non-economic outcomes is relatively obvious, as when employment reduces the likelihood of committing economic crimes. In other cases the causal relationship may be quite complex, as in the claims that employment for women provides a source of meaning that reduces the incidence of both out-of-wedlock pregnancies and lone parenthood (Ladner, 1995).

The amplified conception of human capital development is sequential; if a programme is not implemented at Stage 1, then there can be no learning at Stage 2 and no changes in economic behaviour at Stage 3; if there is no learning at

Stage 2, neither economic nor non-economic benefits can develop at Stage 4; if at Stage 3 the individual is not economically active, or if competencies learned are not used in economic activity – because they are not the required competencies – then for purposes of the programme the learning has been wasted.

The sequential nature of this model also implies that a successful training programme – usually defined as a programme with successful economic outcomes in Stage 4 – requires a number of conditions to be fulfilled, each of which is necessary but not sufficient for success: a programme must be implemented, *and* learning must take place, *and* that learning must affect economic behaviour, *and* that change in behaviour must result in various economic and non-economic outcomes. There are many different places in this chain of events where things may go wrong, and therefore many different reasons why well-intentioned programmes may have no effects.

Conceptions of VET planning often take this conception of human capital development and work backward from desired outcomes. That is, if the desired outcome includes enhanced earnings and employment of some group, then the process of developing a training programme usually involves identifying employment opportunities necessary for Stage 3, identifying the competencies necessary on those jobs, planning the learning opportunities necessary at Stage 2 to teach these competencies, and hiring the instructors and providing the other resources (textbooks, supplies, buildings, administrative support, and the like) necessary at Stage 1. Often, when evaluators conclude that a programme has worked poorly, it is because one or another of these steps was not carefully planned, that somewhere in the *sequence* of necessary stages, something was left out. In particular, there is a marked tendency to pronounce programmes as failures when in fact poor implementation at Stage 1 is to blame. For example, the Worker Demonstration Project in the United States was declared a failure when in fact the wrong type of training was really to blame: preparation for blue-collar jobs was offered to displaced white-collar workers (Bloom, 1990).

It is also important to recognize that some applications of the amplified version of human capital development, particularly by evaluation economists working in the tradition of human capital theory, tend to assume fluid market mechanisms and perfect competition. For example, the hiring process at Stage 3 generally assumes a labour market in which employers hire the most productive individuals from the available pool. If this is not true – if employers hire on the basis of characteristics other than productivity – then several things can go wrong: training programmes that provide no real enhancement of competency may still have high placement rates (and therefore look productive) if there is preferential hiring from a programme. Conversely, programmes that are effective at enhancing the competencies related to productivity may still have low placement rates. (This has often been a problem in training for women, for example, who cannot subsequently gain access to certain jobs dominated by men.)

Similarly, the wage-setting mechanism is usually assumed to pay individuals according to their productivity on the job, allowing wages at Stage 4 to be used as measures of productivity. If this is not the case – if, for example, ex-trainees are paid less than their productivity – then wages and earnings will not completely measure the benefits of the programme. Alternatively, if a training programme gains an individual entry into employment where wages are artificially high, for example, in a state-run enterprise, then a programme will look more effective than it actually is from the standpoint of the wider economy.

Finally, many evaluations implicitly assume an economy in full employment, where wages adjust to eliminate any unemployment. Then the employment of individuals trained must represent a net increase in employment, rather than simply the displacement of one worker by another. But in economies with substantial unemployment the danger of displacement – of a trained individual being hired but displacing another into unemployment – is substantial and cannot be assumed away. Our point is that the human capital conception, so widely used in discussions of VET, incorporates many stages and assumptions, and is therefore more complex than is conventionally understood.

There are, of course, other conceptions of the effects of education and training on employment. One version, usually known as signalling or screening, assumes that only the most able or motivated individuals can complete a programme; employers are assumed to be unable to observe an individual's ability and motivation directly, and therefore hire educated or trained individuals because they are more likely to get motivated, high-ability workers who can better profit from further training, not because they (employers) value the skills acquired in the programme itself.

Acquiring education or training is rational for the individual, for whom it leads to higher earnings, and rational for the employer, whom it allows to hire the more able workers. But signalling is socially rational only if there are benefits, notably increased productivity and reduced training costs from concentrating additional training upon more able and motivated individuals, who can make better use of it, that can outweigh the costs of VET. But because education and training, used as signals of abilities, need not teach new competencies, there has always been a suspicion that signalling is not as valuable socially as education and training in the human capital sense.[8]

In addition, some individuals have asserted that employers do not really understand the value of education and training for their organizations, and hire on the basis of credentials even when it is not rational to do so.[9] In effect, these views of credentialling assume that some problem arises at Stage 3: a programme does not change actual or potential behaviour on the job, though employers believe it will and therefore hire trained individuals. Acquiring education and training may therefore be rational for the individual, but not for the employer or for society as a whole.

In theory, signalling and credentialling situations can be distinguished from the conventional human capital model, either by investigating the nature of learning (Stage 2) or changes in behaviour on the job (Stage 3). Indeed, certain kinds of evaluation, described more fully in Chapter 2, are intended to investigate precisely these possibilities; for example, assessments of learning and inspection methods focus respectively on the outcomes and the process of learning, and could in theory distinguish signalling situations. In practice, this kind of research has been rarely undertaken.

Finally, each of the stages in the amplified version of human capital formation has its own characteristic form of evaluation. The implementation stage is the focus of 'process' evaluation, or implementation studies. The learning stage is the subject of efforts to assess what individuals have learned in a programme, and of efforts to examine the teaching–learning process directly. The economic behaviour aspect of Stage 3 involves the observation or measurement of job search, productivity, and learning curves, as individuals gain experience and training. Final outcome evaluations typically focus on the economic variables of Stage 4, and only sometimes on the non-economic consequences. However, most outcome evaluations ignore the intermediate stages, particularly Stages 2 and 3, though process or implementation studies have become more common. And so most evaluations of VET programmes are partial and incomplete: they tend implicitly to *assume* the amplified version of human development, but they do not usually *investigate* all aspects of it.

Notes

1. See, for example, Gaude and Payne (1994) for the ILO and Van den Berghe and Tilkon Consultancy (1996) for CEDEFOP. See also the articles in Section I of Tuijnman (1996).
2. In most descriptions of education and training, narrowness is usually defined as preparation for a relatively specific *occupation*. In Becker's (1975) influential formulation of human capital theory, specific training is defined as being useful to a particular *firm*. We note that firm-specific training and occupation-specific training are not necessarily the same, though both may be attacked as overly narrow.
3. Notable exceptions include Australia and the United Kingdom, which have both merged at national level the government departments responsible for education and employment.
4. One of the functions of the performance management systems that are built into contemporary training programmes in the United States is to monitor implementation, eg to what extent have participants been drawn from the groups that the programme was intended to serve? See, eg Barnow (1992).

5. While there are many ways to think of different types of competencies, a particularly broad and useful one is that of Gardner (1983), who includes seven competencies or 'intelligences': linguistic, logical-mathematical, spatial, bodily/kinaesthetic, musical, interpersonal, and intrapersonal.
6. For a review of the literature on teaching in vocational education, concentrating on the English and the German literature, see Achtenhagen and Grubb (1999).
7. For example, in the United States evaluation literature a remedial literacy programme in San Diego has been widely acclaimed, yet the evaluation of this programme (Martinson and Friedlander, 1994) fails to describe its approach to teaching.
8. For a model of signalling, see especially Spence (1974). Of course, education and training may include both elements of signalling and of human capital formation, see especially Riley (1979). See also Psacharopolous (1979) on 'weak' signalling, where education is used as a signal in hiring but not in promotion, versus 'strong' signalling, where it is a signal for both hiring and promotion. Signalling theories have rarely been mentioned for job training (as distinct from education), though it is clear in the case of remedial training that marginal employers may hire from job training programmes because they screen out the least motivated and incompetent individuals.
9. There are in reality several different models of credentialing; see especially Rawlins and Ulman (1974), and Berg (1970) for an influential early work. Some models of credentialing are economically rational; for example, employers may hire over-qualified individuals for entry-level work in anticipation of promoting some of them.

2

Why evaluate?

The multiple and conflicting purposes
underlying evaluation

It has become increasingly common to call for evaluations of VET programmes. In the United States, large-scale government programmes are routinely evaluated in some way, and private donors such as foundations often evaluate the experiments they support, sometimes quite formally. The evaluation of VET programmes has become less uncommon in the United Kingdom, and the European Commission has sponsored evaluations of various programmes. In developing countries, major donors like the World Bank and specific agencies, such as the United States Agency for International Development (USAID), also evaluate the projects they undertake, sometimes specifying a standard methodology for evaluation, and the ILO has promoted a form of evaluation for all its projects.[1] In a period of increased accountability, the need for evaluation seems obvious. And evaluation has begotten ever more evaluation: a simple faith in the efficacy of education and training has become more difficult to maintain, partly because previous evaluations (particularly of remedial training) have found many programmes to be ineffective, and have raised the question whether VET programmes in general are effective, or indeed whether education and training are the appropriate solutions to the economic problems of developed and underdeveloped countries alike.[2]

But evaluation is a varied enterprise, and its purposes vary widely too. Evaluations designed for one purpose may not be useful in achieving other goals, and so recognizing these different purposes is important when designing and interpreting evaluations appropriately. In this chapter we examine five purposes for evaluation, and clarify the ways in which they require different information. We first examine the roles of evaluation in improving the decisions made by the three types of sponsors – governments, employers and individuals. We then examine the more general issue of improving the quality of VET programmes. Finally, we shift to a more general and less instrumental conception – one in which evaluation is a mechanism for carrying on public debates about VET programmes and policies.

Informing governmental decisions

Perhaps the most obvious use of evaluation is to improve public decisions. In the United States, for example, the central question in evaluations of remedial job training is whether it increases the employment and earnings of participants, or (for programmes aimed at welfare recipients) if it moves individuals off welfare and into employment. If programmes are successful, then they may be expanded, and indeed the positive evaluations of experimental welfare-to-work programmes during the 1980s were instrumental in expanding such programmes after 1988. If programmes prove not to work, in the sense that they do not enhance employment, or if they enhance employment but their costs outweigh their benefits, then they may be either terminated or improved. In this vision, the results of evaluations are translated directly into governmental decisions about VET programmes, an assumption we discuss further in Chapter 6. In any case, the *intention* of informing governmental policy underlies many evaluations.

For the purpose of deciding whether to expand or eliminate programmes, it is often enough to measure the average or overall effect of a programme. Thus the most sophisticated random-assignment methods have usually calculated the average effects, for example, the average increase in weeks worked, or in monthly earnings, for a sample of participants, and the cost-benefit calculations from these results examine whether aggregate benefits outweigh aggregate costs. Results for groups of participants may be reported, for example, for youth as distinct from older participants, for men versus women, for less educated and more educated individuals, to determine whether certain groups benefit more than others, and therefore whether governmental programmes should be targeted on certain groups rather than others. Often, however, the results for particular groups are less accurate and less extensive than the overall results, and therefore the dominant results answer the question of whether the programme as a whole is worth funding or not. Conventionally, these evaluations emphasize final outcomes – typically, economic outcomes, though sometimes (particularly for youth) non-economic outcomes like criminal behaviour – without examining intermediate stages in training programmes, because information about final outcomes is conventionally thought to be all that is necessary to make decisions about expansion or elimination.[3]

Improving employer decisions about training

Evaluation is also potentially relevant to the training which employers sponsor for their employees, even if it is rarely performed in that context. Employer sponsorship is central to the development of workforce skills in all economies, particularly to skills developed after leaving full-time schooling.[4] In the United Kingdom, employers sponsored around 80 per cent of the training which the adult workforce of the mid-1980s reported having received (DE, 1989). In developing countries, the role of the employer is typically pivotal, dominating the training of employees for both the large enterprises of the formal sector and, through apprenticeship, their smaller counterparts in the informal sector (Fluitman, 1989; Maldonado, 1993).[5] The importance of employer sponsorship is underlined by the broad finding that it contributes more reliably to improved economic outcomes, for employers and workers alike, than do other forms of sponsorship, particularly public labour market programmes (see Chapter 4).

Employer training may be evaluated from two perspectives: the employer's interest and the public interest, including the interests of workers themselves.[6] The employer's interest is in establishing whether training increases profits – that is, whether it contributes more to organizational performance than it consumes in resources. In principle, training should satisfy the same rate of return criteria as investment in capital equipment. The public interest is a wider concept, involving both efficiency and equity. The efficiency test is ideally implemented through a social cost-benefit analysis – the analogue for the public sector of cash-flow analysis in the private sector (see Chapter 3, The challenge of comparison). The equity test is whether training changes the distribution of social and economic outcomes towards the interests of individuals or groups favoured by public policy, typically the disadvantaged.

In principle, information about training patterns and outcomes can be used to improve firm-sponsored training. Decisions affecting the volume, occupational level, and quality of training are made routinely by individuals, employers and governments, often according to impressions and based on *ad hoc* criteria. Efforts to base these decisions more effectively on evaluation findings could yield potentially large returns, by avoiding wasteful training and increasing training where it is under-supplied.[7]

Unfortunately, the centrality of employer-provided training to overall national training efforts has not been matched by relevant evaluation efforts. From the standpoint of employer interests, efforts to evaluate employer training programmes have a long history (Thomas *et al.*, 1969; Ryan, 1980; Kirkpatrick, 1994). Yet even in developed economies only a minority of employers have attempted any formal evaluation of their training programmes, and a still smaller minority have estimated the benefits or outcomes of training (eg DE, 1989; Ryan, 1991a; Plant and Ryan, 1992).

From the public standpoint, systematic evidence on the effects of employer training has in recent years accumulated from various sources, including employee earnings and employer productivity (see Chapter 4). Even here, however, evaluation findings remain partial and fragmentary, and therefore of only limited value as a guide to public policy. Debates over the merits of public intervention to encourage employer training often proceed without much evidence about the benefits of such a policy (Baily *et al.*, 1993; Heckman *et al.*, 1994).

Informing individuals about their options

Yet another use of evaluation is to generate the information that individuals need to make their own decisions about education and training. This is particularly important in pre-employment VET and individual sponsorship of training, of course: individuals completing their compulsory schooling need information to choose among several post-compulsory options, including vocational education in tertiary institutions, private training, and employment opportunities with possibilities for firm-sponsored training. Similarly, when individuals consider retraining for a new occupation, they need to be well informed about the alternatives.

In addition, government policy may emphasize individual initiative. For example, some governments have supported voucher mechanisms for training – like the Youth Credits scheme in Great Britain[8] in the mid-1990s, which funded a variety of options amongst which individuals could in principle choose for themselves. Similarly, welfare programmes in the United States have sometimes allowed 'individual referral', where individuals can put together their own education and training programmes (often subject to some restrictions from the programme itself) and have them funded by a welfare agency. Somewhat like a voucher, this assumes an individual can rationally choose from the options available.[9] In practice, the available evidence suggests that – particularly in the case of remedial training – information about programme effectiveness is almost completely missing, and many individuals seem to make virtually random decisions under these circumstances (Hodkinson, Sparkes, and Hodkinson, 1996; Grubb, 1996b, Ch. 2; Hull, 1993).

The evaluation evidence necessary for individual decisions is much more specific than for governmental or firm decisions, however. Individuals need to know about specific *local* programmes, not national averages, and they need information for several local programmes on a roughly comparable basis if they are to decide among them. For example, a young British person seeking a qualification in electronics might be able to choose between several local providers of vocational qualifications, including Further Education Colleges, secondary schools, commercial training organizations, employer-sponsored apprenticeships and public programmes. Similarly, an individual in the United States might be able to choose from several community colleges, perhaps an area vocational school, several private providers, and (if eligible) several job training programmes. The kind of evidence typically available – that might include non-completion rates for training programmes, job placement rates for courses at community colleges and private providers, and perhaps some data on earnings from colleges – is usually incomplete, frequently inconsistent, sometimes invalid,[10] and often outdated. When the necessary evidence is not available, individuals may have to rely on hearsay from friends and other informal indicators of reputation.

Improving the quality of individual programmes

A central purpose of evaluation has been to improve the quality of programmes – whether they are governmental or firm sponsored. If certain kinds of programmes are found to be more effective than others, for example, if on-the-job training is more effective than classroom training, or if certain approaches to instruction are more effective than others, then ineffective programmes can be either closed or can be reformed by emulating more effective programmes. The widespread method of identifying exemplary programmes, or forms of 'best practice', is another way of identifying the conditions enhancing the quality of programmes and therefore outcome measures.

However, the information required to improve programmes is more extensive than that necessary to decide whether to continue them or not. Improving the quality of programmes requires knowing *why* they work, rather than simply *whether* they work, and usually this requires more information about the processes prior to final outcomes. Because the success or failure of a programme may arise from any of the logically prior stages, decisions about quality may require information on all of the prior stages – the implementation stage, the teaching and learning processes, and the employment effects. For example, one examination of particularly effective job training programmes in Texas – as measured by placement rates and earnings – determined that the most effective programmes targeted jobs with high and growing demand, and counselled potential participants about the occupational fields in which they were most likely to be successful, thus improving the chances that anything learned in the programme would be translated into higher earnings (King *et al.*, 1999). The obvious recommendation is that remedial job training should carefully examine the local labour market and target jobs with the highest earnings levels and growth rates for which their clients can qualify.

This method is fraught with uncertainty because the characteristics that lead to higher quality, and therefore greater effectiveness in terms of outcomes, may be difficult to identify. For example, an evaluation of several programmes for single mothers determined that one specific programme was much more effective than the rest, and concluded that one aspect of its teaching and learning process – the combination of academic and vocational skills training – was responsible (Burghardt and Gordon, 1990). However, this programme differed from unsuccessful programmes in several other ways, including strong connections with local employers and the provision of work-based experience as well as classroom training (Grubb, 1996a: 81–82); therefore it is difficult to know which of several possible recommendations to make for other programmes.[11]

Throughout this report, we stress the special problems of enhancing the quality of VET, rather than simply replacing programmes or changing their size. Government decisions about VET are often stated in terms of quantity (eg number of places provided in particular programmes), rather than quality (eg breadth and depth of services provided) and evaluations are often designed to answer the question of whether a programme is worth doing or not. Issues about quality are much more difficult to address, both in government policy and in evaluations, for several reasons. As we have just pointed out, the factors that influence the quality of a programme are many and varied, and can occur at many different places in a chain of human capital development. Therefore the information required to specify the important dimensions of quality may be extensive. The content of some dimensions of quality is unresolved and disputed. For example, approaches to teaching and learning have been quite controversial in some countries, and the specific combination of competencies necessary in certain jobs is often unrecognized even by expert practitioners (Evans and Butler, 1992). And, when we examine the use of evaluation in governmental policy in Chapter 6, we find that dimensions of quality often prove difficult to incorporate: there is a more vocal constituency (programme providers and potential clients) for the *quantity* of places than for *quality*, and it is often difficult for *central* governments to enhance the quality of *local* programmes. But increasing the volume of low-quality programmes is obviously not a sensible policy, and so there is no way to avoid the need to address quality in both evaluations and in policy-making.

Of course, quality can be oversold too: it is certainly possible to have programmes of substantial effectiveness that are quite expensive, and there is therefore a trade-off between the quantity of training provided and its quality. For example, the Job Corps programme in the United States – a remedial training programme that provides residential, year-long services to disadvantaged youth – has widely been regarded as quite effective, though its high cost (over US$15,000 per trainee in 1993 US dollars) means that it is too expensive to implement on a large scale.[12] But our point is that it is impossible to weigh the benefits of high-quality programmes, or to consider the inevitable trade-off between quantity and quality, without examining quality more carefully than has usually been the case.

A final use of outcome-related data, and therefore of evaluation in its broadest sense, is to improve performance management in VET programmes. Performance management encompasses the variety of decisions intended to improve performance, including the dimensions of quality that we stress throughout this book but also administrative decisions such as tracking mechanisms, accounting systems, and the like. Under the best conditions, performance measures can help make local delivery of VET programmes more outcome-oriented by measuring performance in various ways and providing rewards and sanctions for high and low performance.

For example, the main job training programme in the United States, the Job Training Partnership Act (JTPA), has required the local agencies that deliver its services to collect data on various performance measures, including such 'gross outcomes' as rates of employment and pay after the completion of training. Programmes that fall below certain standards may be reorganized, and those with high performance may receive additional incentive funds. Similarly, Florida is moving towards performance-based funding for several VET programmes.[13]

But the data used for performance management are not generally the same as those needed for programme evaluation. Indeed, the near-term, 'gross outcome' performance measures that are used for JTPA prove to be uncorrelated with evaluation-based estimates of medium-term *net* outcomes (ie outcomes relative to those in a control group; Doolittle *et al.*, 1993: 10; Barnow, 1997). Performance management requires information to be quickly available, on such gross outcomes as rates of training completion and job placement, that focus the attention of managers on immediate problems. Control groups are not readily available and are not considered necessary. As the point is to focus the attention of managers on outcomes, then certain kinds of data are valuable – particularly measures that are calibrated from time to time against findings about net outcomes, so that they lead programmes in the right direction – even though they may not be as valid as data generated from conventional evaluation studies (Barnow, 1992, 1997). Performance management data are therefore one way to improve the operational quality of a programme, but such evidence is far from sufficient to establish whether the programme has worked: that is the task of evaluation proper.

Moreover, performance measurement can backfire if associated with inappropriate incentives. For example, the JTPA performance measures, especially job placement rates, have been charged with causing programmes to 'cream', or select the most able applicants. The use of a 'cost per placement' criterion, designed to encourage efficiency, encouraged local administrators to use short-duration, inexpensive, and ultimately ineffective, services. Therefore, while performance management measures have a part to play in running a programme, and can be one way to redirect attention from inputs to outcomes, they need to be carefully chosen and do not substitute for evaluation proper.

Evaluation as a mechanism of public debate about VET

A final view about evaluation is less specific and purposeful, but perhaps more honest about what evaluation can accomplish. The purposes we have already discussed are 'rationalist' conceptions of evaluation: a programme is evaluated, positive or negative findings are then used to expand, modify, or shut down the programme, and evaluation results therefore have direct consequences. But practitioners of policy-oriented research have noted that their work is not often used in this way. (In Chapter 7 we will summarize some of the ways evaluation can be ignored or abused in the political process.) Therefore a more modest conception of research and evaluation has developed, in which evaluation generates information that is then used in public debate, which may either act on evaluation results, reinterpret them, search for further information, or ignore them altogether. In this conception, evaluation is a way of discussing public programmes, where the information it provides is different from and possibly a corrective to the more political, self-interested, or value-laden positions that would otherwise be taken.

The view of evaluation as a forum for public debate requires that its results be broadly understood, of course: technical discussions among experts are unlikely to help broader groups form views about VET. For public discussion, greater understanding of the purposes of VET programmes and the difficulties they face – particularly governmental-supported programmes that require voter support – should be an important feature. Thus technical reports that simply present conclusions about a programme's overall effectiveness are probably less informative than evaluations that give a deeper sense of what the programme has and has not accomplished.

An exemplary effort along these lines is the evaluation of the New Chance programme in the United States (see Box 3.6), which has been aimed at reducing poverty amongst single mothers on welfare: in addition to a sophisticated random-assignment evaluation (Quint et al., 1994a; Quint et al, 1997), an intensive interview study was also undertaken (Quint et al., 1994b). The quantitative study has so far generated negative results, which are especially discouraging because the programme was carefully designed to provide a variety of services and was quite costly, but the qualitative study helps explain these results by clarifying the variety of problems that single mothers face, such as other family members who impede their educational progress, and mental health problems beyond the reach of VET programmes. This kind of evaluation can therefore contribute to greater public understanding rather than simply fostering the conventional and dismal conclusion that 'nothing works'.

One way to stimulate public discussion of VET is for interested groups to participate in the formulation of evaluations, for example, in specifying what stages of a VET project are to be evaluated, what outcome measures are to be emphasized, or what issues of quality to investigate. In particular, the tripartite discussions about policy that have been effective in certain countries could provide forums for *formulating* evaluation, as well as *interpreting* the results, because, as we will show in greater detail in Chapter 6, tripartite bodies that have not participated in formulating an evaluation may be more likely to react to the results politically and negatively than in the spirit of public discussion. This is *not* an argument that evaluation can be wholly designed by a tripartite or other political process; as we clarify in Chapter 3, evaluation has certain technical requirements if the information it generates is to be useful, and therefore requires a critical role for non-partisan experts. But the role of evaluation in public discussion suggests that debate about purposes, means, and quality should be started sooner rather than later, and joint deliberation about evaluation is one way to do this.

Finally, the bare minimum for evaluation to be useful is that it should add to public debate, rather than simply representing one more time political positions that are already well established. In turn, this means that evaluation is a forum in which certain political and ideological positions must be either set aside, or re-framed in the empirical questions that are the heart of all evaluation. To put it bluntly: if empirical evaluations are dishonest, or twisted by ideological commitments, or skewed to make a programme or a donor or a government look good, then the results cannot inform public debate. They will be worse than useless because they can only mislead the public, often by getting them to think that the outcomes are better than they are. Of course, values can still play a role in evaluation, particularly by being restated in empirical terms. For example, a concern with the equity of training, such as its effects on the most disadvantaged participants, as well as on the less disadvantaged, requires that certain kinds of information for particular groups of participants be collected, as we stress in Chapter 3. Then programmes can be found equitable or inequitable, effective or ineffective, and political decisions made as a result. But evaluation has its own logic and rules of evidence, as we clarify in Chapter 3, and distorting this logic for ideological purposes destroys its value in carrying out principled debates about VET.

It should now be clear that the purpose of evaluation affects the kind of evaluation undertaken. For some purposes, particularly deciding if programmes should be closed, rigorous outcome evaluations may be necessary. To improve the quality of programmes, more information is typically needed on the process underlying final outcomes, that is, on Stages 1 to 3 in the conception of human capital development presented in Chapter 1. For firm-based training, outcomes for individuals are less important than effects on overall productivity. To inform individuals, much more detailed local information is necessary. And to contribute to public debate about VET, evaluations probably need to be more accessible, more qualitative, and (again) more concerned with early stages, not just with outcomes – and the process of formulating the evaluation may be a central part of its contribution. It is therefore impossible to recommend a single approach to evaluation, for example, the common recommendation that pilot programmes be conducted and evaluated rigorously with random-assignment methods, because the purposes of the evaluation should dictate what methods are used.

Notes

1. See Evaluation Unit, *Guidelines for the Preparation of Independent Evaluations and ILO Programmes and Projects*, ILO, May 1997.
2. For a sceptical view from the ILO, see Carnoy and Fluitman (1995).
3. There is a technical problem in using evaluation results to justify expanding VET programmes. An evaluation typically measures the *average* effects of a programme, but expansion requires knowing whether the *marginal* effects of a programme — the effects for those trained as the programme expands — are sufficiently high. If there are declining marginal returns to training, for example, because the individuals trained are less competent as the programmes expands, or because the demand for trained individuals become saturated, or because wages of trainees fall as supply increases, then average effects will overstate marginal effects. This distinction is especially important in considering differences between European programmes, which tend to allow all individuals to be eligible, potentially expanding the numbers of trained individuals substantially and reducing marginal effects, from United States programmes, which tend to restrict eligibility for training.
4. The dominance of employer sponsorship is more marked for adult than for youth training, given that employers typically enjoy unilateral control over adult training at work and that in some countries (notably France and Sweden) schools and colleges play the major role in initial VET.
5. The United States is exceptional in the importance of non-employer sponsorship. Previous receipt of employer-sponsored training ('on the job' and 'apprenticeship') was reported only 40 per cent as often as that of other types of training ('off the job') by young adult workers in 1983 (Lynch, 1992, Table 2), though were adults covered and informal training included, the contrast to other countries would undoubtedly be much softer.
6. A category intermediate between the employer and the economy is also relevant to the evaluation of training: the interests of employers as a whole, whether at sectoral or national level. Arguments for training boards, for example, hinge upon the proposition that the interests of the individual employer diverge from those of the employer collective, primarily as a result of the externalities among employers associated with the 'poaching' of trained workers (Stevens, 1996).

7. On the avoidance of wasteful training, see Heckman *et al.* (1994); on encouraging training that is under-supplied, see Steedman and Wagner (1989); and on changing the mix of training, see Bierhof and Prais (1996).
8. Great Britain refers to England, Scotland and Wales.
9. For the differences between individual referral and vouchers, see Barnow and King (1996).
10. One of the little-noticed findings in the evaluation of the JTPA programme in the United States is that measures of effectiveness determined through random-assignment methods are completely uncorrelated with performance indicators used by programme administrators; see Doolittle *et al.* (1993: 10), and Barnow (1997). The point is that different methods of evaluation yield different, and in this case completely uncorrelated, measures of effectiveness.
11. In theory, evaluations could be designed to answer more precisely questions about which of several practices lead to greater effectiveness, for example, by contrasting programmes varying by both combinations of academic and vocational education and of classroom and work-based learning. In practice, however, such evaluations would be enormously expensive to carry out in the most rigorous ways, and so much more informal assessments of why certain programmes work are necessary.
12. See also the case of the Perry Pre-school Project discussed in Box 6.2, which also represents a programme (in the area of early childhood) that is of such high quality and cost that it could not possibly be widely replicated.
13. The monitoring of programme attributes – much like evaluation research itself – is much less developed in Europe than in the United States (Auer and Kruppe, 1996).

3

Approaches to evaluation
From the ridiculous to the sublime

If evaluation is to be useful for any of the purposes outlined in the previous chapter, it needs to develop new evidence that is both accurate and valid, that is, pertinent to the questions posed by the evaluation. The technical methods for doing this – the logic and rules of evidence governing evaluation that differentiate it from purely political or ideological debate – have been well developed over the last 30 years, and we need only briefly summarize them here.[1] However, because so many different activities call themselves evaluation, we describe what each of these approaches does and does not do. In particular, we clarify the kind of comparison that each method makes – sometimes explicitly, and sometimes (and more dangerously) implicitly – as part of its approach to the task.

Different methods of evaluation illuminate different stages in the amplified conception of the human capital development that is the aim of most VET programmes. The most sophisticated evaluations have concentrated on economic outcomes for individuals at Stage 4, particularly employment outcomes. However, certain purposes of evaluation require more information on the other three prior stages, which often requires different evaluation methods. Therefore we attempt to establish the links between evaluation methods and stages of cause and effect.

Despite the variety of activities that call themselves evaluation, the high ground has been occupied by outcome evaluations that use experimental methods and concentrate on a small number of employment-related outcomes. Such outcomes are surely among the most important results of VET programmes, and deserve priority over fluffier measures (such as satisfaction of participants with the programme). But we argue that, given the inevitable limitations of any one evaluation method, multiple approaches are desirable – particularly in order to use evaluation to improve the quality of programmes and to enhance public debate about VET. And when we consider developing countries, the counsel to undertake the most sophisticated evaluations is likely to be ignored, and so alternatives to rigorous – as well as expensive, technically demanding, and potentially misleading – evaluations of economic outcomes become even more necessary.

The first section considers the range of outcomes that evaluation research can and should embrace, followed by a discussion of their duration and variability across participants and by programme size. The various ways in which the evaluators may try to quantify what would have happened to participants in the absence of the programme is discussed in the third section. We then discuss the problem of establishing the effects of a programme as a whole, particularly when outcomes for individuals must be aggregated. The case for aggregating a programme's costs and benefits across both categories and years by way of cost-benefit analysis is then considered in the next section, along with the roles of the economic criteria of efficiency and equity within evaluation methods. Illustrative examples are provided as appropriate. The case for, and the methods of, evaluation at earlier stages, notably that of programme implementation, are considered in the penultimate section, followed by the conclusions.

Outcome measures: is variety the spice of life?

Because training programmes vary so much in their purposes, the outcomes that have been measured – or *could* be measured – vary as well. In practice, because VET programmes are concerned first and foremost with employment, the employment and pay of ex-participants have dominated the evaluation of remedial training, and productivity has been the dominant outcome for firm-sponsored training. But some of the most interesting results have come when evaluators have turned their attention to other measures, which we review in this chapter. More to the point, a more expansive view of what VET programmes *could* accomplish would lead to a broader variety of measures, which we outline as well. For our purposes, we can classify the different potential outcome measures according to the four stages of the amplified conception of human capital development outlined in Chapter 1, Why should VET work?

Individual outcomes: economic

By far the most common outcome measure has been the increase in earnings of participants – usually monthly or annual earnings, but in some cases hourly or weekly. Earnings have the advantage of being comparable across individuals, and over time (since earnings can be adjusted for inflation). In addition, earnings are comparable for different programmes, and so they can be used to compare the effectiveness of one approach over another, and to compare the effectiveness of different programmes.[2] Finally, changes in earnings are easily incorporated into cost-benefit analysis, whereas other potential outcomes – the stability of employment, for example, or job satisfaction – are much more difficult to value and compare with costs.

Evaluation research in the United Kingdom tends to distinguish regularly between the wage and employment components of earnings, eg the extent to which increases in annual earnings reflect increases in earning capacity (hourly wages) as opposed to job search and access to employment (hours worked per year). The distinction is particularly important for programmes that aim at significant increases in participant skills (eg France's *Contrat de Qualification* programme, whose participants aim to acquire a recognized vocational qualification).

For programmes whose goals are to emphasize not so much skills as labour force attachment and useful activity, outcomes tend to be predominantly employment-related outcomes. Commonly used indicators include the rate and incidence of employment, eg the share of ex-participants in work at a particular date, or the number of weeks participants have worked since leaving the programme. An example was the National Supported Work programme of 1975–81 in the United States, whose services to disadvantaged youths comprised primarily work experience and assisted job search (Couch, 1992).

The importance of employment measures is not only that remedial and retraining programmes aim to enhance employment rates; in addition, many results show that the benefits of remedial and retraining programmes come largely from enhancing the amount and stability of employment, not from increasing hourly wage rates. In addition, from some vantage points employment is by itself a valuable outcome, regardless of the wage level, since it keeps individuals occupied in some socially useful purposes, may lead to on-the-job training and advancement from even low-level jobs, reaffirms a social preference for work over idleness, and may reduce socially undesirable behaviour like crime.

At the same time, if a programme with serious training ambitions does not improve hourly earnings, it will be hard to call it a success even if it increases employment rates. Such a picture was painted by some interpretations of the British Youth Training Scheme in the 1980s (of which more below).

Employment-related outcomes other than earnings, employment and pay rates are used much less frequently. For example, an evaluation of the British Job Training Scheme of the mid-1980s examined 1) the occupations entered by trainees, in order to measure the fit with the occupations at which training had been aimed; and 2) job satisfaction, a measure of economic well-being quite distinct from earnings (Payne, 1990a, 1990b). Other aspects of the quality of employment are occasionally measured – occupational status scores, for example. It is unfortunate that the quality of employment is rarely evaluated, as it may be related to earnings growth and employment stability.

Individual outcomes: learning and skills

Most conceptions of human capital development assume that education and training develop the competencies of individuals enrolled in them. However, these competencies are rarely measured directly in evaluations – even for those programmes (such as remedial adult education) where preparation in basic literacy and mathematical skills is a central element.

There are a few exceptions, however. One study of a remedial education programme for welfare recipients in San Diego, California, examined their scores on the Test of Applied Literacy Skills (TALS), a test of simple reading ability and grammar (Martinson and Friedlander, 1994). Project STEP, an American programme for secondary students, intended to increase their basic academic skills, enhance employment, and reduce the risk of pregnancy, measured reading ability, mathematical ability, and knowledge about contraception (Grossman and Sipe, 1992; Walker and Vilella-Velez, 1992).

When evaluations have measured learning outcomes, the measures have been largely confined to standard tests of academic skills. Obvious though this approach may be, there are at least two serious problems with it. One is that standardized tests tend to measure relatively basic skills in reading, writing, and mathematics – certainly not 'higher-order' skills, such as problem-solving abilities, or the application of cognitive abilities to complex and ambiguous situations. The standardized multiple-choice tests on which such assessments rely are inappropriate for inducing VET programmes to enhance the high-performance skills that many policy-makers and employers in advanced countries have called for. The predominant approach to measuring such skills in the United States has thus far been limited to forms of 'authentic assessment' – including instructor evaluation of projects and portfolios – that are quite time-consuming, embedded in instruction, and difficult to make reliable across different instructors.

In addition, conventional academic tests ignore the fact that most VET programmes – except for the shortest and most job-specific programmes that emphasize a single skill – typically incorporate a broad variety of competencies that are critical to job performance. Vocational education, particularly at the post-secondary level, often includes literacy skills at relatively sophisticated levels, though they are usually job-related kinds of literacy (for example, the ability to look up information in manuals) that are not particularly 'academic'. Similarly, the mathematics taught may be quite applied, and poorly assessed through conventional tests. In addition, depending on the occupation involved,

VET programmes often incorporate: manual skills; visual abilities; the ability to work with others; communication skills of great variety; a broad range of other job-relevant information, including health and safety considerations, and the appropriate use of tools and machines; and a broad variety of 'lore', or informal information about relationships and procedures in real workplaces that may differ from the 'textbook' presentation in training programmes (Achtenhagen and Grubb, 1999). Indeed, successful on-the-job performance is usually dependent on the ability to combine these different abilities in the ways appropriate to particular jobs. But this range of abilities is often unrecognized, even by instructors; there is virtually no literature that describes the extent to which VET programmes consciously incorporate this range, and evaluation efforts in developed countries have traditionally ignored such outcomes.

Among possible learning outcomes, there are several that merit special consideration by those concerned with the well-being of individuals being trained. One of these is knowledge of health and safety conditions. VET instructors often pay special attention to the safe handling of tools and equipment, usually prior to students starting any workshop or work-based component of training, but whether they instruct students in the larger health and safety issues, for example, the hazards of various chemicals, the most prominent threats to safety on the job, or environmental threats, is unclear. Similarly, in the vocational programmes we have examined, occupational instructors typically ignore all aspects of industrial relations and workers' rights – even though vocational training provides unique opportunities ('teachable moments') to introduce these aspects of working life. An obvious question is whether this kind of explicit instruction has any effect, either in the knowledge individuals have (ie in Stage 2) or in behaviour on the job (Stage 3), as measured by accident rates, for example.

Often, as part of the process of enhancing the competencies of trainees, VET programmes encourage or require individuals to apply for particular credentials. The acquisition of such credentials is therefore an obvious outcome measure for evaluations. Thus the General Education Diploma, or GED, which is supposed to be the equivalent of a high school diploma in the United States, has been widely used to evaluate training programmes; the receipt of occupationally specific National Vocational Qualifications (NVQs) is increasingly serving the same purpose in England and Wales (and, in Scotland, SVQs), and craft (*Facharbeiter*) and higher (*Meister*) occupational skill examinations have done so in Germany. Elsewhere occupational licensing examinations could serve the same purpose. Because such examinations are based on various kinds of academic and vocational content, they can sometimes be interpreted as measuring learning outcomes.

In France, both apprentices and full-time secondary students prepare for the same public examinations of vocational knowledge and skill, including the vocational upper-secondary certificate, the *Baccalauréat Professionnel*. Lower pass rates for apprentices than for full-time students (*Ministère de l'Education Nationale*, 1995) might suggest that apprenticeship is the inferior method of learning but any such conclusion requires allowance for 1) the bias of formal examinations towards academic knowledge rather than practical competencies, which disfavours apprenticeship; and 2) any tendency for less able young people to be steered into apprenticeship rather than full-time studies (see section, Programme effects, below).

These different credentials are presumed to be useful outcome measures because they help individuals gain access to employment – that is, they measure competencies gained in Stage 2 that then facilitate employment in Stage 3. In some cases – particularly *Facharbeiter* examinations in Germany – this assumption proves warranted. However, in other cases, this assumption has been quite doubtful. For example, in the United States, the GED certificate is often interpreted by instructors as being equivalent to an eighth- or ninth-grade reading level, not to high school graduation, and its effect on employment and subsequent education is very small.[3]

The extent to which the recently developed system of NVQs in England and Wales (and SVQs in Scotland) provides a comprehensive, valid and reliable measures of job-related learning of use for evaluation purposes has been highly controversial. One problem is that many employers still make no use of NVQs (Robinson, 1996). A more basic difficulty is that the aspiration of the competence-oriented NVQ system to measure only skill outcomes, independently of methods of skill acquisition (Jessup, 1991), has been stymied in practice by high assessment costs, high variance of standards across assessors, and incentives to employers and trainees to certify inadequate learning as adequate (Prais, 1991; Wolf, 1995).

Thus the potential value of credentials as measures of learning achievements and skill outputs is difficult to realize in practice – so much so that it hardly features in the review of evaluation findings in Chapter 4. At the same time, when due allowance is made for such limitations and biases, the acquisition of such credentials can still constitute a potentially valuable ingredient within the wider evaluation of a training programme.

Other agents' outcomes

The outcome measures reviewed so far emphasize the outcomes for the individuals enrolled in education and training. The effects of VET on other individuals and organizations are less often evaluated. For example, a training programme might increase the productivity of individuals on the job without increasing earnings commensurately, thereby benefiting employers as well as workers.

The effects of training on productivity are difficult to measure. The standard approach to evaluation in business recommends that the outcomes of training on business practices be measured with attention to the causal stages involved (Kirkpatrick, 1994). In fact, the vast majority of employers' training evaluations are limited to assessments of the reactions of trainees to the programme; some assess effects on learning, and only a few examine effects on changing practices, including productivity (Plant and Ryan, 1992). Otherwise, evidence on the effects of training on productivity is available only indirectly, from case studies of job training (Jones, 1986), surveys of employer training costs (Ryan, 1991a), and statistical comparisons of productivity in matched plants and sectors (Prais, 1995).

Welfare and social programmes

Because many remedial programmes try to move individuals off welfare, the amount of welfare payments, or continued participation in welfare and other social benefit programmes, are often used as outcome measures. Similarly, a series of experiments in the United States has examined the effects of different subsidies on the length of time that an individual claims unemployment insurance benefits (Meyer, 1995). The relationship between these measures and earnings or employment depends on the institutional details of welfare programmes, of course. If welfare programmes allow individuals to stay on welfare even as their earnings increase moderately, VET programmes may increase earnings without reducing the likelihood of being on welfare. Conversely, if falling welfare payments result from increases in earnings, then a remedial programme may reduce welfare payments and thereby benefit taxpayers, but increase earnings only marginally and actually leave participants no better off – as Project Independence in Florida did.[4] For those concerned more with the well-being of participants than with savings to taxpayers, these are distressing results. However, the methodological point is that the evaluation provided sufficient evidence to reveal this outcome, rather than (for example) collecting evidence only about individual earnings, or only about welfare payments.

Social outcomes

As noted in Chapter 1, Targets of education and training, training programmes – particularly remedial training programmes – may be designed to reduce undesirable social phenomena, such as criminal behaviour and drug use, by providing individuals with employment that then improves other aspects of their behaviour. Youth programmes in particular have often measured these non-economic outcomes. For example, the evaluation of the Job Training Partnership Act (JTPA) in the United States, a remedial training programme, examined arrest rates for youth, as did the evaluation of JOBSTART, an experimental programme for secondary school drop-outs age 17 to 21, and the early evaluation of Job Corps, an intensive residential programme for youth. The JOBSTART evaluation also examined the drug use of those enrolled, hoping that improved prospects of employment would reduce drug use.[5]

For women, sexual behaviour and teenage pregnancy have been greater concerns, since young women who become pregnant without being married tend to stay on welfare for long periods of time. Therefore the JOBSTART evaluation examined whether young women in the programme ever became pregnant and whether they ever gave birth within four years after the programme. Similarly, the evaluation of New Chance, an experimental programme focusing on young mothers, asked those enrolled (as well as a control group) about pregnancies, births, abortions, and levels of sexual activity with and without contraception.

The importance of multiple outcomes

Of course, there is no reason why the various outcomes of a training programme should all go in the same direction – all positive, for example, or all negative. For example, the New Chance programme did increase rates of participation in various kinds of education, training, and life skills classes, and increased the receipt of high school equivalency diplomas (GEDs); but it decreased earnings, increased the stress levels experienced by participants, and increased homelessness problems (Quint, Bos, and Polit, 1997). Some of these results are puzzling, but they clarify the importance of collecting information about multiple outcomes.

A more dramatic example is Florida's Project Independence, an effort to move welfare recipients off welfare and into financial independence. The programme did increase employment rates and it increased earnings over two years by US$227 dollars – a statistically significant but trifling amount. But it decreased welfare payments by US$265, so welfare recipients participating in the programme were made worse off in terms of overall income.

This brief survey of possible outcome measures clarifies how incomplete most evaluations have been. The emphasis on employment-related individual outcomes is understandable, given the motives behind all forms of training, but it has had the effect of neglecting the causal links in VET programmes, particularly the effects of programmes on learning and on characteristics that enable trainees to be hired. Similarly, the emphasis on employment outcomes reflects the relatively specific goals of *training* (as compared to *education*), but that has in turn reinforced the notion that training programmes should be relatively unconcerned with non-economic outcomes.

One obvious recommendation is therefore to expand the kinds of outcome measures collected in evaluations. In many cases, it would be better to gather other indicators in informal and low-cost ways, like informal interviews, to have at least some information about the process by which a programme might work, rather than to emphasize more rigorous evaluation that provides no information about a broader array of outcomes. Particularly if evaluation is to be used to improve the quality of programmes, an array of measures is important for assessing what might be changed.

Programme effects: duration and heterogeneity

When a set of outcome categories appropriate to the evaluation task has been selected, two further problems arise: over what period can and should outcomes be measured, and should a uniform programme effect be assumed?

Duration of outcomes

The issue can be illustrated in relation to the training content of the various labour market programmes on which evaluation research has concentrated. Some programmes are established to solve short-run problems, eg the absorption of former East Germans into the German economy, or the unemployment caused by NAFTA in the United States, or other temporary or cyclical unemployment. In these cases, short-run outcomes are appropriate, and the political process needs to know quickly if these programmes work.

But most programmes have been established to address systemic and enduring problems such as unemployment, poverty, or the difficult transition of certain youth into work. These require long-term solutions, not short-run effects, and any attempt to develop coherent systems of institutions would require a long-run perspective. Therefore a central question is whether programmes have short-term effects that then decline – for example, because the learning in the programme becomes obsolete, or because the programme provides a push into employment (such as through job search assistance) without teaching any skills useful in the longer run, or because individuals in remedial training lack the skills necessary to keep jobs after they get them – or whether a programme puts an individual on an employment path where responsibility, on-the-job learning, and earnings increase over time. Most evaluations in the United States have measured earnings between 18 and 30 months after the programme ended; in the few evaluations that extended the time period to five and six years or beyond, the benefits tend to fall and become insignificant, particularly in years four and five,[6] suggesting that the appearance of earnings increases 18 to 30 months after a programmes ends may be misleading. In contrast, the effects of conventional education programmes on earnings prove not only substantial but also sustained over the working life, as do those of firm-based upgrade training.

Differences between short-run and long-run outcomes may also generate inappropriate conclusions about the types of VET programmes that are the most effective. For example, programmes relying on job search assistance and other methods of getting individuals into employment quickly may have positive short-term results but no long-term results. Conversely, programmes that give individuals extensive education or training have negative short-term results (because individuals earn less while enrolled in VET) but may have more positive long-term results – just as evaluations of conventional education programmes indicate that the benefits of education may take several years to materialize.[7] Several reviews of the evaluation literature have concluded that job search assistance is more cost-effective than more intensive education and training (at least for remedial purposes), but these findings are based on short-term evaluations;[8] the longer-term prospects of job search assistance are poor, and while short-term job training programmes have been no more effective, more intensive VET programmes – those typically considered vocational education – might have better long-term results.

The differences between short-term and long-term outcomes suggest that the competencies necessary for *finding* jobs are not necessarily the same as those for *keeping* jobs. The skills required to find jobs are presumably the competencies necessary on the job, including certain general academic abilities as well as the specific vocational skills built into the design of any VET programme. The difficulty in *staying* employed over longer periods of time may reflect the design of the programme, particularly if it targets jobs that are quite unstable, or where employment varies substantially over the business cycle; thus an important question in understanding why short-run and long-run outcomes may differ is to understand whether the basic conception of the programme, and the jobs it targets, are appropriate or not. But in addition, the skills required to keep jobs may include the ability to get along with co-workers, supervisors, and customers; the ability to understand what a job requires, and to respond appropriately; the flexibility to learn more as job requirements change over periods of months and years; the willingness to show up on time and to put up with the undesirable aspects of most jobs. These are quite different from the academic and vocational skills embedded in most VET programmes, and they are never incorporated into evaluations except for the rare qualitative assessments based on interviews (eg Quint *et al.*, 1994b). The short-term focus of most training programmes therefore skews both the skills they impart and the evaluations carried out.

Variations in effects

The outcomes reviewed in the previous section usually describe the effects of training on individuals in terms of the *average* effect. A different question concerns the *variation* in outcomes across participants; another, whether the programme's effects decline as it gets larger, with the *marginal* effect less than the average.

If, for example, a few individuals benefit substantially from a programme, while most do not benefit or even suffer (eg because they remain out of the labour force), then the average effect might be positive even though the majority of participants did not benefit. Examining the variation in outcomes is technically more difficult than examining the average effect. The usual regression formulation assumes that the programme has a common effect on all participants within the group in question, overlaid by a normal distribution of a set of miscellaneous random influences on individual outcomes. Differentiation is therefore most easily allowed for by estimating the effect of a programme within different groups and comparing the results across groups, for example, by sex, age or schooling level. Evaluations of American programmes tend to find that remedial VET programmes are more effective for adult females than for youths, for example (Bloom *et al.*, 1997).

More detailed findings suggest a 'triage' process, in which programmes are least effective for the best-prepared individuals, who can find employment on their own, and also for the most disadvantaged individuals, who have problems too serious and varied for most programmes to resolve. Those programmes are therefore most effective for the group in the middle.[9] Such results cannot reveal all dimensions about the variability of a programme's effects, but they can pick up differences among the most important groups of participants.

The possibility that a programme's effects vary with its size is often a matter of interest: how big should it aim to be? A small programme may fail to benefit from economies of scale; a large programme may suffer from an induced saturation in the labour market facing ex-participants. The issue bears particularly upon a striking difference between labour market programmes in the United States and Europe. In the United States, programmes typically serve only a fraction of those who meet their eligibility criteria; in Europe, programmes typically cater to the majority of eligibles, and, in the case such youth programmes as Britain's Youth Training, sometimes guarantee access to all interested eligibles.

The extent to which increasing a programme's coverage changes its effectiveness remains an under-researched issue (Friedlander *et al.*, 1997). What can be said is that the similarities in the evaluation findings for American and European programmes that differ more in scale than content suggest that the content of those programmes appears to matter more for their outcomes than does their scale of operation (see Chapter 4).

The challenge of comparison: what would otherwise have been?

After determining the outcomes to be measured, evaluation focuses on the extent to which those outcomes differ from what they would have been had the training not taken place. The problem is to establish *what would otherwise have occurred* – technically, *the counter-factual.*

In this section we discuss with examples the main ways of addressing that problem, starting with economic outcomes, primarily those for individual workers, which are the focus of most evaluation research in practice. The evaluation methods reviewed here do, however, apply in principle to all three categories of VET sponsorship (public, employer and individual), to all points along the spectrum between vocational education and on-the-job training, and to effects on skill learning and behaviour as well as economic outcomes (see Chapter 1).

The examples mostly concern the economic effects of publicly sponsored education and training for young workers, referring frequently to the British Youth Training Scheme in the 1980s. The number, variety and limitations of attempts to evaluate that programme usefully illustrate our approach to evaluation.

That approach is pragmatic and context specific. It is pragmatic in that we emphasize the limitations of all approaches to evaluation, taken individually, and the importance of using multiple approaches when possible. Abandoning as unrealistic the ideal of perfect data, we emphasize the need to live with imperfect evidence. We therefore reject the standard dichotomies between 'scientific' and 'non-scientific', and between 'experimental' and 'non-experimental' approaches to evaluation (eg Dar and Gill, 1995a; Heckman, 1993), preferring to think of scientific merit and experimental status as continuous attributes that in social science can never attain the scientific ideal of laboratory science.

Our approach is context-specific in that it refers to the position of many developing and transition economies, where data scarcity deters evaluation efforts but where what we term 'weakly experimental' methods may still yield useful information.

The problem of determining what would have happened to ex-trainees had they not received training – *what would otherwise have been* – arises because the same individual cannot be observed simultaneously both with training and without training (Heckman and Smith, 1996). Some way has therefore to be found to estimate the experiences of trainees had they not undertaken training. The problem can be approached in many ways. The most popular options are listed in Table 3.1, categorized according to how closely they approximate the experimental conditions employed by laboratory-based science – that is, how effectively they vary the variable of interest (here, training received) while holding constant other influences (like education and ability).[10]

The discussion starts with quantitative methods, beginning with the unsophisticated methods near the end of Table 3.1. The informational limitations of successive approaches are outlined as the discussion climbs the ladder of methodological sophistication to the informationally more demanding approaches at the top of Table 3.1.

Table 3.1 Evaluation methods for economic outcomes, establishing what would have happened in absence of a training programme

	Category	Method	Comparison Category	Evaluation Example
1	Highly experimental	Measure mean difference in outcomes	Randomly Allocated Non-participants	US: New Chance
2a	Quasi-experimental	Adjust outcomes by regression; measure adjusted mean difference	Individuals in standard micro datasets	US: post-secondary Vocational education
2b		Same, with Heckman correction	Same	UK:YTS
2c		Same, with fixed effects correction	Same	UK and US: apprenticeship
3a	Weakly experimental	Measure mean outcome difference relative to:	Participants' own past	Sweden: public training
3b			Similar age group(s)	Sweden: youth programmes
3c			Opposite sex	France: public training
3d			Participants in other programmes	France: VET diplomas
3e			Similar groups in other countries	EU: apprenticeship and employment
3f			Participants' views	UK: YTS
3g			Informed opinion	UK: Investors in People
4	Non-experimental	Measure gross outcomes	None	UK: YTS

Notes: EU: European Union; UK: United Kingdom; US: United States

Quantitative evaluation methods range from the non-experimental to the highly experimental. The least ambitious is what we term the *non-experimental*, which is limited to the recording of gross outcomes. The outcomes in question are typically the employment rates and pay achieved by participants, as surveyed either on leaving the programme or not long thereafter. For example, in Great Britain, the proportion of ex-trainees who attain a 'positive outcome', defined as any condition other than unemployment, and particular more detailed outcomes, such as being in employment, is routinely recorded for the major public training programmes (see Box 3.1). Evidence on gross outcomes has been particularly influential in France, with its long tradition of research into links between young people's qualifications in VET and subsequent employment rates (Affichard, 1981). Simple tracer studies, in which the labour market experiences of ex-trainees are recorded over time, are a popular variant in developing countries (ZIMFEP, 1991).

Box 3.1   Non-experimental evaluation: gross outcomes

Youth Training Scheme (Great Britain)

The Youth Training Scheme of 1983–94 entitled all unemployed 16–17-year-old workers to a programme of training and work experience lasting up to two years. Typically, at least one-fifth of a trainee's time was spent in off-the-job training, the rest in OJT and work experience. Although training plans were formally required, in practice employers faced few restrictions on the use of trainees. Publicly funded training allowances amounted to around 35 per cent of average youth pay. Participating employers received a moderate training grant per trainee. At its 1989 peak, 16 per cent of young people entered YTS (Ryan, 1991a; Dolton *et al.*, 1994b).

Government publications regularly reported the destinations of those leaving YTS, including the proportion of ex-trainees who 1) attained a job; and 2) gained a vocational qualification, or a credit towards one. During 1987-93 the former fluctuated around 50 per cent, the latter around 30 per cent. As no account is taken of the outcomes which participants would have achieved had they not entered YTS, it is impossible to gauge the scheme's success from such data.

Source: DE (1994), p.10

The problem with gross outcomes as measures of success is that, as no explicit estimate of what *would otherwise have been* is made, they indicate little or nothing about the effects of the programme (Simpson, 1990). One interpretation would be to treat *any* favourable employment outcome as evidence of success, but that would be to assume – implausibly – that without training all participants would have remained unemployed. Such methods therefore have little to offer to the task of evaluation, unless there are clear and widely accepted standards of comparison against which to judge the results, or unless the gross outcomes prove so low – for example, few or no trainees found a job – that the programme must be judged a failure because outcomes in the absence of the programme could not have been significantly worse.

The informational weakness of gross outcomes for evaluation purposes is underlined by American-based evidence of low correlations between such short-term indicators and the findings of evaluation methods proper that seek evidence on the counter-factual and measure outcomes over a longer period (Geraci, 1984; Doolittle *et al.*, 1993).

Gross outcomes are potentially more useful for administrative purposes, as part of performance management and, indeed, are often termed performance measures, reflecting their potential role in a programme's management. The short-term 'success' of a programme's implementation from area to area can be assessed against national standards, and local administrators rewarded accordingly. Even in that context, however, informational problems limit the usefulness of gross outcomes: gross outcomes vary from place to place according not only to managerial effort and quality but also according to attributes of participants and local labour markets that are difficult for central programme administration to measure and control for (see Chapter 2).

The next category of evaluation method is the *weakly experimental*. This approach has merit in that it does at least raise, implicitly or explicitly, the question of what would otherwise have been, unlike the non-experimental methods that never raise that question. The estimate of the counter-factual is typically based on the experiences of a comparison group. Common choices of comparison group include: nearby age groups; the opposite sex; participants in other programmes; similar groups in other countries; and participants themselves before entering the programme, ie simple before/after comparisons in which it is assumed that in the absence of the programme nothing would have changed for its participants over time. Alternatively, participants themselves may be asked whether they think their position has improved as a result of training; or informed opinion may be asked whether it judges the programme to have worked. Examples of all seven approaches are provided in Box 3.2.

Box 3.2   Weakly experimental evaluation

Comparison groups are used, chosen on 'rough and ready' grounds, with little or no attempt to control for differences between the groups or for other influences on the outcomes attained by the two groups. The examples of various ways of inferring *what would otherwise have been* (Table 3.1, lines 3a to 3g) include:

a. Before/after comparisons. The difference between participants' earnings before and after participation in public training was taken as the effect of training. The private and the social returns to training were both judged positive and substantial. *Source:* Axelsson and Löfgren (1992).

b. Other age groups. The effect of four public programmes on the unemployment of 16–19-year-old Swedes in the 1980s was assessed by comparison to the unemployment rate of 20–24-year-olds, who were not offered comparable assistance. The fall in the 16–19-year-old relative unemployment rate was interpreted as evidence that the programmes 'served their purpose'. *Source:* Jonzon and Wise (1989).

c. Opposite sex. The effect of public programmes upon young French females was considered by comparison to outcomes for male participants. Lower rates of transition to employment amongst females were taken as evidence that the programmes were failing young women. *Source:* Chevalier and Silberman (1988).

d. Participants in other programmes. The effect of various VET qualifications on young people's chances of unemployment in France during 1973–9 was studied by comparing unemployment rates across diploma levels. In 1979, but not 1973, the possession of higher diplomas was associated with lower unemployment risk, leading to the conclusion that by 1979 more training meant lower unemployment risk. *Source:* Affichard (1981).

e. Other countries. The effect of apprenticeship training on the employment of 16–19-year-olds in European Union countries was studied by comparing apprentice numbers, youth relative pay and youth employment shares across countries. Apprenticeship training was found to raise youth employment rates, even when apprentices were excluded. *Source:* Marsden and Ryan (1991a).

f. Participants' views. The value of training under YTS (see Box 3.1, above) in Great Britain was assessed by asking participants to assess its merits. The high proportion that rated the experience favourably suggested that the scheme had succeeded. *Source:* TA (1989).

> **g. Informed opinion.** The effectiveness of Investors in People (IIP), a government programme which encourages British employers to adopt national procedures and standards for their training, was evaluated by asking representatives of 24 employers in four regions about their reasons for seeking or avoiding IIP recognition. Many employers showed low awareness of IIP; others, concern that obtaining IIP recognition was too arduous. In the absence of an explicit counterfactual, it is difficult to assess the conclusion that 'IIP has made significant progress' (p.i).
>
> *Source*: Rix *et al.* (1994)

The limitations of weakly experimental methods are marked. The difficulty is suggested by the category's descriptor. It is as if, in a laboratory science, the laboratory facilities were so ramshackle that all sorts of extraneous influences on the outcome of an experiment (eg temperature, noise, atmospheric pressure) varied uncontrollably, making it hard to distinguish the effects of the experimental variable itself.

In training evaluation, the problem takes the form of differences between participants and the comparison group that are potentially important for the outcome in question. The problem is magnified by the tendency to compare the fortunes of participants and non-participants at group rather than individual level and without use of statistical techniques to try and remove the effects of inter-group differences. For example, before/after comparisons use participants' own previous situations to suggest what would otherwise have been. The problem is that the labour market may have changed – let us assume improved – during the duration of the programme, making it easier for trainees to find jobs or to earn higher pay independently of training. By making their previous labour market position an overly pessimistic guide to what would otherwise have been, the before/after comparison results then in an overly favourable estimate of the effects of the training. In the absence of a separate comparison group, no correction can be made for such influences.

As weakly experimental methods do not generally correct for such distortions, they implicitly assume them to be unimportant, that is, they assume that, in the absence of training, the experience of the comparison group would have been the same as that of the trainees. The limitations of that assumption may be severe. Consider again the simple before/after comparison. Its usefulness, for the evaluation of public remedial programmes at least, is widely impaired by a second problem: a widespread tendency for trainees' earnings to dip before training, eg as a result of lower employment rates – one reason why many participated in the first place. The effects of training tend therefore to be overestimated by before/after comparisons (Ashenfelter and Card, 1985). Similarly, given intense occupational segregation between the sexes, the outcomes that would have been experienced by females in the absence of training are unlikely to be the same as those which actually faced males in the absence of training.

These weaknesses have led many evaluation experts to neglect weakly experimental methods. We demur, finding some of them potentially valuable for three reasons. First, they offer potentially valuable information: given, as will be found below, that no one method provides conclusive evidence, a variety of sources of information helps paint a fuller picture. Moreover, the list of potential comparisons stretches beyond those in Table 3.1. For example, an evaluation of a training programme in a particular industry in a developing country (eg furniture) might glean some information on what would otherwise have been from either outcomes in the same sector in a similar country or those in a different sector (eg clothing) in the same country.

Second, the informational content of weakly experimental methods may be increased by imitating quasi-experimental methods (see below). For example, the informational content of international comparisons can be improved by drawing on the 'fixed effects' approach to econometric modelling. When an international comparison considers changes in, rather than levels of, national outcomes, it abstracts from the effects of any national attributes, such as culture and institutions, that may be presumed not to have changed significantly over time (Marsden and Ryan, 1991b).

Similarly, other sources of information may help to reduce biases caused by underlying differences between participant and comparison groups. For example, when a before/after comparison is threatened by changes in labour market tightness, other evidence on the labour market, such as unemployment and vacancies, may provide a guide to how the market changed during the period and the likely severity of bias in the results.

Finally, given these attributes, weakly experimental methods may be particularly valuable in developing and transitional economies, where data are scarce and more sophisticated methods may be impossible to implement. The partial evidence produced by weakly experimental methods is better than no evidence, and better than non-experimental methods, such as simply enumerating gross outcomes (see Box 3.1).[11]

At the same time, it is often possible to address the informational limitations of weakly experimental methods by using better data and econometric methods. *Quasi-experimental methods* do both in the attempt to control for potentially disturbing influences on outcomes. Standard datasets, representative of individual workers, are often used to pick a comparison group of non-participants whose experiences provide the backdrop against which the effects of training on participants are estimated. Regression analysis is applied to the pooled participant and comparison groups, relating the outcomes of interest (pay, employment status, etc) to relevant individual attributes (schooling, other training, experience, etc) and training status. The coefficient on the training status variable then provides an estimate of the average effect of training upon participants. The approach is termed quasi-experimental because it applies statistical analysis instead of setting up a social experiment.

The approach is exemplified by the 'earnings function', a key tool in the vast statistical literature, associated with human capital theory, that relates participation in education and training to earnings over the life-cycle (Mincer, 1974). Research into the effects of vocational education on individual careers, in developed and developing countries alike, relies heavily on such techniques. An example is provided in Box 3.3.

Box 3.3   Quasi-experimental evaluation 1

Vocational education, earnings functions (United States)

Much pre-employment VET takes place in community colleges, technical institutes and proprietary trade schools. Its effects have been estimated by regressing subsequent labour earnings on education (years, type, degrees and length of time for drop-outs) and other personal characteristics, including race, sex, disability, family background and experience. The technique implicitly compares individuals with post-secondary VET to those with secondary education only. The data came from a national random sample of employees aged 25 to 65.

The results confirmed the economic benefits to participants of two-year Associate Degrees and one-year certificates, particularly for those who complete programmes in business and technical fields (for men) and health occupations (for women). The benefits are substantially higher for individuals who find employment in fields related to their education, while the benefits of occupational education in unrelated employment are often close to zero.

Source: Grubb (1997)

Quasi-experimental techniques are particularly attractive in using explicit controls for the non-training differences between participants and members of the comparison group that may cause the outcomes achieved by the two groups to differ independently of training, which addresses the main failing of weakly experimental methods. But distorting influences can rarely be removed by simple regression analysis. The problem that impedes them is selection bias: the distortion arising from potentially important but unobserved differences between participants and non-participants. As those differences are not observed by the evaluator, their effects on outcomes cannot be controlled by simple regression analysis, limited as it is to observed differences between individuals. The extent to which differences in outcomes between participants and comparators (after controlling for their observed differences, in schooling, etc) reflect the effect of the programme as opposed to unobserved differences, remains unknown (Barnow *et al.*, 1980). For example, the estimated benefits of two-year vocational programmes (see Box 3.3) might really be generated by differences in the ability and motivation between the typical two-year post-secondary programme graduate and the typical high school graduate who takes no further schooling, rather than by the training itself.

Two factors make selection bias a serious problem. First, a range of individual attributes that are potentially important for labour market outcomes – including ability, motivation, schooling quality and family background – are typically measured only incompletely or not at all by evaluators, and therefore cannot be used as statistical control variables. Although some evaluators envisage a statistical world in which measures have been developed of almost all individual attributes, that happy state is at best a distant prospect even for the home of mass datasets, the United States, let alone for the typical developing country. The measurement of individual qualities may be compared to seeing an iceberg from above rather than below the surface: only the tip is visible, most of its bulk remaining out of sight.

Second, participation in training is likely to be associated with the same unmeasured individual attributes. Selection for training may be based on such attributes. For example, programme administrators or employers may be able to observe them and allocate places according to them (eg when an employer gives training only to the more able within a pool of eligible employees). Alternatively, trainees may know their own qualities and self-select accordingly, whether consciously (eg judging oneself sufficiently able to gain enough from training to make it worthwhile) or unconsciously (eg more motivated individuals being the more prone to take training). Selection effects may be negative (as when a public agency directs remedial training towards the less able and motivated) or positive (as when an employer picks the more able and motivated for on-the-job training). To remove the effect on outcomes of differences in measured attributes alone is then insufficient to establish the effects of training without bias.

For example, the low wage gains apparently associated with training in early statistical evaluations of American public programmes were often 'explained away' by those programmes' supporters as downward biased, on the presumption that (unmeasured) ability and motivation were lower for trainees than for the individuals to whom they were compared, cancelling out benefits and making an effective programme appear ineffective (Levitan and Johnston, 1975). In reality, however, simple quasi-experimental evaluations of remedial training are often upwardly biased because the individuals who enrol in and complete programmes are more motivated, and have fewer barriers to employment, than similar individuals who fail to enrol or who drop out before completing them.

Great ingenuity has been devoted to the removal of selection bias. One line of attack is to improve the sophistication of quasi-experimental methods; the other, to switch to social experiments (see below). The two approaches are now discussed in turn.

Within the quasi-experimental approach, two lines of attack on selection bias predominate: two-step methods and fixed effects models.[12] Two-step methods (or 'Heckman corrections') seek indirect evidence on unmeasured personal qualities, in the participant and comparison groups alike, from other evidence. It is assumed that participation in training reflects unobserved characteristics, such as greater ability or motivation, as well as observed ones, such as years of schooling. Two relationships are estimated. The first is the participation function, seeking to explain the fact that participants participated and members of the comparison group did not. The part of the participation decision that cannot be explained statistically by observed individual attributes (ie the regression's residuals) is then converted into an independent variable for use in an outcome regression, in which pay (employment rates, etc) is explained in terms of observable attributes and this proxy for unmeasured individual qualities.[13] Under particular assumptions, the outcome regression is purged of selection bias. In the case of the British Youth Training Scheme in the 1980s, one application of two-step methods suggested that correction for selection bias radically improves the interpretation of the programme's effects – from failure to ineffectiveness, though not to success (in terms of its training goals at least; see Box 3.4).

A second line of attack on selection bias uses 'fixed effects' models. The *change* in outcomes associated with training is assumed to be unaffected by unmeasured personal attributes, drawing on the assumption that the person before training is the same in all relevant respects – except exposure to training – as the same individual after training. The same assumption underlay the simple before/after comparisons that were encountered above in the weakly experimental category (see Box 3.2). Two problems were noted in that context: that the outside world may have changed between the 'before' and the 'after', and that the 'before' situation may be exceptionally unfavourable for participants in particular. Fixed effects models deal with the former problem by changing the comparison group from the 'participants in the past' to a group that does not participate at all; and by comparing the change in the outcome variable in the two groups. For example, if the economy improves, pay and employment rates will rise in the comparison group and that change can be used to suggest what would have happened to participants had they not entered training. The effect of the programme is then estimated as the 'difference in differences': the difference between the changes in outcomes experienced by participants and non-participants. The estimate is made after prior correction for differences in observable attributes across the two groups, on the assumption that even if selection into training depends on differences in unobservable attributes, the effect of those attributes on outcomes falls out as a result of the double differencing (Ashenfelter and Card, 1985). An evaluation of in-service employee training using a fixed effects model is described in Box 3.5.

Box 3.4   Quasi-experimental evaluation 2: Two-step methods

Youth Training Scheme (Great Britain)

The effects of prior participation in YTS (see Box 3.1) were estimated by regression analysis of weekly earnings in a nationally representative survey of 19–20-year-old young British workers in spring 1986. Observable differences in personal attributes (years of schooling, experience, etc) were controlled directly using a standard earnings function relating pay to participation in training (eg Box 3.3). Participation in YTS was estimated to *reduce* subsequent pay by a statistically significant 10 per cent.

But does that estimate reflect the selection of less able or motivated workers into YTS rather than damage done by the scheme? The question was addressed using two-step methods. In the first step, regression relationships between individual participation in YTS – and, for good measure, prior employment – and observable individual attributes were estimated. The unexplained variance in those regressions was converted into two proxies for unobserved individual attributes, for example, the possibility that less able young people had gone into YTS or had found a job before doing so, given schooling, etc. Those proxy variables were then introduced into an earnings function in order to represent the influence of any unobserved attributes. Participation in YTS was then estimated to have had no significant effect on pay, suggesting that the programme's apparently negative effect in a simple earnings function arose from unseen selection processes – or, in the author's preferred reading, from the success of the programme's efforts to cut the pay aspirations of young workers – rather than from any damage done to human capital. At the same time there was no evidence of improvements in participants' skills from enrolling in YTS.

Source: O'Higgins (1995), Table 3.2

Although researchers who adopt either two-step or fixed effects methods often claim to have 'controlled' for selection bias, such claims should be viewed sceptically. Both methods require restrictive assumptions. The efficacy of two-step methods is limited by 1) the potentially large component of labour quality, potentially relevant to both participation and outcomes, that remains unmeasured in standard micro datasets; and 2) the restrictions required concerning both the distribution of disturbances and the variables that can be included in the outcome and participation equations. Moreover, the effect of such corrections often proves small, even when powerful selection processes may be presumed to have been present.

Box 3.5   Fixed effects model

Youth training at work in the United Kingdom and the United States

The effects of employer-sponsored training on the pay of non-college graduates in the United Kingdom and the United States were studied using two large national datasets to create representative samples of employees aged 23 years (United Kingdom) and 25 years (United States). The prior training reported by interviewees was analysed with a fixed effects model, which assumed that 'self-selection varies only across individuals and not over time for a particular individual'. The change in pay between first job and current job was regressed upon the receipt of training and changes in other potentially relevant measured attributes, including disability, marital status, union membership and local unemployment rates. The effects of unchanging personal attributes, both measured (eg years of schooling) and unmeasured (eg motivation) fall out by assumption. The study found that training in general, and apprenticeship in particular, generated pay gains for participants, particularly when associated with acquiring a vocational qualification, and more for males than for females.

Source: Blanchflower and Lynch (1994)

The fixed effects approach assumes in particular that unmeasured personal attributes are 1) invariant over time; and 2) independent of the programme in determining outcomes. Its results typically prove sensitive to the point at which the 'before' state is measured, and, when that is close to the start date, the extent to which the standard pre-programme dip in participants' earnings is taken to be transitory, and therefore disregarded, or permanent, and therefore taken as given.

The results of both approaches have been shown to be painfully sensitive to choice of both identifying assumptions and membership of the comparison group (LaLonde, 1986; Fraker and Maynard, 1987; Friedlander and Robins, 1995). The same programme has been evaluated variously as a failure or a success according to the evaluator's choices in these key areas. Efforts to improve the accuracy of quasi-experimental methods have concentrated upon two options. First, specification tests are used to try to rule out inappropriate assumptions about outcome-generating mechanisms. Second, non-participants are selected statistically so as to match individual participants as closely as possible, in terms of both geographical location and personal qualities, and thereby to reduce the disparities between the two groups with which regression analysis must grapple (Heckman, 1993; Heckman and Hotz, 1989).[14]

The power of such procedures to resolve the weaknesses of econometric evaluation has been challenged (Friedlander and Robins, 1995). The prospect for truly removing selection bias – as opposed either to escalating the technical complexity of the analysis or to just lodging blandly the standard claim that it has been 'controlled for' – remains limited, and with it the contribution of even the most sophisticated econometric evaluation methods.

Recognition of the difficulty of removing selection bias by econometric methods favours *highly experimental methods*, or social experiments. The social experiment is the social science equivalent of the clinical trial in medical sciences. Individuals eligible for and interested in training are randomly allocated between two groups, the first of which is given the training (the 'treatment' group), the second of which is not (the 'placebo' or control group). The difference in mean outcomes between the two groups is then, in large samples, a good (unbiased) estimator of the effects of the training. Econometric correction is often undertaken for any differences in observables between treatment and control groups, but in large samples the differences become trivial under truly random assignment. The scope for unobserved attributes to generate selection bias is removed by random selection into training.

Social experiments nowadays dominate the evaluation of labour market programmes in the United States. An example is provided by the principal evaluation of the New Chance programme for young welfare mothers (see Box 3.6).

The predominance of social experiments reflects an orthodoxy – especially in the United States – which holds that *only* random assignment evaluations generate meaningful results, given the sensitivity of quasi-experimental methods to data and assumptions, as noted above. Some have inferred accordingly that only experimental results can be trusted.

At the same time, controversy over the merits of econometrics and social experiments has made it clear that neither can identify perfectly the counter-factual. Social experiments themselves face difficulties serious enough for it to be appropriate to categorize them as 'highly experimental', not 'fully experimental' nor simply 'experimental'.

Box 3.6   Highly experimental evaluation: social experiment

New Chance (United States)

New Chance, conducted at 16 sites between 1989 and 1992, served mothers aged 16 to 22 and receiving public income support; almost all were high-school drop-outs. A range of support, health and job-finding services was provided in addition to remedial education and job training. The programme offered up to 30 hours of services weekly for up to 18 months, well beyond the norm for American remedial programmes.

The programme evaluation involved the randomized allocation of eligible women either to participation or to an 'untreated' control group. Programme effects were estimated by the difference in mean outcomes between the two groups, in terms of employment, earnings, educational achievement, public welfare support, fertility, physical and mental health, the behaviour of their children, and various attitudinal measures. Effects, measured 3 1/2 years after entering the programme, were found to be favourable only for educational achievement. As the credential involved (the GED certificate) has little economic value and as other effects were essentially zero, the programme could not be called a success.

A separate, implementation-oriented, qualitative evaluation is described in Box 3.12, below.

Source: Quint *et al.* (1994a, 1994b, 1997)

The fundamental problem is that social experiments cannot achieve in practice the purity of the laboratory ideal. Just as the placebo effect impairs clinical trials, so in social experiments it is often found that many non-participants have gained access to services similar, even identical, to those given to participants. The evaluation then captures at best the effects of the difference between the average amounts of training received by the two groups, not those of training as opposed to no training (Kempel, Friedlander and Fellerath, 1995). There is also the problem that some of those who are randomly assigned to training drop out at various stages along the path from assignment through enrolment and participation to completion. As the attrition is unlikely to be random, selection biases can be expected when the evaluation compares outcomes for participants and non-participants (Heckman and Smith, 1996). Moreover, even when there is random assignment to programmes as a whole, participants may be non-randomly assigned to particular services so that overall effectiveness is influenced by various selection and self-selection effects. And the selection of sites for an evaluation study is unlikely to be random, given the well-known reluctance of many administrators to assign to training on a random basis.

Second, when a difference between outcomes for the treatment group and the control group is found, the reasons for it may not be apparent, and it may be necessary to supplement experimental methods with either econometric research or qualitative research in order to investigate mechanisms.

Third, social experiments tend to be restricted to public programmes, since employers and individuals do not readily accept randomized allocation in any training they sponsor. There are similar problems in public training, too. The ethical and political acceptability of refusing training to some when offering it to others is widely questioned, particularly in Europe. Such considerations encourage programmes to cater to all eligible individuals, in which case random assignment becomes impossible. In the United States, examples include whole-school reform, vocational education in secondary schooling and the devolution of programme responsibility to states and communities.

Finally, social experiments are costly to undertake and slow to yield results. It is not possible to start an evaluation during the life of a programme, turning to retrospective data in order to conduct a quasi-experimental evaluation. The evaluation must start at the front, with the locus and accuracy of the initial random assignment as a matter of crucial importance.

For all these reasons, the orthodoxy in favour of experimental methods has been hotly contested. Social experiments produce valuable results, and deservedly constitute the centrepiece of the American evaluation industry, the most elaborate in the modern world. But the recognition that they too have limitations has led many evaluators – including the organizations that carry out large-scale evaluations in the United States – to prefer multiple methods and to tailor the choice of methods to the particular questions being asked.

The applications considered in this section have for the most part concerned economic outcomes for individual workers – that is, at Stage 4 of our amplified conception of human capital development (see Chapter 2). Their applicability is, however, more general. The problem of determining *what would otherwise have been* applies in principle to the previous stages as well, where the problem again is to determine, variously, what services the individual would have received, what he or she would otherwise have learned, and how he or she would have behaved in the absence of training, in order to identify training-induced changes in skills and behaviour.

In sum, we advocate a pragmatic approach to the problem of setting the keystone of the evaluation arch: what would have occurred in the absence of the programme. The case for using the more sophisticated methods when data and other resources permit is clear. At the same time, when that is not possible, the alternative need not be to abandon the effort altogether, eg by relying only on gross outcomes in tracer studies. Weakly experimental methods may still yield clues to the effects of a programme, and it may be possible to go further still. In the example in Box 3.7, a simplified 'fixed effects' comparison of changes in labour market outcomes for participants and for members of a rough and ready comparison group provides at least some sense of the likely effects of the programme, even if the probable weakness of the comparison group and the absence of econometric controls for changes in observable individual attributes make it difficult to draw firm conclusions.

Box 3.7   Pragmatic evaluation

The Chile Joven programme

The programme has since 1994 offered semi-skilled occupational training to young Chileans who are school drop-outs, unemployed or lack a stable job. The programme was evaluated by comparing the change in annual earnings of participants between the pre-participation and the post-participation periods to that of a comparison group (whose selection and composition were not outlined) over the same period. This pseudo 'fixed effects' method removes the effects of differences between participants and non-participants in unchanging personal attributes, although no attempt was made to adjust for changes in measured personal attributes. The programme was judged successful. The increase in mean participant earnings net of that in the comparison group amounted to 10.2 per cent of participants' average pre-programme earnings.

Source: Caceres Cruz (1997), Table 9

Aggregation: the programme as a whole

The various ways of estimating the effects of training on individuals that were outlined in the previous section are typically added up across participants when it comes to estimating the effects of the programme as a whole. Even if accurate evidence could be obtained concerning the effects of training on individuals, there would still be the problem of determining effects upon non-participants. Even a small programme may have effects on other economic agents. For example, a participant might take a job that would otherwise have been filled by another worker (the problem of displacement), or one firm's trainees may be hired by another firm (an externality, in this case a benefit to the firm that did not make the investment in training). The effect upon the two agents taken together then differs from that upon the participant alone.

Under standard human capital theory, such 'external' effects are either trivial, in the case of displacement, or absent, in the case of externalities. Perfect competition rules out by assumption any external effects of training upon non-participants (Stevens, 1996). It makes displacement a second-order phenomenon: full employment in all labour markets would mean that ex-participants would not displace other workers from employment, and training would simply alter wages marginally as it varies the relative supplies of trained and untrained workers.

If analytical convenience certainly encourages the adoption of competitive assumptions, that hardly justifies the practice. Labour markets are so widely characterized by imperfect competition, involuntary unemployment and segmented pay structures – even in the United States, the closest approximation to the competitive norm – as to make displacement and externalities matters of potential importance in the evaluation of training (Katz and Summers, 1988; Lindbeck and Snower, 1990; McNabb and Ryan, 1990; Card and Krueger, 1995; Stevens, 1996). Under such conditions, displacement becomes a potentially first-order phenomenon. The problem is most pressing for programmes which simply recycle participants within low-skill labour markets in which participants and non-participants are likely to be close substitutes for each other. Under those conditions, it is particularly dangerous to simplify the evaluation task by assuming perfect competition and adding up outcomes for participants.

If, however, a training programme takes participants from surplus to deficit markets, eg from glutted markets for low-skill labour to shortage markets for skilled labour, then displacement is likely to be low, and aggregated individual gains a better guide to aggregate benefits. Work experience and low-quality training programmes typify the former category, occupational training for certified skills the latter (Johnson, 1979; Solow, 1990; Ryan and Büchtemann, 1996).

Aggregation problems may be addressed in two ways. The first is to estimate displacement and externalities directly within an 'aggregative' approach, adding up evidence that refers to individual workers. The second, 'aggregate' approach estimates the outcomes of training directly at some higher level of aggregation, such as the plant, the employer, the sector or the economy, at which outcomes may be expected to include the effects of at least some displacement and externalities. Both methods are discussed briefly here. Not surprisingly, each approach has contributions to make and problems to face.

Direct estimation of displacement

Two methods are noteworthy. First, the parties involved may be asked what they would have done in the absence of the programme – a method whose limitations were discussed in the previous section. For example, extensive displacement during training has been suggested by interviews with employers concerning the British Youth Training Scheme: around 80 per cent of their YTS trainees simply displaced other employees or apprentices, leaving only 20 per cent as a net addition to employment and training (see Box 3.8).]

Box 3.8   Aggregative methods

Youth Training Scheme (Great Britain)

Representative samples of employers that both participated and did not participate in the British Youth Training Scheme (see Box 3.1) were asked to indicate the employment patterns that would have prevailed in the programme's absence. The displacement of regular employment and training by subsidized trainees, as measured by the proportion of YTS traineeships which would otherwise have been regular jobs or apprenticeships, was estimated to have risen from one-third to four-fifths during 1983–89. As managers faced incentives to conceal displacement, which was formally against the rules, its true incidence may have been even higher.

Sources: Deakin and Pratten (1987), Begg *et al.* (1991)

Second, it is sometimes possible to estimate displacement from statistical evidence. For example, the substitution of participants for regular employees in work-based programmes can be investigated by estimating statistical relationships between employment (as a ratio to output or population) and trainee numbers across time and sector (Crane and Ellwood, 1984). Similarly, inflow and outflow rates from unemployment in relevant categories (sectors, occupations or regions) may suggest whether, for example, a public training programme has increased the inflow of experienced workers into unemployment, suggesting significant displacement in the market for trained workers (Disney *et al.*, 1992).

Another variant uses macroeconomic modelling and simulation, for programmes that are large enough to affect employment in the relevant labour markets (Lindley, 1996). For example, Eyssartier and Gauti (1996), using a macroeconomic model of the French economy, estimate that between two-thirds and three-quarters of the places provided for young people by public training and employment programmes during 1985–94 represented losses of regular youth employment – again suggesting that when it comes to aggregative evaluations, the whole can be much less than the sum of the parts.

None of these methods is truly satisfactory, let alone definitive. But all of them can provide some sense of the extent of displacement, and therefore of the validity of simply aggregating outcomes for participants without taking displacement into account.

Estimation of net aggregate outcomes

The second approach is the 'aggregate' one, relating economic outcomes to training activities at a level high enough to capture the effects of displacement and externalities without having to estimate them directly. For public training this might involve examining the extent to which government programmes have affected the relative unemployment rates of affected and unaffected groups of workers, both during and after training (see Box 3.2).

A method that has proved influential in the United Kingdom compares productivity, equipment, and workforce skills in matched establishments – those producing similar products – in the metalworking, furniture, clothing, food, and hotel sectors of the British, German, French and Dutch economies (Prais, 1995). Extraneous influences on productivity are reduced by matching product lines across establishments. Differences in average labour productivity between the nationally defined sectors in question are then estimated and, after allowing for capital equipment, related to differences in workforce skills (measured by educational attainment and possession of intermediate vocational qualifications). The clothing industry study is summarized in Box 3.9.

Box 3.9   Aggregate evaluation 1

Productivity and skills in matched plants (Germany and the United Kingdom)

Average labour productivity was estimated from company records for a sample of matched German and British plants producing women's outerwear, and checked against national official statistics for the sector. German plants showed a substantial productivity advantage despite shorter product runs. Their superior performance was attributed primarily to a much higher incidence of craft-level vocational qualifications amongst employees, particularly in production. The benefits of training for productivity accrued primarily through higher product quality, faster turnaround and learning times on new products, and less machine downtime. Although YTS trainees were present in British plants, their training was geared to semi-skilled work, unlike the craft-level apprenticeships that predominated in German plants.

Source: Steedman and Wagner (1989)

One difficulty is the reliance of these studies on qualitative rather than quantitative assessment of the contributions of capital, technology and management to labour productivity, making it difficult to estimate explicitly the contribution of training to productivity (Cutler, 1992). That difficulty has been avoided in a parallel line of research, concerning the association between workforce skills and sectoral performance in national statistics. The performance indicators in question are productivity and export shares. Inputs of physical capital and technology (R&D) are specifically accounted for (Oulton, 1996; O'Mahoney and Wagner, 1996; Cörvers, 1997). Again, sectoral skill stocks are found to contribute strongly to economic performance, supporting the findings of the matched plant studies. A British-German comparison of skills and trade is summarized in Box 3.10.

These two lines of research are clearly more useful for assessing the economic effects of workforce skills, and indirectly the national VET system as a whole, rather than those of any particular training activity, public or private. Their strength lies in their ability to capture any displacement and externalities associated with training.

That marked economic effects are found for training in aggregate evaluations is reassuring evidence that displacement and externalities do not render meaningless any favourable outcomes found in aggregative (ie individually based) ones. As aggregate methods are more useful for analysing the economic effects of employer-based training and skill stocks in general than for those of labour market programmes, the value of both approaches in relation to the question 'does training work?' is clear.

Box 3.10   Aggregate evaluation 2

Trade and skills in national statistics (Germany and the United Kingdom)

The relative export performance of 30 British and German manufacturing sectors during 1978–87, compiled from national statistics, was related by regression analysis to the relative skill content of the sectoral workforce, as measured by the share of employees holding four levels of qualification (in both general education and VET). British trade performance was generally poorer than German in terms of levels and growth of exports. The national gap in performance was significantly larger in sectors in which the skills of the British workforce, particularly at craft level, were lower than their German counterpart, suggesting that an inferior training effort has damaged British trade performance.

Source: Oulton (1996)

Cost-benefit analysis, efficiency and equity

Aggregation of the effects of training involves one further step, after considering displacement and externalities. As noted in the section Outcome Measures, above, it is often desirable to consider multiple outcomes in any evaluation of training, particularly when the training is part of a wider public labour market programme. The problem is this: having assessed impacts on a variety of outcomes of interest, both economic (eg employment, earnings) and non-economic (eg criminality, pregnancy, dependence on public income support) across some time period, how are these diverse effects to be compiled so as to establish whether the programme is a success – and whether it is more of a success (or less of a failure) than alternative programmes? And even if there are benefits from training, are they enough to outweigh its costs?

Cost-benefit analysis is the standard method of aggregating benefits and costs across outcome categories and across time. Economic values are assigned to the various categories of benefit; non-economic ones are assigned money values ('shadow prices') where possible. The value of benefits net of costs is then calculated for every year of the evaluation period, and cash flow analysis (discounting) is used to convert the stream of annual net benefits into a single 'measure of merit' – either the present value of net benefits of training, or the rate of return on the investment in training – for the programme as a whole.[15] Diverse projects with diverse cost and benefit streams can then in principle be ranked in order of merit.[16]

The method can be illustrated using a landmark example: the cost-benefit analysis of the Job Corps, a long-running, intensive programme of remedial education, training and other services for highly disadvantaged youth in the United States (see Box 3.11). A summary of the results is presented in the final column of Table 3.2.

Box 3.11   Cost-benefit analysis

Job Corps (United States)

Job Corps is a residential programme that provides VET and other services to disadvantaged youth who have left school. It has been one of the most expensive remedial training programmes (about US$15,000 per participant year in 1993 dollars). An evaluation using quasi-experimental measures found positive effects on employment rates and earnings per week, though not on hourly wages; the programme also reduced crime rates. Effects on earnings and crime were then incorporated into a cost-benefit analysis (Table 3.2). Equity effects were considered by including reductions in welfare payments, as benefits to taxpayers and offsetting losses to participants, with no overall effect on net benefits. The finding of positive net benefits was widely interpreted as showing that expensive programmes can work even when cheaper ones do not. On the distributional side, the programme was found to benefit participants while imposing small losses (US$214 per participant) on taxpayers.

Source: Long *et al.* (1981)

Table 3.2 Benefits and costs per participant, Job Corps, United States (1977 US dollars)

Component	Participants (1)	Rest of Society (2)	Whole Economy (1) + (2)
Benefits			
Output produced by members	3 397	1 255	4 653
Dependence on transfers	-1 357	1 515	158
Criminal activity	-169	2 281	2 112
Drug and alcohol use	0	30	30
Utilization of alternative services	-49	439	390
Other benefits	+	+	+
Total benefits	1 823	5 520	7 343
Costs			
Operating expenditures	-1 208	5 351	1 449
Opportunity cost of participant labour	728	153	881
Unbudgeted expenditures[a]	-185	231	46
Total costs	-665	5 736	5 070
Net benefits			
Net present value (benefits less costs)	2 485	-214	2 271
Benefit-cost ratio	1.82	0.96	1.45

Notes: Benefits not assigned a US dollar value are shown as +
[a]. Other than those on participant labour
Source: Long, Mallar and Thornton (1981), Table 6

The benefits of the programme comprised the increased output produced by members, estimated as the increase in earnings caused by the programme (US$4,700), as inferred from statistical analysis of outcomes for participants relative to members of a carefully matched comparison group (section The challenge of comparison, above).[17] The other important area of benefit was a reduction in criminal activity, a social benefit that lacks a ready market price for valuation purposes, but for which a shadow price was developed from evidence on the costs imposed on society by criminal activity. Second-order benefits were estimated to arise primarily from reduced use of drugs and alcohol, to which are added the savings in resource costs associated with reduced dependence on public income support and social services. Other benefit categories were considered too marginal or too difficult to cost, but programme effects upon them were generally favourable. Total quantified benefits to the entire economy, after discounting across the evaluation period, were estimated at US$7,300 per participant. Against those had to be set the resource costs of running the programme, at US$5,100 per capita, leaving a net benefit to the economy and society of US$2,300 per capita. The Job Corps has subsequently been considered a rare success in the category of youth programmes – though with reservations, in view of the use of quasi-experimental rather than highly experimental evaluation methods (see section, The challenge of comparison, above).

Cost-benefit analysis estimates the effects of training upon economic efficiency. When the criterion of a positive present value of net benefits is satisfied, a programme is judged to yield to the economy benefits in excess of its costs, and as such to represent a worthwhile use of scarce resources.[18]

An important ingredient is the comparison of benefits to costs. That is, a programme may be effective, in the sense of creating economic and non-economic benefits for participants, but these effects may not be worthwhile if they are less than the costs involved. The criterion that benefits should outweigh costs is an application of the concept of economic efficiency; thus a programme may be *effective*, in the sense of creating net benefits for participants, but not *efficient* if its costs outweigh the benefits.

The use of multiple benefit categories and the comparison to costs make cost-benefit analysis more meaningful than the 'single outcome' evaluations (eg the effects of a training programme on earnings) that dominate the academic evaluation literature. It has accordingly become the norm for public evaluation of public labour market programmes in the United States (Grubb, 1996a, Ch. 5), though it is still rarely used for the evaluation of training in other countries.

The other extensive application of cost-benefit methods concerns education in developing countries, for which internal rates of return are frequently estimated, on both a private and a social basis.[19] The results have led to several recommendations, including the idea that countries should invest first in expanding primary education, which has the highest rate of return, rather than secondary or post-secondary education, and the idea that countries should emphasize general or academic schools in preference to vocational education (see Chapter 7, Special issues in developing and transitional countries). As, however, the difference between social and private rates of return is typically limited to allowing for public subsidies to education and taxes on the earnings of more educated labour, such studies do not aim very high in terms of a key cost-benefit goal: the inclusion of multiple outcomes (see section, Outcome measures).

The limitations of cost-benefit analysis itself must also be recognized. At the practical level, major empirical problems arise in such areas as: identifying a suitable range of outcome categories and estimating effects within each; finding suitable 'shadow prices' with which to value benefits, particularly those measured in physical units (eg employment rates, crime rates); identifying displacement and externalities; establishing the appropriate discount rate to use to aggregate across time; and establishing and valuing the costs associated with the intrinsic uncertainty of project outcomes (conceived, eg as the potential variability of net benefits around 'best estimates' such as those in Table 3.2). A humble but appropriate response to this range of problems is not to ignore them, but rather to bring to bear on them whatever information is to hand (eg using the resource costs of imprisonment as a guide to the value of reductions in criminality) and, when that information is particularly weak, to estimate the sensitivity of net benefits to alternative assumptions about key imponderables, such as the social discount rate or shadow prices for non-economic benefits, rather than either making unique arbitrary assumptions or excluding them altogether.

A further objection to cost-benefit analysis runs along the lines: economic efficiency is all very well, but training should be assessed on other criteria as well.[20] Alternative objectives include the distributional, the educational and the fiscal. For example, a training programme may help the disadvantaged even if it is a loss for the economy as a whole, and, in Europe in particular, this may be regarded as a sufficient merit for it to be supported. Or, as vocational education, training may contribute to personal development by encouraging young people who would otherwise have left school to stay on, learn more and enjoy more and better personal development, quite apart from any associated economic benefits. Or, again, a training programme's effect on public revenues, local activity, etc, may be politically important even when it has no efficiency or equity effects to speak of.

The need to expand the range of evaluation criteria is important. To some extent cost-benefit analysis can deal with the need, to some extent it cannot. The area of its competence overlaps with distributional issues, while the area of its unsuitability concerns educational ones. Cost-benefit analysis has found no ready way to include purely educational objectives and outcomes; and it excludes strictly political objectives from consideration.

Cost-benefit analysis can in practice accommodate consideration of the distributional effects of training in two ways. The first is to calculate net benefits for different groups of participants. For example, cost-benefit analysis of JTPA Title II programmes in the United States has found that net benefits were highest for adult males, followed by adult females, while net benefits for youth were actually negative.[21] Such evidence is, however, usually of more interest for efficiency and implementation issues than for distributional ones, as sex and age are not usually related closely to economic disadvantage within the client groups for public training programmes.

More pertinent is the degree to which the programme has at least benefited its participants, whether or not it has benefited the economy as a whole. Cost-benefit analysis addresses that issue by distinguishing benefits to participants from those to the rest of the economy. In the case of the Job Corps evaluation in Table 3.2, above, columns 1 and 2 reflect the division of the programme's overall costs and benefits between participants and other members of society – with the latter comprising both the taxpayers who fund the programme and other public services, and, in this case, the citizens who suffer from the criminal activity that the programme reduces.[22]

Other members of society are seen to gain more from the Job Corps, in terms of gross benefits, than do participants. Non-participants enjoy benefits from: 1) the higher output of ex-participants, by way of the latter's increased income tax payments; 2) the reduced requirement for public spending on income support and other services to participants; and 3) the lower criminal damage done to them by participants. But as non-participants have to pay the taxes required to set up and run the programme, they lose marginally from it overall (US$200 per participant), and the net benefits of the programme accrue primarily to participants (US$2,500 each).

It is worth noting that in a cost-benefit accounting framework such as that in Table 3.2, some benefits to non-participants are treated as transfers from participants, as those benefits lack any equivalent from the standpoint of the economy and society as a whole. For example, the loss to participants arising from a reduction in their welfare income (US$1,400 per head) is closely paralleled by the gain in income (US$1,515) attributed to non-participants, resulting from their correspondingly lower tax requirements. The difference between the two, US$1,585, represents the savings in resource costs arising from the reduction in welfare transfers – and only that part is relevant to the efficiency assessment (column 3 of Table 3.2).

The distinction between participants and non-participants matters from the distributional standpoint primarily for public programmes of remedial training that are targeted on disadvantaged groups, as participants can then be taken to be poorer than non-participants. For training more generally, the distinction between the two groups is of secondary or no importance for distributional concerns, and other methods must be used.[23]

In the best of all possible worlds, of course, publicly funded VET programmes provide net benefits to both participants, in the form of future earnings, and to taxpayers, in the form of enhanced future taxes and decreased social costs (of crime and the like). In practice, different programmes produce different mixes of efficiency and distributional effects. The various possibilities can be illustrated from youth-related outcomes in three remedial programmes in the United States: Supported Work, Jobstart, and the Job Corps (see Table 3.3).[24] In terms of efficiency (row 5), cost-benefit analysis suggests that only the Job Corps produced net benefits for the economy as a whole. In terms of equity (row 3), Supported Work and the Job Corps succeeded, in that both increased participant incomes relative to what they would otherwise have been, but Jobstart failed here too, as participants were found to have been made worse off during the programme as a result of reduced access to employment. The verdict on Supported Work depends therefore on the importance attached in public policy to equity relative to efficiency, but Jobstart is judged a failure and Job Corps a success on both criteria.

Table 3.3   Evaluation criteria and outcomes in three remedial labour market programmes in the United States

	Supported Work	Jobstart	Job Corps
1. Participants: income during programme	+	-	+
2. Participants: total earnings after programme	0	0	+
3. Participants: all income (1+2)	+	0	+
4. Non-participants	-	-	-
5. Whole economy (net benefits)	-	-	+

Notes: + statistically significant gains; 0 insignificant effects; - significant losses
Source: Derived from Ryan and Büchtemann (1996), Tables 2, 3

Viewed as a whole, cost-benefit analysis is a politically powerful method of evaluation. It summarizes an enormous amount of information in a simple concept and a simple number – notably the cost-benefit ratio or the internal rate of return.[25] In several cases, including the Perry Pre-school project (see Box 6.2), cost-benefit ratios have been widely discussed and accepted, promoting social programmes that might otherwise have been eliminated. Finally, cost-benefit analysis has sometimes been valuable simply by forcing analysts and policy-makers to think about the variety of costs and benefits a programme entails – a way of systematically arraying effects, even if actual figures cannot be developed.

But these benefits do come at a cost. The need to put money values on benefits has discouraged effective consideration of a wide range of benefits. And the very simplicity of the cost-benefit ratio or internal rate of return, powerful though they may be in the political arena, is itself a problem in that it summarizes so much information, and thereby short-circuits the process of understanding how VET programmes work.[26]

Evaluation of implementation and other stages

The final aspect of evaluation method considered here involves evaluation at earlier stages in the process of human capital development, primarily at the first stage: the implementation of training. There are two strands to implementation-oriented evaluation of training. The first is the investigation of activity patterns in order to establish to what extent the intended and actual constituencies for training coincided: did the training reach those whom it was intended to reach? If not, the training cannot be judged the success that it might otherwise have been, however useful it proved to those who actually received it.

At stage one, the implementation of training, the determination of *what would otherwise have been* is in principle a different kind of issue: the relevant comparison is between training as actually delivered and training as planned or proposed. The evaluation methods appropriate to the task boil down to investigating the steps which have been taken to deliver training and establishing the extent to which the services delivered have corresponded to those proposed by the programme design. Appropriate methods include the inspection of facilities and activities (quantitatively where possible), interviews with trainers and trainees, and questionnaires concerning the activities of trainees and their assessments thereof (eg Levin and Ferman, 1986). The quantitative side of the work overlaps with performance management, though the two are distinct in that performance management considers gross outcomes for participants as well.

The second strand seeks to find out why particular outcomes occurred. When training is found to have failed at any of the later stages of human capital development (learning, behaviour and, most commonly, economic outcomes), it may be important to find out why, not least in order to suggest a more promising design. The failure of public training programmes for disadvantaged youth, indicated by negative net benefits to society (and for some, little or no benefit even for participants), has prompted just such an interest in the United States (Heckman, Roselius and Smith, 1994; Bloom *et al.*, 1997). Conversely, when training works, understanding the reasons for its success can help make it better still (US Department of Labor, 1995).

The preferred research method for this strand is the qualitative investigation of motives and experiences in training, typically through case studies of particular training programmes and intensive interviews with participants, providers and administrators. Detailed interviews can explore a wider range of topics than can quantitative methods like surveys, which require that the topics explored be specified in terms of multiple-choice questions. An example is provided by the New Chance programme for young welfare mothers in the United States, which a highly experimental evaluation of outcomes found to have broadly failed its participants (see Box 3.6). The reasons for that failure were investigated by intensive interviews with participants. The results suggested a series of barriers to employment – including the actions of family members, problems associated with depression and drug abuse – that the programme could not address (see Box 3.12).

Box 3.12   Qualitative, implementation-oriented evaluation 1

New Chance (United States)

In addition to the highly experimental evaluation of outcomes (see Box 3.6, above), New Chance was studied through intensive interviews with 50 participants, focusing on their views of the programme, its non-economic effects, and related life conditions. Participants were found to have appreciated the innovative services offered, particularly community-based mentors. The main sources of disappointing outcomes were found to be: abusive and demanding family circumstances; high cost and low availability of childcare; difficulty of holding down jobs for both personal and job-related reasons; significant incidence of clinical depression; and unplanned pregnancies. The programme emerged as carefully designed and effectively implemented but incapable of overcoming such difficulties in only 18 months.

Source: Quint *et al.* (1994b)

Similarly, the apparent failure of the British Youth Training Scheme (YTS) to generate consistently higher pay or employment rates in quasi-experimental evaluation of its economic effects (see Box 3.4, above) might have remained a disappointing puzzle in the absence of other evidence. Implementation-oriented research found that, at least in the programme's early years, most placements were in occupations with low skill requirements, and that most training was short-lived and informal. Many trainees complained of being either used as cheap labour or left with little to do – termed 'dogsbody' and 'noddy' placements, respectively (Box 3.13).

Box 3.13   Qualitative, implementation-oriented evaluation 2

Youth Training Scheme (Great Britain)

A sample of trainees, employers and training providers involved in the early days of the British YTS, drawn from one English town, was interviewed to establish the experiences of trainees and the context of their training. The responses suggested that the majority of traineeships were low quality, on such criteria as the existence of a training programme, educational content, integration of on-the-job with off-the-job training (where the latter was present), repetitive work tasks and access to a qualification.

Source: Lee *et al.* (1990)

As a final example, an evaluation of the British Job Training Scheme for adult workers used open-ended questionnaires to ask participants about their views of the programme; they reported gains in self-confidence, ability to act decisively, and motivation. These (at most semi-quantitative) effects were particularly notable amongst women returning to work after a career break (Payne, 1990a, 1990b).

If implementation-oriented research therefore offers access to valuable insights into mechanisms and processes, what about a strategy confined to implementation issues? When the implementation of training is defective, implementation-oriented evaluation can provide valuable warning signals even in the absence of evidence on outcomes. The British YTS of the 1980s again provides an example: the programme's implementation was widely recognized to be defective even before outcome-oriented results became available.

At the same time, implementation-oriented evaluation shows some clear limitations in practice. It is only too easy for such research to share the tendency of the journalistic methods with which it overlaps to generalize from a few individuals of unknown representativeness, and describe 'success stories' with little effort to determine what happens to other participants, or what would have happened to any of them in the absence of the programme (Levin and Ferman, 1986).

Moreover, qualitative methods not only offer limited evaluative power when used on their own, but are particularly open to abuse by interested parties. When carried out by independent evaluators, qualitative research may be useful in understanding the changes that VET programmes can make and, conversely, the influences that are difficult for public programmes to affect (such as personal relationships or motivation). However, qualitative evaluation has developed a bad reputation in some circles because it has often been carried out only informally, by administrators whose interests lie in making the programme look good, and because results have been reported without clarifying the evidence on which they are based. Under these conditions, informal assessments of outcomes, particularly non-economic ones, may not be useful for any purposes of evaluation.

An example is provided by the official evaluation of a European Commission training-related programme. The limitation of evaluation to qualitative methods and implementation issues allowed interested parties – notably the official sponsor and its commercial contractors – to promote a favoured programme (see Box 3.14).

Box 3.14   Qualitative, implementation-oriented evaluation 3

COMETT programme (European Commission)

The European Commission's Community Action Programme for Education and Technology promoted industry–university cooperation in training matters. A series of four evaluation exercises involved separate reports from several independent experts, all member governments and a European consortium of national consultancy organizations. The evidence was however limited to qualitative implementation issues, such as the development of intended intermediary bodies, the setting up of relevant projects, and the like. The enthusiastic summary assessment, with its emphasis on outcomes ('COMETT II has been an undoubted success'; p.10), cannot be sustained on the basis of such evidence.

Source: CEC (1996)

Finally, although studies of implementation are reasonably common, evaluation at stages two and three – skill learning and economic behaviour – remains rare. A few of the American evaluations have measured scores on tests of reading and mathematical ability, as mentioned in the section, Outcome measures. A study of a remedial education programme using random assignment methods examined scores on a test of reading, grammar, and simple mathematics (Martinson and Friedlander, 1994). However, none of these evaluations have looked into implementation issues at each stage, such as processes of teaching and learning, to identify any problems with the way instruction is delivered and to specify where improvements might be made. Such studies have been indeed carried out by ethnographers (eg Hull, 1997) or those interested in the quality of teaching (eg Grubb *et al.*, 1999) but they have not been linked to outcome-oriented evaluations.

Conclusions

In sum, we emphasize several attributes and requirements of evaluation methods:

- the importance of considering a range of outcomes, particularly in public training programmes;
- the value of cost-benefit analysis as a means of including a range of outcomes in different periods and condensing them into a single measure of the training's merit;
- the centrality of the problem of the counter-factual, ie, estimating what would have happened to trainees in the absence of training;
- the variety of potential sources of information concerning the counter-factual, ranging from the sophistication of social experiments and the econometric analysis of micro-data to the rough and ready use of the experiences of similar groups, eg, in other programmes, sectors or countries, and informed, expert opinion;
- the informational limits of all sources, including the most sophisticated, and the corresponding value of multiple sources of information;
- the potential implications of training for *non*-participants, through displacement and external effects, and the corresponding value of aggregative approaches to evaluation;
- the potential importance of implementation-oriented evaluation, along with the potential for its abuse when evaluation is limited to implementation issues and conducted by parties whose interest is served by a favourable assessment.

Our approach can be illustrated with the help of the classical dictum, *all roads lead to Rome*. Sadly, so optimistic a proposition cannot be fully sustained for evaluation methods, if by Rome is meant the 'truth': non-experimental methods offer little or no mileage. Actually, in our view *no one road gets to Rome*: all evaluation methods are informationally imperfect. The consolation is that *most roads lead towards Rome* – and that at least some credit for travel towards Rome (road miles?) can be acquired along almost all roads, including the neglected dirt tracks of weakly experimental research.

Finally, our approach can be exemplified by bringing together the evidence on the British Youth Training Scheme in the 1980s. This programme has, like most European training programmes, not been subjected to the highly experimental, cost-benefit evaluation methods that are familiar in the United States, but has undergone instead a series of partial assessments by various official bodies, non-profit organizations and academics.[27] Putting the results of outcome-oriented evaluations, both individualistic and aggregate, together with those of learning-oriented and implementation-oriented ones (as reported in Boxes 3.4, 3.8, 3.9 and 3.13 above), a clearer picture of YTS emerges: as a generally low-quality programme incapable of dealing with training needs, both individual and national – as opposed to simply keeping many young people active and providing some employers with cheap labour. The inadequacies of the programme's design and implementation help both to buttress and to explain the evidence that the programme did not increase its participants' skills. YTS is therefore a classic example of a training programme whose evaluation benefits from – indeed, requires – multiple sources of evidence.

Notes

1. One of the earliest approaches to evaluation was Campbell and Stanley (1963), which still repays careful reading; it has been updated in Cook and Campbell (1979). For other works covering a variety of evaluation methods, see Rossi and Freeman (1993) and Schmid, O'Reilly, and Schömann (1996). On process evaluation or implementation, see especially Grembowski and Blalock (1990). In the United States, there is even a Joint Committee on Standards for Educational Evaluation that has issued a set of 30 standards for evaluating education and training programmes: *The Programme Evaluation Standards: How to Assess Evaluations in Educational Programmes*, 2nd edition. Thousand Oaks, CA: Sage Publications, 1994.
2. Indeed, the meta-analysis of American programmes carried out by Fisher and Cordray (1996) confines its analysis to earnings and employment effects because they are so common in training evaluations and because they are easy to standardize in the effect sizes required for meta-analysis.
3. Murnane, Willett, and Boudett (1995) found a very small effect of earning a GED on earnings; Cameron and Heckman (1993) found essentially no effect.

4. See Kemple, Friedlander and Fellerath (1995), with some results reprinted in Grubb (1996a), Table 4.10.
5. These studies are reviewed in Grubb (1996a).
6. See Friedlander and Burtless (1995), especially Table 4.2, reprinted in Grubb (1996a), pp. 76-77. See also Couch (1992), US GAO (1996), and the meta-analysis by Fisher and Cordray (1996), which found that effect sizes for earnings increase gradually until quarter 9, at the beginning of the third year, but then decay rapidly.
7. For example, Freedman and Friedlander (1995) have compared the 'labour force attachment' approach, which emphasizes job search assistance and other methods of getting individuals into work quickly, and the 'human capital development approach', which provides longer-term education and training so that individuals can develop more substantial skills. The early results, two years after the programme, show modest positive results for employment and earnings for those in the labour force attachment approach but zero or negative (though insignificant) results from the human capital approach. But results after two years do not reach the period 3–4 years after the end of a programme where reduced earnings tend to set in. Updated results will be available soon, but even they will not extend long enough.

    The results in conventional age-earnings profiles in the United States indicate that the earnings differentials associated with more years of schooling do not materialize until individuals are in the early thirties. For youth in particular, one school of thought is that they 'mill around' in the labour market until their early twenties when they are able to get 'adult jobs' – so that the benefits of any training programmes would take several years to materialize. Klerman and Karoly (1994) have challenged this presumption, but their results indicate that many high school drop-outs do not find 'adult' employment – defined as employment lasting at least two years – within three years of leaving school, and these proportions are surely higher for low-income and minority youth.
8. See, for example, Fay (1996) and OECD (1994), restated in Dar and Gill (1995a). The OECD Jobs Strategy has been based on this reading of the available data, as have some recommendations of the World Bank. However, the conclusions about job search assistance are based on a misreading of the evidence, in our view. In the American evaluations cited, the evidence is too mixed to conclude much about the effectiveness of JSA versus job training (Grubb, 1996a, Ch. 5). A recent report found that (Quint *et al.*, 1997) 'intensive receipt of education and training services' made for better outcomes in a programme for teenage mothers on welfare, compared to counselling and mentoring only. The review of job search assistance strategies by Meyer (1995) does not contrast JSA with job training but instead measures the effects of JSA only, finding effects that are by any measure small – even though the benefits outweigh costs. And the causal mechanism is unclear: it's possible that the positive effects noted by Meyer are due not to JSA but to the more frequent review of eligibility in these experiments.
9. Grubb (1996a), Ch. 5. See also Friedlander (1988) for earlier results.
10. The classification in Table 3.1 draws upon Ryan and Büchtemann (1996).
11. Weakly experimental methods have been widely used in case-study evaluations of the productivity effects of employer-sponsored 'in service' training. Those effects are typically estimated by simple before/after methods. Individual output is compared before, during and after training, along a measured 'learning curve'. The increase in productivity is then taken to be the effect of training. A slightly more sophisticated variant infers the increase in productivity caused by the formalization of training

from the difference between the learning curves under formal and informal training methods. As trainees are compared to participants in other programmes, such studies involve a weakly experimental approach (eg Thomas *et al.*, 1969).

12. A third approach involves the use of instrumental variables. A variable that is correlated with participation but not with outcomes is used to remove statistically the association between participation and the unexplained component of outcomes (Friedlander *et al.*, 1997).

13. The requisite assumptions are that random disturbances to both the participation and outcome equations share a joint normal distribution, and that the sets of observable attributes used to explain participation and outcomes are not identical.

14. One approach looks to matching to remove entirely the need for regression analysis, but this assumes implicitly – and implausibly – that unobserved attributes are either unimportant for outcomes or unrelated to selection for training (Dar and Gill, 1995a).

15. The rate of return on training has the advantage, relative to the present value of net benefits, of ready comparability to rates of return on alternative investments, including other VET programmes, and also in financial and physical assets. Implicitly, then, calculating internal rates of return suggests a particular source of funding: instead of coming from general taxation, the resources used for training displace investment in a different programme or physical capital. The need to specify whether a public training programme is financed from taxation or borrowing, and the implications of these alternatives for the discount rate used either to calculate the present value of net benefits or to compare to the programme's internal rate of return, are discussed by Brown and Jackson (1990).

16. On the methodology of cost-benefit analysis, see Brown and Jackson (1990), Layard and Glaister (1994), Gramlich (1981) and Sugden and Williams (1978).

17. The implicit assumptions are that pay is an accurate index of marginal product and that displacement and externalities are both negligible – assumptions more suited to perfectly competitive than to segmented labour markets (see section, Aggregation, above). The programme's effects on earnings were assumed to be sustained after the period to which the evaluation evidence was limited.

18. The efficiency criterion underlying cost-benefit analysis is a modified version of the Pareto criterion, holding that, when those who gain from a programme are able to compensate out of their gains those who lose from it, and still be better off than were the programme cancelled (ie aggregate net benefits are positive), the programme is economically desirable. (Were the compensation actually to be paid, the strict Pareto criterion for an increase in efficiency – that nobody loses and at least one person gains from the programme – would be satisfied.)

19. These studies are summarized, for example, in Psacharopoulos and Woodhall (1985) and Middleton, Ziderman, and Van Adams (1993). There has been considerable debate about the results and their interpretation; see, for example, Bennell (1996).

20. The classic article on this problem is Wildavsky (1966).

21. Bloom *et al.* (1994), exhibit 16; reprinted in Grubb (1996a), Table 5.8.

22. Further examples are presented in Grubb (1996a), Ch. 5.

23. A sophisticated but informationally demanding alternative is the distributional weighting of costs and benefits. In principle, the incidence of costs and benefits across households could be estimated and related to the income position of the household – establishing, for example, the degree to which the benefits were received by low income groups and the costs incurred by high income ones. Then

the same pattern of costs and benefits could be weighted in relation to household income status. On egalitarian values, higher weights are assigned to benefits and costs that fall to lower income households; the intensity of egalitarian values can be reflected in the strength of the relationship between the weights and household income.

24. All three programmes functioned during the late 1970s at least; all catered to disadvantaged young Americans, mostly high school drop-outs. Supported Work was the only one not to offer remedial education and training; all offered support services and job search assistance. Job Corps was the most intensive and the only one to offer a residential programme.

25. Technically, cost-benefit ratios are inferior to the present value of net benefits (Gramlich, 1991), but the ratio is a simple and politically more potent number.

26. A case for opening up cost-benefit analysis to popular public scrutiny is argued by Campen (1986).

27. Additional outcome-oriented evaluations of YTS are reviewed in Ryan and Büchtemann (1996). See also Jones (1988) and Marsden and Ryan (1991b).

4

Evaluation findings

We now review the leading findings of contemporary evaluation research on VET. The material refers largely to advanced economies, particularly the United States and western European ones, as that is where the bulk of evaluation research has been conducted. The findings may nevertheless be informative for decision-makers in other economies, both developing and transitional, who wish to learn about the successes and failures associated with VET elsewhere.

We discuss evaluation findings for the three types of training sponsorship identified in Chapter 1: public, employer and individual. We maintain as far as possible the approach to evaluation outlined in the previous section: in particular, the desirability of considering a range of outcomes, the difficulty of reaching exact conclusions, and the value of multiple evaluation methods and sources of evidence.

Our evaluation criteria are unavoidably influenced by the criteria used in the research which we now survey. Official American evaluations of remedial training and retraining typically concentrate on the efficiency criterion, as implemented through cost-benefit analysis. Most academic research implicitly adopts a narrower criterion, requiring evidence of – hopefully lasting – gains to participants. (We treat academic research on training as part of the evaluation literature, though most of that research does not aspire to a fully fledged evaluation.) Equity is rarely considered important in either literature, let alone sufficient to pronounce a programme a success. So we are pushed towards single outcome evaluations. At the same time, we attempt to keep wider issues of efficiency and equity in view throughout.

Findings for publicly sponsored training, including remedial programmes, vocational education and adult retraining, are discussed in the first section ; the next sections consider individually sponsored training and employer-sponsored training, both 'in service' training for current employees and apprenticeship for young people. The chapter ends with conclusions.

Publicly sponsored training

Evaluation research has concentrated primarily on publicly sponsored training in general, and remedial programmes for disadvantaged workers in particular. The great bulk of the vast evaluation effort in the United States concerns such programmes. For youth, remedial training is but one part of pre-employment insertion and training programmes for young workers in general, a category of particular importance in European evaluation research. For adults, remedial training shades into retraining and other programmes for adult workers. We consider these three categories in turn.

Remedial programmes

During the past three decades, the United States has adopted a succession of programmes to help disadvantaged workers, offering a variety of services, including occupational training and remedial education alongside job search, work experience and counselling. Smaller, more targeted programmes – some of them explicitly experimental, like Jobstart and New Chance (see Chapter 3) – have also appeared, albeit usually only briefly (Grubb, 1996a).

The range and sophistication of evaluation methods increased steadily throughout the period, from the weakly experimental methods of the early 1960s, through the quasi-experimental ones of the 1970s and 1980s, to the highly experimental ones that have become the norm since the mid-1980s. Aggregative methods, which simply add up outcomes for individual participants, have predominated, using cost-benefit analysis. Outcomes for recipients have typically been tracked for three years or less and assumed to persist unchanged thereafter.

The consensual view of mainstream programmes in the United States is that they have yielded 'modest gains in annual earnings for adult men and women... but no increases or even losses in income for youths' (Grubb, 1996a: 38). The group with the greatest gains in subsequent earnings has been adult females, with adult males generally registering lower gains and youths either no gains or losses. Such patterns characterize in particular the experimental evaluation of the largest of contemporary American remedial programmes, under the Job Training Partnership Act (JTPA), Title II (see Table 4.1). The picture is particularly dismal for young males, whose training cost nearly US$2,000, and whose earnings fell by a further US$1,000 as a result of embarking on the programme.[1] (The loss of earnings caused by the JTPA reflected the fact that members of the control group earned that much more over the relevant 30 months than did participants: some 'controls' found jobs during the time that the programme took up for participants). A cost-benefit analysis concluded that social net benefits were negative for young workers, and only moderately positive for adults.

Table 4.1 Outcomes under JTPA Title II programmes, United States, circa 1990

Outcome	Adult Females	Adult Males	Young Females	Young Males
Labour earnings (%):				
All services	+10*	+5	+1	-4
Classroom training	+6	+7	+9*	+2
Job training and search	+15	+10*	-4	-13*
Educational achievement (GED, %)	+12*	+8	+8*	+1
Arrest rates (%)	n.a.	n.a.	+2	+7*
Total net benefits (US$):				
Participants	1,650	2,080	-80	-620
Whole economy	532	570	-1,170	-2,900

Notes: * statistically significant (p = .10)
Outcomes are measured 30 months subsequent to entry to programme as a percentage of outcomes for randomly assigned control groups; net benefits to the economy are measured as earnings gains minus training costs; estimates are per person assigned; outcomes for young males refer only to those with no prior arrest record.
Source: Bloom *et al.* (1994)

Such results have encouraged the impression that nothing works in dealing with the problems of disadvantaged workers (Heckman, Roselius and Smith, 1994). That view is excessively bleak, even for young workers (Ryan and Büchtemann, 1996). 'Not much works' certainly applies to youth, but what does appear to work includes the Job Corps, the most expensive and intensive youth programme of all (see Box 3.11, above) – though even there the benefits appear fragile. Gains to Job Corps participants consist of more frequent employment rather than higher pay rates; gains to society depend on small declines in criminal activity to which high shadow prices are attached (see Table 3.2, above). Moreover, as the results of the current experimental evaluation have yet to emerge, many commentators prefer to reserve judgement on the programme.

The evaluation literature sheds light on several aspects of remedial programmes in the United States. First, different programmes offer different services, including different types of training. In some programmes adult participants tend to gain more from on-the-job training (and job search) than from short-term classroom (ie, off-the-job) training. This finding is consistent with the low educational achievements of disadvantaged workers, though classroom training surprisingly proved the only training medium from which young male participants in JTPA did not lose out (see Table 4.1). Simple work experience appears less effective than job-based training (Maynard, 1984) – again, no surprise given the limited developmental content of most work experience. However, it is difficult to generalize these findings across the entire spectrum of American remedial programmes (Ehrel et al., 1996) and the issue will be taken up again in later sections.

Second, the effects of training may also change with the passage of time, whether declining from disuse and obsolescence, or increasing from deepening and renewal. Most evaluation research has been too short term to illuminate the issue. Longer-term evidence is unfortunately restricted to programmes with little or no training content (Couch, 1992), but it appears likely that for remedial training, unlike mainstream education, its benefits, even when positive, decay within five or six years at most (Grubb, 1996a).

Third, American research also reveals that within any one programme different sites produce different outcomes, particularly amongst young males. Moreover, they do so in ways that are not readily explained by observable local conditions (eg unemployment), underlining the need for evaluation at earlier stages, notably implementation. Outcome-oriented evaluations simply report the differences between participants and similar individuals who have not been through the programmes, but they shed no light on which strengths or weaknesses of the programmes might be responsible for the results. Similarly, that line of research typically measures the effects of programmes relative to a control group that typically has access to some services. Therefore evaluation results sometimes fail to distinguish which services are responsible for any outcome difference.

Finally, the superior outcomes that are regularly reported for adults rather than for youths, and for female rather than for male adults, are paradoxical from a human capital standpoint – if training benefits one age-sex group it would be expected in any well-functioning labour market to benefit others similarly. Inter-group differences in outcomes are often taken for granted in evaluation research, instead of becoming the subject of further evaluation at the earlier stages of implementation, learning and behaviour. Clearly, a great deal has still to be learned even in the United States, the centre of contemporary evaluation research, about what does and does not work, and why, in the area of public remedial training.

Evaluation results for remedial programmes in Europe have only recently become available. As those studies rely on quasi-experimental rather than experimental methods, their findings are correspondingly less well grounded than is the case for the United States. The range of benefits considered is typically confined to single labour market outcomes, and cost-benefit analysis is avoided. The story told by European research proves none the less broadly similar to its American counterpart: remedial training tends to increase the employability of disadvantaged participants but to leave their earning power unchanged, and its efficacy for young workers is again dubious.

For youth, public training programmes in Europe cater typically to a larger slice of the labour force than simply its most disadvantaged segment. At the same time, as they often guarantee a place to all those eligible, those programmes implicitly favour the disadvantaged, whose access to regular employment and training is lowest of all. The relevant question then is whether public training does more for the most disadvantaged than for other young workers. The evidence focuses primarily on employment effects, for which different conclusions have been reached concerning both France and the United Kingdom. Amongst the many public programmes available to young French workers, those oriented towards training not only raise the subsequent employment of participants, but in some results do so more powerfully for young people who lack prior qualifications than for others (Bonnal, Fougère and Sérandon, 1995a, Table 5). At the same time, the potential benefit is not widely available amongst disadvantaged youth: most are steered into job creation in the public sector, which has little or no training content, rather than into training-oriented programmes in the private sector (Balsan, Hanchine and Werquin, 1996). Similarly, some evaluations of the British Youth Training Scheme (YTS) in the 1980s (see Box 3.1, above) found stronger effects upon employment prospects amongst more disadvantaged young people (Main and Shelley, 1990; Dolton, Makepeace and Treble, 1994a), but other studies have found no effect (O'Higgins, 1994). Pay effects have been invariably either insignificant or negative (eg Box 3.4, above). The evidence is therefore too partial and mixed to permit the inference that remedial training actually works for youth in Europe, unlike the United States, but the possibility remains open.

Findings for the remedial training of adults in Europe are potentially even less favourable than for the United States, where modest gains in earnings characterize mainstream programmes. An example is provided by the British Employment Training programme (ET), which during 1988–93 offered courses of training and work experience lasting up to six months, primarily to adults in long-term unemployment. Various attributes of the programme point to an unfavourable verdict. A quasi-experimental evaluation concluded that participation increased employment rates, but not pay rates (Payne *et al.*, 1996). As in the case of its youth equivalent, the YTS, the ET's inability to raise earning power is consistent with what is known about its design and implementation, notably the brevity of the training period and its dominance by work experience, the low incidence of both off-the-job training and acquisition of vocational qualifications, lax public regulation of training content, and a high drop-out rate.

Moreover, remedial programmes of that stripe, which provide little training, largely recycle participants within markets for less skilled labour where, given substantial unemployment, the likelihood of displacement of other workers by ex-participants is high (see Chapter 3, Aggregation). It is unlikely that any employment benefits to participants are matched by comparable aggregate ones; more likely, the jobs filled by ex-participants would otherwise have been filled by other unemployed workers. Any aggregate benefits can then be no more than second order, arising from any reduction in how long it takes employers to fill unskilled vacancies – a period which is short anyway in surplus labour markets.

Such an interpretation is supported by two other pieces of evidence. The first is an aggregate-level evaluation of German adult training programmes. By relating programme activity levels to total flows into and out of unemployment, it concluded that, in contrast to job creation programmes, training programmes have no overall effect. The implication is that any favourable effects upon participants are offset, largely or wholly, by associated losses for non-participants in the competition for jobs (Disney *et al.*, 1992, Ch. 5). The second consideration is the direct estimates of high displacement in youth programmes in France and the United Kingdom (see Chapter 3, Aggregation). So, whether remedial training does or does not increase access to employment for its participants, aggregate employment effects appear to be weak – and the pay effects that might suggest skill enhancement largely absent.

Any claim that such programmes might lay to public approval must therefore concentrate on redistributing inactivity away from the disadvantaged, including the long-term unemployed. That criterion certainly has appeal on grounds of equity, and possibly even of efficiency too, but its limitations from the wider standpoint are clear. Moreover, it has status only when participants themselves benefit in the first place, and that has not always been the case (see Chapter 3, Cost-benefit analysis).

Pre-employment training

In much of Europe, remedial training for disadvantaged youth is contained within wider systems for the training of young people who have yet to secure employment. Two stages are involved. Prior to entry into the labour force, vocational curricula may be offered in full-time secondary education, as notably in France, Sweden and Japan. (Post-secondary vocational education will be considered separately, under individual sponsorship.) After entering the labour force, *insertion* contracts may be used to provide unemployed young workers with a foothold on employers' premises from which they may try to clamber into a regular job. We discuss the two in turn.

Vocational secondary education
Vocational studies in secondary schooling have been evaluated extensively in both the United States and, more recently, France. Controversy rages over the merits of vocationalizing secondary education in developing countries (Psacharopoulos, 1987; Bennell, 1998). The conventional conclusion in both contexts has been that vocationalism has failed. On closer inspection, however, that conclusion proves difficult to sustain.

American and French evaluations have both relied heavily on the earnings functions favoured by human capital theory, using quasi-experimental methods to study the links between pay and schooling. As selection bias is potentially powerful – less gifted and motivated students tend to be tracked towards vocational courses – and most studies do not attempt to counter it, evaluation findings must be treated with caution.

Nevertheless, a range of studies have concluded that the 'voc ed' traditionally offered by American high schools, which comprises such occupationally specific skills as machining, typing and car repair, does little or nothing to benefit its clientele. Some studies have found gains in pay for males or females when working in the occupation for which they trained in school, but more generally the picture is bleak (eg Meyer and Wise, 1983; Rumberger and Daymont, 1984; Boesal and McFarland, 1994). Correction for selection bias, in so far as it was possible, led one study to conclude that only commercial courses raise subsequent pay, and then only for females (Altonji, 1992).

At first blush, more favourable findings emerge from the French literature. The vocational qualifications traditionally offered in secondary education – *CAP* and *BEP*[2] – are both associated with higher employment rates and higher pay after leaving school, even when selection effects are considered (Elbaum, 1988; Goux and Maurin, 1994). The good news for vocationalism is, however, limited. Increased unemployment has during the past decade swamped the fragile craft of vocational secondary qualifications – including even an ambitious innovation, the *Baccalauréat Professionnel* in upper secondary studies – in the face of competition from more qualified young people for dwindling employment opportunities (Eckert, 1995; Veneau and Mouy, 1995).

Moreover, the key problem of *what would otherwise have been* must be considered more carefully than has often been the case. Holding a vocational qualification should not be compared to holding none at all, but rather to holding the qualification the young person would have attained had he or she taken a different route, which in France has increasingly become a general, academically oriented *Baccalauréat*. Otherwise the benefits of vocational studies will be overestimated.

Given evidence of both more precarious benefits and higher costs in vocational rather than general courses, vocational secondary schooling has been widely judged a failure (Psacharopoulos, 1987). But, in so far as they refer only to traditional, unambitious 'voc ed', such conclusions are premature. More ambitious variants seek not simply to give young people a jump start in learning job skills, but rather to fuse general and applied learning, to the potential benefit of both (Grubb, 1995a). Some evaluation findings suggest favourable results. Students in American high schools who take specialized vocational programmes end up earning less than those who take more integrated programmes – though selection effects may again contribute to the difference (Kang and Bishop, 1989). Career academies and magnet schools, two innovations that embody greater educational aspirations, have been found to improve educational outcomes, including participation, attendance and learning, though later effects in the labour market have yet to be estimated (Crain *et al.*, 1992; Stern *et al.*, 1989). Thus it is important not simply to evaluate vocational education, but also to determine – from direct observation of the teaching–learning process – what kind of vocational education is involved.

'Insertion' contracts

The large EU economies in which youth unemployment rose strongly after 1974 all developed special contracts under which employers sponsored programmes of training and work experience, for unemployed young people, lasting from six months to two years, and without any obligation to offer an employment contract. Cases in point include the British YTS, France's *Contrats de Qualification*, Italy's *Contratti formazione-lavoro* and Sweden's Youth Teams programme. Such insertion contracts have been made available to unemployed youth in general, not only to the most disadvantaged young people (Garonna and Ryan, 1991; Ryan and Büchtemann, 1996).

Research on the various French *mesures jeunes* has focused on the contemporary proliferation of pathways between secondary school and regular employment – involving various sequences of work experience, unemployment, and short-term employment contracts, as well as activity in the *mesures* themselves

(Béduwé and Espinasse, 1995). Evaluation methods have evolved rapidly. Descriptive, tracer-type comparisons of gross outcomes along different pathways have been joined by quasi-experimental analysis of the effects of particular programmes upon labour market outcomes. Attempts to control for selection bias have also appeared (eg. Couppié, 1992; Bonnal *et al.*, 1995a). The focus of attention throughout has been how long it takes to obtain a regular employment contract of indefinite duration. Research on the leading British counterpart, YTS, has involved a wider range of methods and outcomes.

Evaluation findings for insertion contracts tend to replicate on a larger scale those for remedial training: they help participants gain access to jobs, but not higher pay once in work. Most quasi-experimental studies in both countries find significant employment effects for participants, at least in programmes with a significant training content (eg Magnac, 1996; O'Higgins, 1994). In France, training programmes are estimated to reduce the time taken to find a regular job, as well – surprisingly – as the duration of the first job (Sérandon, 1994; Pénard and Sollogoub, 1995).

Evidence on pay effects is still rare in France, but the best evidence available suggests adverse effects from insertion contracts. Young people who lose more income while in a training scheme end up with lower pay when in work – the opposite of what human capital theory predicts (Balsan *et al.*, 1994; Forgeot, 1997). Similarly, in Great Britain, negative pay effects predominate in quasi-experimental evaluations of YTS, with and without controls for selection bias (eg Whitfield and Bourlakis, 1991; Dolton *et al.*, 1994b).

Negative pay effects could reflect damage done to the skills of participants, a paradoxical outcome even for programmes that often have little training content. A more plausible interpretation might be that employers view participation in an *insertion* programme as evidence of low labour quality. There are two problems with such an interpretation. First, corrections for selection bias should then remove the negative pay effect, and, while that happens in some accounts (O'Higgins, 1995), it does not in others (Dolton *et al.*, 1994b). Second, negative screening for new hires according to participation in a public programme might be expected to lead to negative employment effects too, and that is not generally the finding.[3] A third line of interpretation would be that such programmes steer young people towards jobs of lower quality than they would otherwise have been willing to accept, or than they would eventually have found, had they avoided participation (Balsan *et al.*, 1994; O'Higgins, 1995). A further possible reason is suggested by implementation-oriented research: any training content in the programme may be widely wasted as a result of occupational switching when entering employment (Foudi *et al.*, 1993).

Similar evaluations of Swedish youth programmes, which previously offered more training and relied less on employers than do the insertion contracts to which they have given way during the 1990s, found no effects on earnings in the early 1980s and *negative* effects on near-term re-employment rates in the 1990s (Ackum, 1991; Ackum Agell, 1995). The former finding offers no comfort for public sponsorship. The latter is not surprising, however, given the depressed state of labour markets in the 1990s and the loss of time while in training that might otherwise have been spent in job search. Moreover, Swedish youth training programmes appear to have increased the duration and stability of subsequent employment amongst participants, relative to a matched comparison group, thereby speedily compensating participants for reduced access to employment while participating in the programme (Korpi, 1994).

In sum, the conclusions reached for insertion programmes are similar to those reached above for the remedial programmes that often form part of them: they can indeed help participants get jobs but they do little for skills and earning power. Moreover, employment gains for participants come to a considerable extent at the expense of other workers (Eyssartier and Gautié, 1996; Skedinger, 1995). Evaluations that consider only participants' subsequent employment rates – and this is the case in much technically sophisticated research, particularly in France – miss the wider picture and reach unduly favourable conclusions.

Adult retraining

For adults as for youths, public training programmes are often available to a clientele wider than the disadvantaged. Public programmes to increase adult skills are much more extensive in Europe than in the United States, and in Scandinavia and Germany than in the rest of Europe.

Interest in the United States focuses on retraining for workers displaced from particular sectors and occupations. In much of Europe, however, retraining the displaced is just one component of adult training programmes, which typically offer retraining also to people who wish to change career, and basic training and upgrade training to those who lack skills or wish to increase existing skills, including females returning from child-rearing. We therefore consider publicly sponsored adult training as a whole, while excluding non-vocational adult education.[4]

One influential view holds that, when properly evaluated, public training is even less successful for adults in general than for disadvantaged adults alone, ie it does them little or no good individually, wasting valuable resources in the process (Dar and Gill, 1995a). That view derives primarily from the experience of retraining programmes for displaced workers in the United States. Certainly, sophisticated evaluations, both highly experimental and quasi-experimental, of four demonstration projects in various American cities during the 1980s found that training, whether off-the-job or on-the-job, typically contributed nothing (over and above the contribution of job search services) to the quest by displaced workers to find a job and earn income (Leigh, 1994; Bloom, 1990). An evaluation of Hungarian retraining programmes reached similarly pessimistic conclusions (Dar and Gill, 1995b).

Closer inspection of a wider range of evidence suggests a less pessimistic assessment about retraining's *potential*, however. The first point is that the American evidence is less persuasive than is sometimes realized. Most programmes in the United States have offered only short and cheap training courses to displaced workers. Some have offered courses ill-suited to the background and interests of trainees, as when non-manual workers face options dominated by manually oriented courses (Bloom, 1990). European programmes have, by contrast, typically aimed higher, notably in Germany, where retraining is generally geared to the attainment of the same craft-level occupational qualifications as is apprenticeship (Johanson, 1994). The one American programme to offer longer and deeper training (under the Trade Adjustment Assistance Programme) showed the anticipated pattern, of lower earnings during training turning into higher earnings after training, relative to members of a comparison group.[5]

Second, although public training programmes in Europe have, relative to their American counterparts, traditionally been subjected to less evaluation – and that largely by the non-experimental methods (placement rates, etc) that tend to produce unduly rosy impressions – the handful of evaluations that have been performed using less crude methods have also reached more favourable conclusions than have American studies. The evidence comes primarily from Sweden and the United Kingdom, which have long offered publicly funded training to adults. The programmes in question are Sweden's Employment Training (ET) programme and the British Job Training Scheme (JTS; 1985–8). Both concentrated on off-the-job training – 'classroom' training in American parlance – ie training with broad occupational content, offered to a range of customers, including but not limited to the unemployed and the displaced. Both offered training of a duration, depth and cost well beyond those typical of programmes in the United States (Alfthan and Jonzon, 1994; Payne, 1990a).

The two evaluations of Sweden's ET programme have involved weakly experimental and quasi-experimental methods. The former, based on a comparison of participants' earnings before and after training for a 1981 cohort, found increases of 13 and 21 per cent for the first and second post-training year relative to the pre-training year. Interpreting those gains as the effects of training, high private and social returns were inferred (Axelsson and Löfgren, 1992; reported in Alfthan and Jonzon, 1994). The problem with such 'before/after' methods is that, while they promise to hold constant the troublesome unobservable personal qualities of participants, they cannot control for changes in either the wider labour market or in participants' own fortunes before training, and typically overestimate the benefits of training (see Chapter 3, Programme effects). Fortunately, Sweden's ET programme has also been evaluated quasi-experimentally, comparing the change in participant outcomes to those in a matched comparison group. A 1994 cohort of trainees was estimated to have improved its labour earnings by 3 per cent within six months of leaving the programme. The increase is not large, and is certainly less than was suggested by weakly experimental methods, but it is still statistically significant and comparable in size to the effects (in Sweden) of a full year of schooling. On the other hand, no earnings effect was found for a previous (1992) cohort, and a drop in employment rates was associated with training in the 1994 one (Tamas et al., 1995). Even so, traditional adult training in Sweden appears to avoid the label of failure that is commonly attached to public training programmes.

Similarly, a quasi-experimental evaluation of the British JTS, using a matched comparison group and adjusting for differences in observable personal characteristics (only), has suggested overall success. JTS improved significantly the three outcomes measured: employment rates, hourly pay and job satisfaction. Pay and job satisfaction rose particularly strongly for those who found employment 'in trade', ie in the occupation for which they trained. Generally favourable assessments by trainees contributed to the conclusion that 'adult training had a marked impact on many people's lives, and some saw it as a major turning point' (Payne, 1990a, 1990b).

Selection bias may well make such conclusions over-optimistic, though participants and non-participants were at least carefully matched according to prior unemployment experience. Nevertheless, JTS suggests that public training for adults can work. The similarity of the findings to those for Sweden's ET and the contrast of both to those for the successor to JTS, the British Employment Training (discussed earlier in this section), are suggestive: ET (Sweden) and JTS involved relatively ambitious courses delivered largely off-the-job; ET (Great Britain), shorter courses delivered largely through on-the-job training and dominated by work experience. While there is nothing intrinsically worse about on-the-job training – and indeed many countries have been attracted to work-based learning (see section, Employer-sponsored training) – public programmes that rely on it are often short and cheap, fail to give trainees access to qualifications, and lack effective quality control. Such programmes may lead to zero or even negative results while more substantial programmes may not.

Both the Swedish and the British evidence suggest that occupational training works at least as well for disadvantaged as for other adult trainees. The benefits of both ET (Sweden) and JTS were higher for participants with lower educational achievement than for other participants, indicating a case for such programmes on grounds of equity as well as efficiency. On the other hand, in Germany the contribution of traditional retraining to equity is limited by the fact that the most disadvantaged adults tend to be ineligible for it in the first place, given the gap between its educational requirements and their educational attainments.

The most ambitious adult training programme of all, the German, has been relatively little studied. Until recently, most evaluation was non-experimental and limited to gross outcomes (Hofbauer and Dadzio, 1984; Johanson, 1994). Weakly experimental methods followed, in the shape of two studies that used for a comparison group drop-outs from the programme and those who completed shorter training courses (Hofbauer and Dadzio, 1987; Blaschke and Nagel, 1995).[6] Both studies attributed to retraining the finding of higher downstream subsequent employment rates for those who completed their courses. The conclusion is precarious, however. Although the difference between the employment rates of completers and non-completers was as much as 15 percentage points in the former study, negative selection around non-completion must account for at least some of it. The one study to adopt an explicit comparison group, for an evaluation of adult training in Hamburg, did, however, find markedly higher employment rates amongst participants than amongst controls nine months after the end of training. For retraining, the rates were 65 per cent, as against 39–56 per cent for controls. Even then, the threat of inadequately controlled selection bias hangs over the results (Kasperek and Koop, 1991).

More sophisticated evaluation of German adult training programmes has emerged only in this decade, in association with the effects of national unification on the eastern German labour market. The massive training effort offered to eastern workers – comprising further and upgrade training as well as retraining – has been studied quasi-experimentally using regression analysis and, in most cases, controls for selection bias. The results have varied greatly. In some accounts, adult training leads to improved employment and pay for participants (Pannenberg, 1996; Schömann *et al.*, 1996); others find no favourable effects or even adverse ones (Fitzenberger and Prey, 1995; Lechner, 1995).

The difference in findings for so important an episode of public intervention vividly illustrates the sensitivity of the results of sophisticated evaluation methods to the assumptions made about selection processes. (Similar, even identical, data were used in the various studies.) It is also clear that the wider implications of even uniformly negative findings for adult training in eastern Germany in this decade would be strictly limited. The average course being short: a median duration of less than a month (Lechner, 1995) means that the eastern German effort has resembled more the United States' than traditional western German methods. More fundamentally, in a labour market as depressed as in eastern Germany in the 1990s, surplus labour floods skilled as well as unskilled labour markets. Under such conditions, even a high-quality retraining effort would be hard pressed to improve outcomes for participants, let alone workers as a whole.

Finally, there is some aggregative evidence that active labour market policies – a category covering all public programmes, as well as purely training-oriented ones – improve the functioning of the labour market by reducing the rate of unemployment at which inflation pressures increase (Jackman, 1994). We conclude, from admittedly only partial evidence, that public training often fails, particularly when it involves short, low-cost courses of remedial training and retraining, and when the criterion of success is a lasting gain in earning power, and not simply a short-term increase in employment rates for participants who continue to inhabit low-skilled labour markets. At the same time, public training can work when it sets its sights higher, aims at occupationally relevant needs in shortage labour markets and takes training quality seriously. The case is strongest for adult training, but it may well apply to youth and remedial training as well.

Individually sponsored training

We move now to private sponsorship of training, starting with the training that individuals sponsor for themselves, ie VET conducted largely or wholly apart from employment. We include in self-sponsored training all vocational courses taken in post-secondary education, such as secretarial vocational courses at American community colleges, technical institutes and proprietary schools, *Brevet de technicien* courses at French colleges, teacher training courses in British universities, and upgrading courses for *Meister* qualifications in German *Fachschulen*.

Two features require comment: the scale of activity and the age of participants. The importance of self-sponsored training varies greatly across countries (see Chapter 1, Why should VET work?). In the United States it accounts for nearly three-quarters of the private sector training experiences reported by young adults, dominating training for the 'mid-skilled' labour market in particular (Lynch, 1992; Grubb, 1996b). In the United Kingdom, by contrast, only one-fifth of privately sponsored training episodes are sponsored by individuals; the rest are sponsored by employers. Second, sponsorship of one's own training is a predominantly youth affair in many countries, its incidence declining sharply with age (eg DE, 1989) – though in the United States there has been a steady increase in numbers of older students, particularly in community colleges.

The evaluation of self-sponsored training has relied heavily on quasi-experimental methods and single outcome criteria. The standard human capital earnings function applies more directly to self-sponsorship than to other categories of training. Individual pay and employment rates are related statistically to the various types of post-secondary VET, using regression analysis to remove the effects of other individual attributes such as race and sex (see Box 3.3, above). Although the selection biases potentially associated with unobserved attributes – notably ability and motivation – have occasionally been addressed (Willis and Rosen, 1979; Goux and Maurin, 1994), the effectiveness of such 'controls' remains dubious and, in any case, most studies simply ignore selection issues.

American research suggests private returns to two-year Associate degrees of the order of 20 to 30 per cent – somewhat lower than to a four-year first degree – and returns to one-year certificates of 10 to 20 per cent. The benefits are higher in particular areas, notably business and technical fields for men and the health field for women. When students complete occupational subjects in community colleges, the private returns tend to be higher than for the equivalent general subjects if they find employment related to their area of training, and lower (even zero, particularly for women) if their employment is unrelated. A smattering of evidence indicates that the returns to the highly vocational courses offered by proprietary schools and technical institutes are lower than those in comprehensive community colleges. Finally, people who take but fail to complete post-secondary programmes, taking only a few courses, receive small net returns, generally less than 10 per cent (Freeman, 1974; Grubb, 1996b, Chapter 2; 1995a; 1997).

Such findings are probably affected by selection bias. For example, lower returns to vocational than to general subjects in community colleges may reflect lower student ability in the vocational category. One study found that correction for selection bias removed the earnings effect of vocational Associate degrees for American men, though not for women (Zilbert *et al.*, 1992). Another found that the marked effects of self-sponsored training on the pay of young American adults survived both the two step and the fixed effects corrections for selection bias (Lynch, 1992).[7]

The parallel French literature on the links between qualifications and employment (see section, Publicly sponsored training, above) suggests similarly that the possession of vocational post-secondary qualifications, notably the *Brevet de technicien* and the *Diplôme d'école d'ingénieur*, confers substantial private benefits, in terms of access to employment, relative to the less *vocationally* qualified at the same level of attainment. During 1970–93 such training reduced the incidence of unemployment, and of employment on fixed-term contracts, during the first year of labour market experience, as well as increasing life-cycle earnings powerfully. The findings survived attempts to control for unobserved selection processes (Minni and Vergnies, 1994; Goux and Maurin, 1994). They are not, however, capable of indicating whether such training is a success on wider efficiency criteria.

Finally, evidence has begun to emerge on the private returns to formal upgrade training in Germany, which we treat as sponsored by individuals rather than by employers. Skilled German workers who wish to upgrade their qualifications from *Facharbeiter* to *Meister* or *Techniker* level do so typically by taking part-time courses outside working hours, relying on local public technical colleges (Münch, 1991). The training might be expected to pay substantial dividends, given large pay differentials between these qualifications, together with strong employer demand for higher vocational qualifications.

Quasi-experimental evaluations of adult training in Germany unfortunately tend not to distinguish between upgrade and further training (*Fortbildung, Weiterbildung*), on the one hand, and retraining (*Umschulung*), on the other (eg Lechner, 1995; Pannenberg, 1996). Moreover, those who make the distinction have studied effects on employment rather than pay. In any event, positive effects on employment have been inferred by two studies. The first used a comparison group to analyse adult training in Hamburg, finding even stronger effects for upgrade training than for retraining (Kasperek and Koop, 1991). The second dealt with eastern Germany, finding that part-time adult courses are associated with lower exposure to unemployment, and full-time ones with the opposite. To the extent that upgrade training is conducted part time, and retraining full time, the implication is that upgrade training reduces the probability of entering unemployment. However, this conclusion too is endangered by selection problems (Schömann *et al.*, 1996, Tables 6, 7).[8]

In sum, in its highly varied national forms, individually sponsored training appears to improve markedly participants' subsequent labour market fortunes, even allowing for unobserved positive selection into such training. That is perhaps no surprise – and it is just as well that it is the case – given that the individuals who take the training have to invest their own time and money while doing so. It is not easy to establish the merits of such training from the efficiency standpoint, as most studies use only partial outcome measures and ignore costs. Its merits from an equity standpoint are intrinsically limited, in so far as individuals must typically already possess resources in order to undertake such training. Public subsidies do, however, reduce the costs to individuals of some forms of VET, notably community college courses in the United States, helping less advantaged individuals to undertake training.

Employer-sponsored training

Research into training organized wholly or primarily by employers has mushroomed in recent years. The category may usefully be divided into two: in-service training for existing employees, typically adults; and pre-employment training, typically for youths taken on under contracts of apprenticeship rather than employment. The former category applies to all economies. The latter applies primarily to Germany and neighbouring countries (Austria, Switzerland and Denmark), although some apprenticeship can be found in practically all advanced economies and it dominates training in the informal sectors of many developing countries (Fluitman, 1989).

The evaluation of employer-sponsored training is more complex than that of other types of training. Much is on-the-job training (OJT) in the literal sense of the term, ie it involves the joint production of skills and saleable output, which makes it difficult to separate training from production in general, and to determine how the costs and benefits of training are shared between the employer and the trainee. Measures of the value of an individual employee's output are typically poor or non-existent (Ryan, 1980). Indeed, the informality of much OJT even makes it difficult to establish whether training has occurred or not: the correlation between reports of the incidence of training made by employers and employees in the same workplace is typically low (Barron *et al.*, 1997). Few employers evaluate their own training activities, even with non-experimental or weakly experimental methods (DE, 1989; Kirkpatrick, 1994).

Above all, the simple analytical framework used in mainstream evaluations of publicly and individually sponsored training, in which benefits are measured through changes in the employment and pay of individual participants, is particularly inadequate for in-service training. It is true that under particular assumptions – notably that skills are highly transferable between employers and all markets are perfectly competitive – such methods would be appropriate. However, as soon as skills are allowed to be at least partly specific to the employer that provided the training, the method breaks down. Pay gains for participants no longer measure productivity gains for the economy, if they ever did in the first place. Both the employer who provides the training and any other employer who hires the trained workers then share in the benefits. Such is the classic training externality (Becker, 1964; Stevens, 1996). The point has been recognized even by economists otherwise happy to live with the simplifying assumptions of competitive economic theory (Barron *et al.*, 1997).

Training evaluation must therefore consider productivity effects as well as – if not more than – pay changes. Aggregate-level evaluations are particularly valuable in the face of the potentially large training externalities associated with the recruitment of employer-trained workers by other employers ('poaching').

In-service training

The training that employers provide to employees comprises induction training for new hires, initial training for new jobs, and upgrade training and retraining for promotions and transfers within the organization. It varies in formality, from learning-by-doing to courses at external institutions; and in transferability, from the purely company specific to the 'general' skills of an occupational labour market. Academic research by economists typically treats these various types of training as an undifferentiated whole, drawing upon national data on individual workers and implicitly comparing those with training to those without. The comparisons in question therefore straddle occupations and sectors, in the case of individual workers and employers, respectively (eg Blundell *et al.*, 1996). By contrast, business academics and practitioners tend to evaluate the formalization of training, by comparing formal and informal training within particular jobs in particular enterprises (eg Thomas *et al.*, 1969).

Selection bias is again potentially important. The difference from public training is again that the employees selected for such training are likely to be higher rather than lower than average in terms of unmeasured 'labour quality'. Employers have incentives to pick more rather than less trainable employees; public programmes, particularly remedial ones, are often slanted towards the less trainable. Moreover, as training is typically associated with promotion along the job ladders and career promotion lines of the organization in question, part of any pay increases associated with training may be spurious, reflecting more the hierarchical structure of pay than the direct effect of training. Similar difficulties arise in isolating the benefits of training to employers (Auer, 1994).

These reservations notwithstanding, most evaluations of in-service training indicate positive results for employees and employers alike. For employees, higher pay has been found to follow employer-provided training in economy-wide data for the United States, the United Kingdom and Germany – although in the case of the United States, the effects become small, even insignificant, after quasi-experimental controls for selection bias. Moreover, the pay effect appears to operate only marginally through the reduction in pay during in-service training that is predicted by human capital theory (Lynch, 1992; Barron *et al.*, 1997; Blundell *et al.*, 1996; Büchel and Pannenberg, 1994).

Looked at in detail, the benefits of in-service training to employees show up primarily in wage rates, and not simply in employment rates, as in many public programmes. The difference undoubtedly reflects the fact that in-service training is provided mostly to the already employed, and public training to the unemployed, but there may also be differences in skill content and quality as well. The benefits of in-service training also appear to be long-lived, like those of formal education, and unlike those of remedial training. Recent American and British studies have both found that benefits persist for at least a decade after training (Lengermann, 1996; Blundell *et al.*, 1996).

The benefits of in-service training overlap with those of promotion, and in some American – though not in British – evidence disappears when selection bias is addressed (Lynch, 1992; Blundell *et al.*, 1996). In some results, in-service training generates larger benefits for workers than does self-sponsored training; in others, the reverse (Tan *et al.*, 1992; Lynch, 1992). It is also clear that the disadvantaged enjoy little access to in-service training, but it is not clear whether the minority that does so enjoys higher benefits than do more advantaged participants (Ryan, 1990: Barron *et al.*, 1997).

Finally, the benefits of training to workers appear highly transferable: pay gains following training are typically not reduced, and may even rise, when an employee changes employer (Blundell *et al.*, 1996; Lengermann, 1996). The implication is again that in-service training generates economic benefits, particularly within the training company, over and above any effect on trainees' subsequent pay (Bishop, 1996).

Pay effects are therefore only the beginning of the story of in-service training. Productivity effects have also been studied, at various levels of aggregation. Starting at the lowest level, it is no surprise to find that the productivity of individual employees is usually increased by training, even within particular job categories. More interesting is the finding that training increases productivity more than it does pay – in one study, ten times more strongly during the first three months of a typical job (Barron *et al.*, 1989; Bishop, 1994; Barron *et al.*, 1997: de Koonig, 1994). The latter conclusion is, however, fragile, as employee productivity is typically measured by supervisory ratings, an ordinal index prone to subjective errors and biases (Bartel, 1995).

Moving up the ladder, training also proves statistically associated with productivity at company and sectoral levels, where externalities are in principle captured at least in part. Research here typically investigates total factor productivity, using a production function to link output to training flows (or, more appropriately, skill stocks), holding constant other inputs, including physical capital and labour hours. Simple estimates sometimes do and sometimes do not find a relationship (O'Mahoney and Wagner, 1996), but selection bias and the interdependence of training and productivity potentially distort such results. Selection bias could occur were the companies that provide more training the 'better' ones in various unmeasured ways – better managed overall, for example. Statistical estimates would then attribute to training the effects of unmeasured company virtues. Mutual dependence is also plausible: high productivity may lead firms to do more training, whether or not more training leads to high productivity. Alternatively, low-productivity companies may have to do more training in order to survive. In the former case, the effects of training on productivity reinforce the positive relationship between the two; in the latter, they offset it and may lead to the apparent absence of any relationship in a cross-section of employers.

Using simple controls for selection bias, quasi-experimental analysis of employer surveys in five developing countries has found positive associations between indices of employer training efforts – typically the presence of a training programme, formal or informal – and total factor productivity. The size of the training effect is, however, implausibly large in some countries, as well as uncomfortably variable from country to country (Tan and Batra, 1995). Similarly, research on productivity in matched plants in various British, German and Dutch sectors has pointed to workforce skills, particularly at craft/technician level, as a major source of productivity differences (Prais, 1995; see Box 3.9, above). Finally, when time lags are used to distinguish the effect of training on productivity from that of productivity on training, both relationships emerge. In the United States in the 1980s, low productivity in particular companies led them to increase their training efforts, as measured by the presence of formal training programmes; those higher training efforts in turn subsequently increased the same companies' relative productivity – though such an account is perhaps too good to be fully convincing (Bartel, 1994).

Finally, evidence on implementation again assists the task of evaluation. Case studies are particularly valuable here, illuminating here both selection processes and the disparity between pay and productivity effects. On the former, it was found useful to divide professional training in one large American company into three categories: core, developmental and technical. Core training was offered primarily to those with potential for promotion, while developmental training went to under-performers. Statistical analysis without allowance for these underlying *and opposite* selection processes suggested that the effect of training on pay was higher for core than for developmental training. When selection was considered, however, developmental training proved unrelated to pay, whereas the effects of core training were still greater than in the simpler analysis (Bartel, 1995).

The disparity between the effects of company training on pay and productivity is difficult to explain in standard human capital terms (Barron *et al.*, 1997). Case study evidence suggests, however, that such disparities may be generated by 'non-economic' forces, as the effect of two pervasive employee norms. The first is that pay differentials within a particular job category or organizational rank should be limited in size, or even absent altogether. The second is that trainee status does not by itself constitute a legitimate source of pay differentiation (Ryan, 1984).

In sum, the evidence points to important links between in-service training, on the one hand, and pay and productivity, on the other. The conclusion is hardly surprising: employers have every reason to use training to their own benefit, and to do so sparingly in view of the threat which labour turnover poses to their ability to use the asset. But the pattern of the evidence – the combination of distinct benefits to the trained employee and to the training employer, as well as the potential benefits to the non-training employer – suggests a case for public intervention.

Apprenticeship

Apprenticeship differs from 'in service' training in its orientation to youth entrants to the labour market, and in involving specialized, training-related, fixed-duration contracts rather than work-related, indefinite-duration employment contracts.

Apprenticeship is highly heterogeneous. Two polar types may be distinguished, which we term for convenience the 'modern' and the 'traditional'. In its continental European variants, modern apprenticeship involves structured programmes of education, training and work experience, sponsored primarily by employers, and secondarily by other interested parties – employer associations, trade unions, educational authorities and public training agencies (Münch, 1991).[9] The training is geared to skills with an educational and occupational rather than simply a job-related content; and to craft, technician and even higher skills, rather than to immediate job requirements at semi-skilled level. Under traditional apprenticeship, things are more informal. Young people receive whatever training and work experience the employer cares to offer. The training typically lacks educational requirements and external regulation (Fluitman, 1989).

The difference in the amount and quality of the VET involved in modern and traditional apprenticeship is therefore considerable. As apprenticeship programmes may be located in practice anywhere between these two poles, it is inappropriate to conceive of apprenticeship as a single entity. The findings discussed here refer primarily to the modern end of the spectrum in developed economies – though even there apprenticeship is pretty heterogeneous.[10]

Evaluation methods
The evaluation of apprenticeship faces at least two problems additional to those noted above for in-service training (Ryan, 1998a). The first applies to the training of all young labour market entrants: the absence of a prior earnings and employment record from which to glean information on unobserved personal attributes for an attack on selection bias. The second is specific to large-scale, quasi-entitlement apprenticeship programmes along German lines: non-participants are neither numerous enough nor similar enough to apprentices to permit effective statistical correction for differences in the attributes of participant and comparison groups. In Germany in particular, the experiences of apprentices after training cannot be compared to those of highly similar young people without training or with full-time vocational education instead.[11] Both the untrained and the more educated – the obvious constituencies for the choice of comparison groups – are either too few or too different from apprentices to permit effective statistical analysis, whether by individual matching or by regression-based correction for differences in personal attributes.[12]

The latter difficulty is symptomatic of a deeper problem: it is more difficult to evaluate *systems*, with their multi-dimensional goals and multiple, intertwined characteristics, than it is to evaluate specific public *programmes*, with their typically unidimensional goals and simple attributes. It is also the case that no social experiment involving apprenticeship has ever been conducted. Consequently, while quasi-experimental evidence remains valuable, weakly experimental methods (notably international comparisons) become more important for the evaluation of apprenticeship than for other VET categories, particularly the more *ad hoc* types of public programme discussed in the section, Publicly sponsored training, above.

Evaluation findings

We consider first the findings of evaluations oriented to economic outcomes, first, for individuals and, second, for employers and the economy. A variety of evidence suggests widespread benefits to individuals from undertaking apprenticeship (Ryan, 1998a, 1998b). The evaluation may involve either full-time vocational education, or employment and simple job training as the alternative, depending on whether apprenticeship is viewed primarily in educational or economic terms.

In terms of *pay*, quasi-experimental research attributes gains to apprenticeship, particularly in relation to regular labour market activity, and particularly for males in the United States and the United Kingdom. In comparison to full-time schooling in France and Germany, however, pay benefits are negligible, and in the case of females in the United Kingdom and the United States, negative, even in studies that attempt to control for selection bias.[13]

In English-speaking economies, the benefits of apprenticeship to workers have traditionally been associated with access to occupational labour markets subject to trade union regulation – such as unionized construction in New York City. Nowadays, however, the returns earned by ex-apprentices in non-union firms prove no lower than those earned in union ones (Blanchflower and Lynch, 1994).

Looked at from a different standpoint, the apparent similarity of the returns to apprenticeship and those to full-time vocational education in Germany suggests that in that country at least apprenticeship belongs at the educational end of the VET spectrum, where substantial gains in pay result from training, rather than at the public training end, where pay gains are generally absent.

The benefits of apprenticeship for pay in Germany appear to depend partly upon the presence of an occupational 'fit' between training and subsequent employment, at least for males (Witte and Kalleberg, 1995). The finding may well reflect the occupational mismatch associated with surplus training by artisanal (*Handwerk*) firms, many of whose 'graduates' move into semi-skilled jobs in large firms, generating the notorious tendency for automobile companies to employ more qualified bakers, primarily on assembly line work, than does the baking industry itself. Artisanal apprentices in particular may have to remain in their occupation – where by law they do at least enjoy the status of skilled worker – in order to benefit from their training.

As is the case for public programmes, the absence of marked effects on pay in apprenticeship promotes interest in its *employment effects*. Apprenticeship lays stronger claims here. Our review starts with quasi-experimental studies. In France, apprenticeship is associated with superior employment outcomes in early working life relative to both alternatives, after attempts to remove selection bias (Sollogoub and Ulrich, 1997). Similarly, after controls for observed personal attributes only, German apprentices are found to experience lower rates of unemployment after training than do both the untrained and graduates of full-time vocational education (Winkelmann, 1996). Indeed, the transition from training to employment in Germany proves less dependent on observed personal attributes than is the earlier one from school to apprenticeship (Palmidis and Schwarze, 1989).

Weakly experimental evidence contributes here as well. Comparing gross outcomes across different French programmes, the first jobs found subsequently by apprentices prove more stable than those found by graduates of full-time vocational secondary education, suggesting that apprenticeship encourages stable employment (Affichard *et al.*, 1992).

Similarly, international comparisons suggest favourable apprenticeship effects on youth employment and unemployment. In one study, unemployment rates in Germany, relative to those for similarly qualified French workers, prove lower for intermediate qualifications, which are produced primarily by apprenticeship in Germany and by full-time schooling in France, than for either higher and lower levels of qualification, which in both countries depend primarily on full-time schooling. As this inverse-U relationship between relative national unemployment and level of worker qualification is more marked for young workers than for all workers, apprenticeship may be presumed to increase employment rates most strongly in early working life – though demographic and other differences may also play a part (Möbus and Sevestre, 1991). Other comparative research also suggests favourable contributions from apprenticeship to youth employment rates.[14]

Little attention has been devoted to the link between apprenticeship and socio-economic disadvantage. The sign of any such relationship is not clear *a priori*. On the one hand, the motivating effects of practical learning may be particularly valuable for academic low achievers; on the other, the same low achievers may find the knowledge requirements of craft and technician courses too demanding and either drop out or fail to be taken on in the first place. The absence of interaction terms in the regression models of quasi-experimental research typically leaves this important issue uninvestigated.

More information is also needed on the implications of apprenticeship heterogeneity. Apprenticeship has been found particularly valuable for subsequent careers when it is associated with a vocational qualification, and particularly with higher vocational qualifications. Such effects have been found in relation to pay in the United Kingdom and in relation to employment rates in France (Blanchflower and Lynch, 1994; Romani and Werquin, 1997; Sollogoub and Ulrich, 1997). But, more generally, little is known concerning the degree to which the benefits of the informal, traditional apprenticeship fall short – as might be expected – of those of its formal, modern counterpart.

Unfortunately, evaluations from more aggregate standpoints – those of the employer, the sector and the economy – are rarer for apprenticeship than for in-service training. Comparisons of economic performance in matched plants and sectors of British and German industry (Prais, 1995; see Boxes 3.9, 3.10, above) involved the entire qualifications of the relevant workforces, rather than apprenticeship training *per se*. As, however, the key linkage between skills and performance concerned intermediate qualifications, and as apprenticeship has provided the dominant route to intermediate qualifications in both countries, the research suggests a powerful link between apprenticeship, on the one hand, and productivity and trade performance, on the other.

The assessment of apprenticeship can also draw upon research at earlier stages of our concept of human capital development. A key issue involves the learning stage: to what extent does apprenticeship fulfil its pedagogical ambitions, as the leading vehicle for the *alternance* ideal in VET, and lead to learning and development superior to that produced by full-time schooling followed by in-service training? While traditional apprenticeship might be expected to fail on this count, little evidence is available concerning modern apprenticeship. To some extent the gap in evidence reflects the difficulty of measuring learning, particularly in the more subtle forms – core skills, key skills, etc. – that are prized by vocationalist ideals. Nevertheless, implementation-oriented evidence, based upon direct inspection, questionnaires and interviews, often points to poor integration of the classroom and the workplace as sources of learning, in some German and French apprenticeship programmes at least (HMI, 1991; Lemaire, 1993; Baudelot and Creusen, undated). To that extent, both the educational and the economic potential of apprenticeship is sometimes only inadequately fulfilled.

Finally, implementation issues are particular important for a system as elaborate and complicated as modern apprenticeship. In fact, the key question for the evaluation of apprenticeship is arguably not 'does it work?' but 'can it be set up in the first place?' The obstacles are daunting. An intricate, multi-level network of social partnership at various levels sustains apprenticeship in German industry (Streeck *et al.*, 1987), an extended historical development lies behind it (Taylor, 1981) – and even then the sources of its coherence remain a matter of debate and its future a matter of concern (eg, Franz and Soskice, 1995; Harhoff and Kane, 1996). The absence of comparably supportive institutions has contributed to the decline of apprenticeship in English-speaking countries (Marsden and Ryan, 1991b; Gospel, 1995). Moreover, attempts by developing countries to adopt variants of German apprenticeship have all failed for lack of suitable institutional support, whether by public education, employer associations, trade unions, tripartite bodies, etc (Böhm, 1994; Jeong, 1995).

On the other hand, the French government's recent efforts to tie apprenticeship more closely to educational qualifications and to entice large employers to sponsor it may yet revitalize a low-status, declining VET channel. If so, it will become clearer that German-type institutions need not constitute the only viable support system for apprenticeship (Combes, 1988; Lemaire, 1993; MTDSP, 1995).

We conclude that, while apprenticeship appears to make distinctive and separate contributions to the interests of workers, employers, and the economy as a whole, a better understanding of the conditions for its implementation remains an important objective and therefore an appropriate topic for further research.

Conclusions

While the evidence provided by evaluation research is necessarily partial, the diverse sources of evidence still paint a broadly coherent picture, even if the impossibility of controlling fully for selection biases suggests caution. The evidence suggests first that particular types of training work well, for both participants, employers and the economy in general, while others work poorly or not at all. The category of largely ineffective programmes includes most public remedial training, particularly that aimed at disadvantaged young workers; public programmes that promote the insertion of young people into employment, although some French programmes do help participants to gain work more easily; and most traditional vocational education in secondary schools. The effective category is dominated by privately sponsored training, both post-secondary VET sponsored by individuals, and in-service employee training and apprenticeship sponsored by employers.

Second, both the content and the context of training can make a big difference to its effects. Publicly sponsored adult training programmes have succeeded, at least in terms of benefits to participants, under two particular conditions: when they provide occupational training and access to vocational qualifications, and when skilled labour is scarce in the occupational markets towards which training is oriented. Moreover, displacement is expected to be low under such conditions. When, however, all that a public programme has to offer is informal, low-level 'training', and its clientele is predominantly disadvantaged workers who face low-skill, overstocked labour markets, evidence of failure hardly comes as a surprise.

The tendency for more favourable evaluation results in private than in public sponsored training has become widely recognized. It has encouraged the privatization of training provision and finance in many economies, both developed and developing. The contemporary popularity in policy circles of promoting training partnerships between governments and employers has been encouraged by such evidence (ILO, 1998, Chapter 3).

There is much to commend in such policies, At the same time, some flies can be seen struggling in the ointment. First, adverse assessments of public training programmes have relied excessively on evidence from the 'shoddy' end of public efforts, notably the short and cheap programmes that have dominated provision for disadvantaged and displaced workers in the United States. The most intensive American programme, the Job Corps, appears to provide benefits to both participants and the economy. The deeper, occupationally oriented training that had, until the present decade at least, dominated adult programmes in Sweden, Germany and the United Kingdom appears to have helped its participants, particularly until the recent intensification of unemployment. Public training is by no means doomed to failure, even if it is all too often used as a palliative for unemployment. And public regulatory participation is a key ingredient in the successful German apprenticeship training system.

Second, the goals of public programmes are not limited, and should not be limited, to the efficiency-oriented criteria to which evaluation is typically limited. Programmes for the disadvantaged in particular are widely intended to offer an activity-based alternative to idleness and personal decay. Even programmes judged failures on efficiency grounds can achieve that goal – though from the equity standpoint there is then no particular case for focusing participant activities upon training, as opposed to education or useful and interesting work.

Third, even if company training generally provides benefits for employers and employees, that does not necessarily make it a superior vehicle for public training objectives. Public programmes that harness employer training to public goals, such as contemporary insertion programmes in France and the United Kingdom, have the merit of linking training to immediate economic needs and of encouraging employers as a whole to offer more training. However, evaluations of such programmes have typically found them ineffective on the tougher, skills-oriented criterion of increasing participants' earning power. Two factors appear to limit those programmes' contributions. First, much in-service training is narrowly job specific, suiting the interests of the employer more than those of the trainee or the wider economy. Second, little training is often provided in the first place. In the absence of effective quality control, less scrupulous employers are encouraged to sign up for cheap trainee labour. The difference between the results of the British Employment Training programme and its Job Training Scheme, as between those of the Youth Training Scheme and apprenticeship, vividly illustrate this neglected problem.

The underlying difficulty is that public policy has in some countries adopted reactive, rushed, and institutionally shallow responses to skill and employment problems, preferring the quick fix to the long haul, the catchy acronym to the established institution, the politically partisan innovation to the consensual development of an agreed and durable training system.

Notes

1. There are differences, in these and other evaluations, between the benefits per person *assigned* to the programme and benefits to those *enrolled* – because many people assigned never enrol. Benefits per enrolee are therefore higher than benefits per assignee, and evaluators disagree about which measure is more appropriate.
2. *Certificat d'Aptitude Professionnelle* and *Brevet d'Etudes Professionnelles*, respectively.
3. Only one of four quasi-experimental evaluations of the employment effect of YTS found that it reduced rather than increased subsequent employment rates for participants (Ryan and Büchtemann, 1996, Table 10.5).
4. These distinctions are unavoidably blurred. Many adult education courses (eg photography) appeal to some customers for vocational reasons, but to others for purely recreational reasons.
5. Corson et al. (1993), cited by Leigh (1994).
6. The former study addressed the manifest threat of selection bias – probably ineffectively – by excluding from the comparison group all non-completers who had been judged unsuitable for training.
7. The category 'off-the-job training' appears to denote in Lynch's study training that is not sponsored by an employer; it is taken here to be dominated by individually sponsored training.
8. It seems unlikely that retraining *increases* exposure to unemployment. More likely, the retraining 'effect' is caused by uncontrolled negative selection effects, given that no attempt was made to counter such bias. Similarly, the upgrade training effect may also reflect positive selection, to the extent that more able and motivated workers are more likely to undertake such training. Incidentally, the authors interpret the difference between the effects of part-time and full-time courses in terms of the pedagogical benefits of combining learning and working, but differences in the constituency and type of training offer a more plausible line of explanation.
9. The primacy of employers in sponsoring apprenticeship can be illustrated from the efforts of the British Government to resuscitate apprenticeship under its Modern Apprenticeship scheme. The key difference between apprenticeship, on the one hand, and full-time vocational education with work experience content, on the other, was seen as the initiatory role and overall responsibility for training of the employer in apprenticeship – although in practice, public colleges of further education have been allowed by default to sponsor apprentices under the programme.

10. In Germany, apprenticeship in small *Handwerk* firms differs considerably from that in large industrial and commercial firms. The lack of an agreed picture of apprenticeship is particularly marked in contemporary France. Some commentators accord low status to apprenticeship, presenting it either as a low-quality relic associated with artisanal production or as just another contemporary training scheme to deal with youth unemployment (Romani and Werquin, 1997; Bonnal *et al.*, 1995a). Others treat it as the leading alternative to full-time upper secondary vocational education, emphasizing its educational content and institutional resilience (Lhotel and Monaco, 1993).

11. In the Netherlands and France, however, apprenticeship and full-time schooling provide in at least some occupations alternative paths to particular vocational qualifications (eg Van der Velden and Lodder, 1995).

12. Evaluations that ignore these problems are prone to error. For example, the wage gains attributed to British apprenticeship by Blanchflower and Lynch (1994, Tables 6, 8) apparently involve the use of first-year apprentice pay as an index of the apprentice's prior state – in which case, what is measured is not just the effect of training on pay, but also the extent to which the trainee pays for the training through a lower training wage in the first place.

13. Lynch (1992), Blanchflower and Lynch (1994), Payne (1995), Büchel and Helberger (1995), Sollogoub and Ulrich (1997). Negative pay gains for women in the United Kingdom and the United States presumably reflect both low female access to apprenticeship (to the hairdressing sector in the United Kingdom, to practically nothing in the United States) and low returns to skills as feminized as hairdressing.

14. Two studies may be mentioned here. In one, the vast difference in the importance of apprenticeship in school-to-work transitions in Germany and the United States is associated in panel data with lower unemployment and a better match between skill supply and demand in Germany during the first 12 years of working life (Büchtemann *et al.*, 1993). In the other, the EU countries that made more extensive use of apprenticeship for initial training in industry showed, in the 1960s and 1970s at least, higher rates of youth employment than did those that relied instead upon full-time secondary schooling and informal job training (Marsden and Ryan, 1990).

5

Judging evaluation
The limits of the evaluation enterprise

Only in the United States has the recommendation to evaluate become routine, at least for remedial job training. There, the evaluation enterprise has generated an argument that reinforces the need for evaluation: because there have been so many negative evaluations, particularly of short-term and remedial training, the simple faith in education and training cannot easily be maintained. When the suspicion of ineffectiveness becomes widespread, then it becomes necessary to evaluate everything in order to maintain public and private support. And so in the United States evaluation has become a new article of faith, replacing the older faith in education and training itself: only if a programme is evaluated rigorously and found effective can it be maintained. Under these circumstances, VET programmes (like other government programmes) have to prove themselves before they can continue.[1]

In other countries, evaluation has been increasing, partly as a way to justify public spending, and we stress that there are many other potential benefits to evaluation, as described in Chapter 2. However, before other countries go down the path of the United States, there are two large qualifications to the new faith in evaluation. The first, explored in this chapter, is that under certain conditions evaluation can give incorrect or misleading results – not just for specific programmes, but for VET as a whole. Policy-makers, administrators and researchers undertaking evaluation need to be aware of the larger problems associated with evaluation, and structure their approaches to both VET and evaluation accordingly.

The second qualification, taken up in Chapter 6, is that evaluation may not be used in policy-making in ways that researchers and evaluators envision. Rather than informing the decisions of governments and employers, it may be ignored, distorted, or used for overly political purposes. Or evaluation results may simply be missing and incomplete, in which case there are other ways of making decisions, some of which pay attention to the underlying logic of VET programmes and some of which simply replicate familiar political decisions. Once we have discussed these two limitations, then we can understand what evaluation can and cannot accomplish and under what conditions it helps to improve the understanding of what VET can do.

Of course, evaluations of VET programmes may be individually misleading because they are done 'incorrectly', essentially because they fail to consider the methodological issues reviewed in Chapter 3. For example, evaluations that fail to consider selection effects, or the strength or weakness of employment demand at various points in the business cycle, cannot provide accurate results except by chance. But here we discuss not *individual* failures of evaluation, but *systemic* problems, where evaluation is likely to be misleading because the technique is poorly suited to the larger issue of what VET can accomplish. We concentrate on four problems in particular: the distinction between short-run and long-run results; the quantity/quality dilemma; the incentives that evaluation itself creates; and the partial nature of evaluation, particularly where a complex of institutions and policies may affect the results of education and training.

Short-run results in a long-run world

There are at least two timing problems that affect many evaluations. The first of these is the problem (sometimes referred to as 'maturation') of whether a programme has been completely implemented – whether the programme is in place, with the academic and vocational instruction and other services intended, with trainees enrolled and completing and who are the targeted trainees. If a programme is evaluated prematurely, before it is truly in place, then a negative evaluation may result, but that may be a false conclusion, due not to the ineffectiveness of the programme but to the fact that there is no real programme.

In theory, a 'process' evaluation, or careful description of what has and has not been put in place, can determine whether this is true or not.[2] Therefore a conventional recommendation is that evaluators undertake a process evaluation before moving to outcome evaluation. However, the assumption underlying this standard recommendation is that the period of implementation is finite: a programme can be put in place within three months, or two years, or some other relatively fixed period of time. If it has not been implemented by then, it is declared a failure for reasons that may range from idiosyncratic to systemic. A different view, however, is that something as complex as a VET programme does not emerge completely implemented within a finite and relatively short period of time, but instead develops over time, with a particular culture, a set of distinctive norms and practices, a particular way of preparing its instructors, just as educational institutions have typically evolved over many decades.

The short-term focus of most process evaluation in effect works against the notion of institution-building: a programme is conceived of something that can be created relatively quickly, introduced among the other institutions of a society, evaluated as a discrete entity, expanded or contracted. We call this a 'project' or 'programme' view, because of its tendency to think of a VET programme as self-contained and independent. Then, what is convention-ally called 'programme evaluation' assesses the effects of the programme only, independently of any surrounding policies and institutions. We con-trast this with what we call a 'systems' view, a perspective that is more common in general education, where institutions have developed over rela-tively long periods of time in systems of articulated institutions and programmes, for example, pre-school programmes leading to elementary schools, leading in turn to secondary schools preparing individuals for various post-secondary options. Most evaluation is consistent more with a 'programme' view than with a 'systems' view: conventional outcome evalua-tions like those described in Chapter 3, The challenge of comparisons, have most often been applied to discrete projects, and the short-term perspective of both process and outcome evaluation in many ways reinforces the 'programme' conception of VET. We return to the question of 'programme' versus 'systems' views later in this chapter.

The second timing problem involves the period of evaluation. Conven-tionally, evaluations of VET programmes examine employment within a rela-tively short period of time after completing the programme, within 30 or 90 days, in many cases, or within two years in some of the most sophisticated ran-dom-assignment evaluations.[3] But, as we have noted in earlier chapters, short-run results are not necessarily related to long-run results: the evaluations in the United States that have taken the longest perspective have uniformly suggested that the benefits of remedial training vanish over five or six years, and short-run evaluations give misleading perspectives about the value of small interventions like job search assistance compared to more substantial forms of education and training. In effect, the short-term focus of most evalua-tions mistakenly confirms the value of those services intended to have quick effects, and conversely devalues those (like more substantial education) whose benefits can materialize only after several years.

The obvious solution to this timing problem is to extend all evaluations over longer periods of time – five or six years at a minimum.[4] Of course, this increases the cost and complexity of evaluation, and means that results about effectiveness cannot be quickly available – a special problem given the impa-tience of many policy-makers and the short-term requirements of many political systems. Such a recommendation is more in keeping with a 'systems' perspective than with a 'programme' focus: it would require policy-makers to think about VET programmes in a longer-run sense – as efforts to generate benefits over a longer period of time, and to create institutions that can endure and improve as more information is generated about their effects on trainees, employers and others. But if evaluations have a shorter-term focus, then they may be misleading in several ways, no matter how technically competent they may be.

The quantity/quality dilemma revisited: the biases of evaluation

Issues of programme quality are unavoidable. The most common statement among proponents of education and training as solutions to various economic problems is that countries ought to sponsor both *more* and *better* education and training. If programmes are found to have negligible effects, the most obvious reason (after the possibility that they have not been implemented properly) is that they are of low quality – a particular danger where programmes are short, or of low cost and intensity, or emphasize services (like counselling and job search assistance) that do not substantially improve job-related competencies. And of course evaluation is sometimes intentionally used to improve the quality of individual programmes, or to identify promising practices for others to follow.

Unfortunately, for a variety of reasons it is much more difficult to enhance quality than it is to focus on the numbers of individuals trained and educated. As argued in Chapter 3, Outcome measures, dimensions of quality often involve arguments about which there is little evidence. For example, should vocational instructors have more experience or more preparation in teaching methods? Should VET take place in school-based settings (or in other institutions unconnected to work) or in work-based settings? Are more resources per trainee (including smaller class sizes), and longer or more intensive training, preferable to shorter and cheaper programmes? Should VET instruction follow competency-based approaches that have become popular in a number of countries, or does this narrow teaching inappropriately? Should instruction focus on relatively job-specific procedural knowledge, or emphasize instead greater conceptual understanding of work processes and machines? Is basic literacy more important than technical skills? These kinds of debates about the quality of programmes all involve Stages 1 and 2 of the human capital model outlined in Chapter 1, stages that are rarely the subject of evaluation.

In theory, these kinds of question should be resolved by empirical research. For example, experiments or other analyses could be undertaken by comparing the effectiveness of instructors with more experience versus those with more teacher training;[5] or examining the effects of more resources or more intensive programmes on subsequent outcomes. In practice, however, dimensions of quality are often matters of faith, as is, for example, the preference for occupational experience over formal training in hiring vocational instructors, or the preference for the dual system in German and Swiss education. And when such analyses have been undertaken they are often inconclusive, either because of methodological flaws,[6] a short-run focus,[7] or simply an inability to capture all the potentially important dimensions of quality that may be important. As a result there is little evidence about the effects of varying quality in VET programmes, though virtually all the ongoing debates – including some that we review in Chapter 7 – are debates about quality.

In addition, many evaluations have been designed so that dimensions of quality are simply uninvestigated, or unreported, or otherwise hidden from view. Typically, process evaluations asked whether a programme is up and running, whether the target number of individuals are enrolled, and how long they remain enrolled, but these are largely quantitative indicators that ignore whether instructors are appropriately qualified, or what kind of teaching takes place, or specifically what services a trainee receives. In many experimental and quasi-experimental evaluations, those enrolled in the programme are treated as a homogeneous group receiving the same services, ignoring the variation in their experiences; similarly, the control or comparison group is treated as if they received no services at all, which may not be true.[8] By treating the programme being evaluated as a black box, dimensions of quality are effectively ignored.

One particular dimension of quality that is difficult to incorporate into evaluations is the breadth of a VET programme. Many countries have become interested in broader and less job-specific forms of vocational education, better integrated with underlying academic competencies, closer to 'education' than to 'training'; this interest has been generated by the failure of narrow forms of vocational education and by calls for higher-order competencies that cannot be taught in narrow, skill-specific job training. But broader and more general programmes are more difficult to evaluate. If such programmes are indeed broader, individuals completing them are likely to go into a wider array of occupations; thus it is more difficult to tell what a job-related placement is. The benefits of such programmes are likely to develop over longer periods of time, as individuals are able to adjust as the economy changes and their careers progress; thus, short-term evaluations are unlikely to capture the full range of benefits. Part of the benefit of broader VET programmes is likely to be captured by employers (see Chapter 4, Employer-sponsored training), and these benefits are notoriously difficult to measure. Similarly, broader training is less likely to result in displacement than is narrow and skill-specific training, where there are typically many individuals who have obtained such skills in many ways; but in the absence of efforts to measure displacement, this benefit will not be clear. Finally, the learning that takes place in broader and more integrated programmes (ie at Stage 2) is more difficult to measure, particularly with standardized academic tests. Indeed, the efforts to develop broader forms of occupational education have foundered on precisely these kinds of problems (Grubb, 1995a, especially Vol. II): a system that has been created for narrow and job-specific VET will reinforce narrow programmes and impede broader programmes in many ways.

In addition, governments typically have found it difficult to control the quality and breadth of VET programmes. Enrolments can usually be increased by providing additional funding, but quality is much more difficult to influence. It requires various combinations of instructor training, external incentives, and standards (like performance measures and student certification), more precise targeting on the most promising occupations, discussions with advisory boards including employer and worker representatives, and technical assistance to enhance any of these. In many countries, there are active debates about quality, but they take place with different intensity in different parts of the VET system precisely because of the institutional divisions mentioned in Chapter 1, Conceptions of education and training. For example, there is serious concern in the United States about the quality of instruction in secondary education, but almost no mention in post-secondary occupational education or in remedial job training.

Finally, it is difficult to signal dimensions of quality to employers, so that they know if their applicants are better prepared for their kind of production.[9] The effort to signal quality has largely taken the form of specifying licensing examinations or qualifications, for example, the *Facharbeiter* in Germany, or NVQs in England and Wales (and SVQs in Scotland), or licensing examinations for health technicians in the United States. However, while some of these (like the German *Facharbeiter*) appear to have worked well – in the sense that they have become widely accepted as reflecting high-level mastery – others (like the NVQs) have yet to become effective signals of quality.[10] In still other cases, particularly in countries hostile to regulation, such standards are voluntary, and their use by employers is difficult to judge. Furthermore, remedial training and retraining for unemployed workers often convey their own *negative* signals, because individuals completing such programmes by design come from the ranks of the unemployed and underemployed, and employers may suspect them of being low-ability or unmotivated workers. Under these circumstances it is difficult to create a signal of high quality to counteract the suspicion of negative selection.

For all these reasons, then, it has been difficult to improve the quality of VET programmes. Many countries have followed a *quantity* rather than a *quality* strategy, trying to increase the numbers of enrolments in VET rather than improving its quality.[11] (The main exceptions tend to be countries in the tradition of the German dual system, which embody several mechanisms of quality control and have been widely if incompletely emulated.) To be sure, evaluation has been only one part of this problem, but it may be particularly influential because it has the potential to provide evidence about the effects of varying quality. When we turn in Chapter 8 to recommendations, we will return to the issue of quality as well.

Incentives for VET programmes and policies

In addition to providing information to policy-makers and to employers, evaluation also creates various incentives for VET programmes. Some of these are intended, of course, for example, the performance measures in American job training programmes are intended to improve placement rates, by creating targets for programmes to meet and (in theory) penalizing them if placement rates fall below a particular standard. Positive incentives can also be used: for example, in the United States the basic remedial training programme (JTPA) reserves funds for state governors to allocate on the basis of high performance; in Tennessee a small amount of funding is distributed to secondary vocational programmes that demonstrate above-average performance; and Florida is moving towards allocating some funding (15 per cent) on the basis of common outcome measures like placement rates.

The downside is that evaluation and performance measures may create perverse incentives, rather than enhancing the quality of programmes. The most obvious of these is 'creaming': if programmes are judged according to their performance, this creates incentives to enrol only the most able, motivated, and experienced individuals. This is a standard and intended feature of employer-sponsored upgrade training, where employers generally choose their most promising employees for further training. However, creaming in remedial and retraining programmes undermines the typical purpose of providing training for the most disadvantaged individuals. In the United States, evidence of creaming has been countered by various requirements, for example, requirements to spend a specific proportion of funding on youth, or hard-to-serve adults. Unfortunately, this creates administratively complex programmes, with incentives and counter-incentives of different kinds.

Another possibility is that, if evaluations have substantial consequences, programmes will simply manipulate the data in order to look as effective as possible. For example, local JTPA programmes in the United States often admit that, under the pressure of performance measures that stress placement rates, they tend to wait a week or two before formally enrolling individuals.

Therefore individuals who are unmotivated, who are likely to drop out within the first few days or weeks of a programme, are never counted as enrolled and do not reduce the placement rate. Similarly, when placement rates are collected through tracer studies that contact former students, programmes may not try very hard to find students from whom they do not get immediate responses; because students who are not successful in finding employment are more likely to leave the area and be difficult to contact, this strategy eliminates some of the least successful students from the calculation of performance measures. It is impossible to know precisely how data are manipulated, of course, since the whole point is to fool evaluators and programme administrators. While a study of performance standards found little evidence of widespread manipulation (Dickinson *et al.*, 1988), this remains a danger whenever performance measures have serious fiscal consequences.

Yet another example involves the common problem of timing. The measures of success in job training programmes have been short-term job placement, measured initially over 30 days and now extended to 90 days; the measure of success in job training for welfare recipients is usually movement off welfare. These outcome measures generate incentives to move individuals quickly into employment – any employment at all, even low-quality employment that can be expected to last only short periods of time – since long-term employment effects are unmeasured and therefore irrelevant to conceptions of success.

In addition, some incentives may backfire in unforeseen ways. For example, during the 1980s, one performance standard applied to American remedial training was the cost per placement, intended to get programmes to provide effective programmes at lower cost. In practice, however, this standard caused programmes to offer short and cheap programmes, oriented to short-term results (eg job search assistance), rather than more extensive training. When federal administrators realized the problem, this particular measure was eliminated.

The lesson of these cases, therefore, is that individuals designing evaluation – particularly the kinds of evaluation used to improve the quality of programmes, like performance standards – must take special care in the specific measures chosen. The good news is that programmes do respond to the incentives they face. The bad news is that there may be ways of achieving those objectives that undermine the effectiveness of VET programmes.

Evaluation creates incentives for particular programmes, then, but there are still larger ways in which evaluation enterprise affects VET policy as a whole. One of these is unambiguously good: evaluation forces programmes to become aware of outcomes, to make them self-conscious about what they can accomplish. However, problems for VET *systems* can arise if some programmes are evaluated while others are not. For example, in the United States, publicly funded remedial training programmes have been evaluated more persistently than education programmes, while upgrade training sponsored by firms has almost never been evaluated except in the most casual ways. This has resulted in a situation where the articulation between public-sponsored short-term training and longer-term education is more difficult, because educational programmes are not used to being evaluated on the basis of their employment and earnings effects: vocational educators insist that they provide 'education, not placement', and have developed a reputation among training programmes for being unconcerned with outcomes. For their part, training programmes often think of themselves as outcome oriented, and policy-makers often refer to them as effective because they are governed by performance standards – even though the performance measures by which outcomes are judged are not necessarily good measures of effectiveness. And upgrade training sponsored by firms has been widely interpreted as effective, because of its close connection to employment, even though its real value to firms has rarely been appraised. Thus the perceptions among different types of VET programmes are skewed by the differential application of evaluation.

These perceptions about effectiveness and evaluations have led policy-makers in the United States to extend performance measures to a variety of other VET programmes beyond short-term job training, including vocational education, adult education, and various smaller remedial training programmes. In theory, a more even application of performance measures should lead all programmes in the system to be more outcome oriented, and should eliminate the variation in the perception of different VET programmes.[12] And, in the long run, a more uniform approach to evaluation would help create a more coherent system out of what is now a series of independent and disconnected programmes, as we consider in the following section. Unfortunately, performance measures are one of the non-experimental and most suspect kinds of evaluation, as clarified in Chapter 3, The challenge of comparison, and therefore it is important to be concerned about the distortions of the evaluation measures developed. Thus, improving the quality of evaluation measures is as important as extending them to the various programmes and institutions in the VET 'system'.

'Programme' versus 'systems' evaluation

As mentioned above, most evaluation takes what we might call a 'programme' approach. A VET programme is conceived, implemented within a defined period of time, and then evaluated by asking whether and how it benefits those enrolled in it – assuming that other institutions in a society stay the same. The outcomes focus on the benefits to individuals, or (particularly for in-service training) to employers in the form of productivity and profits. Presumably, if the evaluation is positive, the programme might be replicated or expanded, particularly as part of a process of experimenting with alternative programme designs. But only rarely do the evaluations of VET programmes conceive of a larger *system* of programmes that might apply to large numbers of individuals or employers, a system that might develop slowly over time. Instead they examine relatively isolated programmes or projects, designed for relatively small numbers of individuals. Indeed, the conventional approach is usually called '*programme* evaluation', as if to emphasize that it evaluates only an individual programme.

It is plausible that the development of a style of fragmented, short-run and isolated evaluation research reflects the decentralized and fragmented political system that the United States has. As Wilensky (1985) has argued:

> fragmented and decentralized political economies like the United States foster isolated, single-issue research, typically focused on short-run effects and used for political ammunition rather than policy plans; more corporatist systems such as those of Sweden, Norway, Austria, and perhaps Germany foster dialogue between researchers, bureaucrats, and politicians in which a wide range of issues are considered, and research findings are more often used for policy planning and implementation as well as budget justification.

A corollary is that, in the United States, and to a lesser extent in the United Kingdom, more energy is put into developing new programmes and evaluating them – and then abandoning innovations or trying new approaches – rather than continuing to develop institutions over longer periods of time. In essence, this kind of programme evaluation substitutes for systems development in VET: evaluation begins too soon, before individual programmes are well established, and certainly well before they have created links with other programmes, and then negative or equivocal results are used as ammunition against the programme (as Wilensky points out) rather than as guidance in improving its quality. This suggests that the entire evaluation enterprise, in its 'programme' focus, is part of an incoherent and fragmented approach that is unlikely to lead to more effective VET policies over time.

A 'systems' perspective would, on the other hand, encourage thinking not about individual projects, but about widely available programmes that are linked to one another and institutionalized. This in turn would lead to asking several different questions in any evaluation.

First, could this programme reasonably be part of an existing system of institutions within a country? Sometimes, evidence from evaluations have been used to make recommendations that are difficult to implement for large numbers of people, because of the lack of the other institutions in a society that are necessary if a particular VET project is to work. The most obvious example is the widespread admiration for work-based learning, based on the apparent success of the German dual system, or (in developing countries) on the success of the Botswana Brigades, with their emphasis on creating employment with training. But in countries without a history of work-based learning, it has proved difficult to find enough work-based placements to expand such a system, even though a small pilot programme may work well. The case of the Republic of Korea being unable to emulate the dual system, reported by Jeong (1995), is instructive, and the school-to-work programme in the United States is currently foundering on this problem (Hershey *et al.*, 1998). Similarly, certain kinds of innovations are notoriously difficult to implement because they are inconsistent with, or just different from, existing practices. Thus the various efforts to integrate academic and vocational education in developed countries, or to create diversified schools in transitional and developing countries, represent such departures from standard practice that they have been difficult to implement. To some extent, this question is simply one facet of the implementation stage of any new programme, but our point is that it should be asked with an understanding of what common practices and conventional institutions currently exist in a country.

Second, could this project be expanded into a system of similar programmes, applicable to large numbers of individuals? Often, positive evaluations are followed by recommendations for expansion, particularly if their purpose is to inform government policy. However, certain kinds of programmes could not conceivably be expanded, or if expanded they would not work as the original experiment did. Many innovative programmes depend on the charisma of a single director, or (for work-based programmes) the generosity of a particular company, and are therefore difficult to replicate. One of the most successful remedial job programmes in the United States depends in part on its longevity in the community, so that employers turn to it rather than other sources for employees.[13] It could not be quickly replicated, therefore, although one implication of its success may be that job training must be stable in order to form the durable links with employers that lead to long-run success – as distinct from the common practice of opening and closing training projects every few years. Sometimes programmes are simply too expensive to be widely replicated – the case of the widely cited Job Corps programme described in Box 3.11, for example – though they could be part of a graduated system in which intensive programmes are reserved for individuals with the greatest barriers to employment, while others receive less intensive training and related services. There are, then, many different issues in the expansion and replicability of programmes, but the issue is whether an evaluation asks the right questions to determine whether any one programme could be expanded into a system.

Third, is this programme linked to other VET opportunities, or is it a stand-alone programme without such connections? Sometimes stand-alone programmes are desirable for specific goals, but – from the perspective that learning should be relatively continuous, including the popular conception of 'lifelong learning'[14] – any particular programme should be linked to other opportunities. For example, some exemplary employers provide relatively continuous training opportunities for their employees. On the contrary, many remedial training programmes and adult education are short-term efforts to get individuals into employment quickly, but since they do not lead to subsequent VET programmes they provide no mechanism for an individual to continue learning and therefore usually leave trainees with skill levels too low for decently paid employment. Many VET programmes provide only vocational skills training without the complementary 'academic' instruction, or provide remedial language skills without vocational skills, so that trainees leave without all the competencies necessary at work. A systems perspective would make sure that each programme is linked to others, so that individuals and employers can achieve both the levels and the varieties of competencies necessary throughout their working lives.

Fourth, would the system implied by this programme work well? If a programme could be replicated and converted into a VET system, would it be desirable? Sometimes, a small programme may work well, but its expansion might not be consistent with a country's other practices, values and institutions. For example, some programmes are selective – either choosing the best potential trainees, as employers often do, or selecting those in greatest need, as remedial programmes do – in ways that would be undesirable in a larger system. Other efforts might reinforce school-based approaches to training in a country that wants to move toward work-based approaches, or might widen rather than narrow the division between training programmes and employers. This kind of question can often be answered only by thinking carefully about the characteristics of an imagined system, perhaps with the help of comparisons with other countries.

Finally, does this programme contribute to, or detract from, the transparency of a country's VET system? Transparency refers to the ability of prospective workers and employers alike to understand where they can get access to VET opportunities, what role a specific programme serves, and how it relates both to other VET opportunities and to employment opportunities. In some advanced countries with a tradition of experimentation, like the United States and France, there are so many programmes with so many different purposes that prospective students, employers, and policy-makers alike are often bewildered; this may also be the case with a transitional country like China, which has some forms of VET linked to the public enterprises that dominated in its past, while other forms are emerging as part of its transition to a more market-oriented economy. In general, transparency is a valuable characteristic of any VET system.

Within a 'systems' approach, a programme might be considered successful not because of its effectiveness for initial cohorts of students, but for its ability to be replicated, articulated with other VET programmes, connected to employer hiring practices, and otherwise related to other established practices. Conversely, a programme with high employment and earnings among its graduates might still be judged ineffective if it requires special conditions – a particularly charismatic director, or an unusual relationship with an employer – that could never be replicated or institutionalized. More generally, a 'systems' perspective would ask not whether an individual programme serves the needs of trainees and employers, but whether a complex of institutions does (Marsden and Ryan, 1991b; Grubb and McDonnell, 1996). But this kind of evaluation is quite different from the conventional approaches outlined in Chapter 3, and no country has yet developed such an approach.

It is difficult to find examples of systems-oriented evaluation. However, a step in the right direction is the effort to develop data and measures of performance that are comparable across programmes. For example, the United States Department of Labor funded several states to develop common data and core measures of performance for various federal and state VET programmes (Trott and Baj, 1996); Florida has moved towards a common set of outcome measures to use in performance-based funding; Oregon has developed guidelines called Oregon Benchmarks for all programmes; and Washington is using a common data source to measure the effectiveness of several independent programmes (Grubb, 1998; Grubb *et al.*, 1999). In addition, the development of human investment councils coordinating a variety of programmes can lead to more coherent systems (King, 1988; Grubb *et al.*, 1999). Although there is a substantial gap between developing common outcome measures and a 'systems' evaluation, these are necessary preconditions that indicate systems-oriented thinking.

Evaluating VET programmes alone: the limits of partial analysis

Evaluation is intended to reflect the effectiveness of a particular programme independently of the other social practices and institutions that surround it. The basic evaluation question is: what is the difference – for individuals, for employers, for other workers, for an economy as a whole – due to having a particular programme in place, assuming that other programmes and policies stay the same? While this is certainly an important question, it may generate misleading answers if other policies or institutions are necessary for a VET programme to be successful. Thus evaluation is not a good technique for assessing whether a *complex* of changes is necessary in order to enhance and utilize human capital, or to promote economic growth, or to reduce unemployment.

There are some obvious candidates for changes that are complementary to the enhancement of VET.[15] One often overlooked relationship, *within* the complex of VET programmes, is that education is often complementary to training. Individuals may be able to benefit from relatively job-specific training only if they have sufficient education, in both 'academic' capacities like literacy and in certain general vocational competencies, for example, knowledge about electricity, or mechanical forces. The empirical evidence is not particularly strong, though an evaluation of Colombia's *Servicio Nacional de Aprendizaje (SENA)* programme found its rates of return higher for better-educated workers (Jimenez, Kugler and Horn, 1986). Other results are also consistent with education and training being complements rather than substitutes: employers who tend to provide more training for their best-educated workers behave as if upgrade training is complementary to education, and the weak effects of remedial training (see Chapter 4, Publicly sponsored training) can be interpreted in terms of an inability to substitute training for more fundamental education. If workers need both general competencies and job-specific skills, then the most effective approach may be to increase both what is normally considered 'education' along with 'training' but conventional evaluations will typically find that either one independently is ineffective.

The most obvious requirement for VET to be effective is, of course, employment itself. In a high-unemployment economy a VET programme is particularly likely to involve displacement, at the expense of increases in aggregate employment. As a result, some countries – Germany and Denmark, for example, and the United States during the 1970s – have provided public employment in addition to training, in effect creating demand for the greater supply of skills. In other contexts, policies to enhance the availability of capital may be necessary, as in efforts to provide micro loans and training for the informal sector in developing countries; stable labour-management relations are another obvious complement. The improvement of health and nutrition is often necessary before individuals can take advantage of either education or training programmes (Schultz, 1995), and agricultural development and education are often complementary to one another. Perhaps the greatest success story of the post-World War II period, that of Japan, has been attributed to a complex of changes including the development of flexible management, government-directed strategies to integrate the efforts of research and industry, co-operation between the government and large groupings of private enterprises, and rejection of foreign investment as a technology transfer strategy – in addition to a high-quality education and training system (Freeman, 1989). And of course basic stability and peace are necessary for any kind of progress. The factors that are complementary to VET have not yet been systematically elaborated, and they may vary from country to country;

but – aside from cases where skill shortages are acute – it is difficult to think of cases where VET can be effective in stimulating growth by itself.

These complex complementary relations are not well described by conventional statistical analysis (Singh, 1994). They require a deeper understanding of the process by which skills are incorporated with other influences to enhance productivity – what we have described as Stage 3 of human capital development – and they are usually described by country-specific case studies. Unfortunately, this stage is rarely examined in conventional evaluations, and so the complementary policies that may be necessary to make a VET programme work are unlikely to be uncovered. This is yet another argument for expanding the range of questions that evaluation considers, lest it miss the central issues that may lead to greater effectiveness.

Conclusion: improving the understanding of VET

The limits of evaluation – and of social science research in general – cannot always be overcome, but *if* the central assumptions and constraints are kept in mind, incorrect conclusions and inappropriate policies can in theory be avoided. Indeed, debates over evaluation results often take precisely this form, with alternative explanations proposed and debated even when evidence cannot be improved. In practice, of course, the political process often constrains debate, as we investigate in the next chapter, so that the full discussion that might prevent misinterpretation and inappropriate policy cannot take place, at least in the policy arena. Therefore it is important to be clear at the outset about the limits of evaluation developed in this chapter: its short-term focus; its tendency to reinforce a 'project' rather than a 'systems' view of VET; the difficulty in examining quality and breadth in VET; the inappropriate incentives it can generate; and its emphasis on a specific programme rather than a complex of institutional policies that may be necessary. Under certain circumstances, when these issues are especially important, evaluation can be worse than useless: it may drive policy in the wrong direction.

This is not, we should stress, an argument against doing evaluation. Instead, this is plain talk about evaluation itself, a plea for a deeper understanding of evaluation no matter what specific kind of evaluation a programme or country or donor undertakes. As we have stressed throughout, evaluation cannot be a 'cookbook' procedure, undertaken by following certain steps mechanically. Instead, policy-makers and administrators need to think hard about what they want from their VET policy, and design evaluations accordingly.

Notes

1. See especially Aaron (1978). He describes the decline of faith in government in the United States as a result of disappointments over the Great Society and Watergate. The attack on government during the Reagan years was a continuation of this process. The declining faith in government has shifted the burden of proof in the United States, from a situation where a simple faith in the effectiveness of government dominates to one of general suspicion of government. In other countries, declining faith in the Welfare State led to the same result.
2. A process evaluation overlaps with implementation-oriented evaluation (see Chapter 3, Evaluation of implementation and other stages): both consider who has been served and with what gross results, but the former is oriented more to delivery mechanisms and the latter more to participant experiences.
3. Evaluation over 30 or 90 days, as has been common in American programmes, may be more appropriately considered a form of performance management rather than evaluation.
4. This is not *necessarily* true. For certain types of short-term training, disappointing short-run results almost certainly would not become positive over the longer run, so short-term results might seem sufficient. However, because positive short-term results might be reversed, as we saw in Chapter 3, Outcome measures, long-run effects would still need to be measured. Note that in earnings functions estimated across a population of various ages – for example, those in the labour force from 25 to 65 years of age – a longer time horizon is built into the analysis. Analyses of single cohorts, for example, the analysis of earnings and employment patterns of a group four years after leaving secondary school, typically revert back to a short-term perspective, though some long-term datasets have become available (eg the United Kingdom's National Child Development Survey, that has by now followed a population cohort born in 1958 through the first 40 years of its life).
5. When this has been done in the United States, the results suggest that the dominant emphasis on occupational experience may be suspect. While some occupational experience appears to improve the quality of teaching, a review of studies over 40 years suggests that extensive experience does not improve the quality of vocational teaching; however, formal post-secondary teacher training is associated with desirable teacher and student outcomes (Lynch, 1997).
6. There is a large literature in the United States on 'education production functions', relating measures of learning (like test scores in language and mathematics) to resources. In the terms discussed in Chapter 1, Conceptions of education and training, these relate measures of learning in Stage 2 to resources in Stage 1 (see, eg Hanushek, 1986 and Hanushek *et al.*, 1994, and the interchange in *Educational Researcher* of February 1992, Hanushek, 1992). But these results are flawed because they do not consider the process of teaching (ie Stage 2). It is therefore impossible to know whether an experienced teacher is a more skilled instructor or is simply burned out, or whether smaller class sizes lead to different and more effective approaches to teaching or simply allow teachers to continue a standard lecturing approach with fewer students. At best, the results of this literature show that more resources are not by themselves sufficient to improve learning, but they cannot show the conditions under which resources make a difference.

7. There has been some effort to determine whether less intensive job search assistance is more or less effective than more intensive classroom training. The World Bank and the Organisation for Economic Co-operation and Development (OECD) have concluded that job search assistance is more cost-effective than classroom training. Most of these evaluations are, however, quite short term and exclude aggregation problems (see Chapter 3, Aggregation). The effort to contrast the effects of a less intensive 'labour force attachment approach' with a more intensive 'human capital development approach' in the JOBS programme has yet to generate conclusive results.

8. Technically, enrolment in a programme has been represented by a binary variable, ignoring all variation in quality. In the evaluations of the American welfare-to-work experiments in the 1980s, the differences in services received by experimental and control groups were often not reported. More recent evaluations have been more careful about documenting the services actually received, from which it is clear that control groups may receive almost as much remedial and formal education (because of the widespread availability of such programmes) as do experimental groups.

9. This is possibly not a problem for upgrade training, where an employer presumably knows the effects of firm-sponsored training. However, even here the tendency to contract with independent training providers means employers and supervisors may not know whether upgrade training is of the desired quality.

10. See Chapter 3, Outcome measures.

11. There is, of course, an even more subtle policy problem about the trade-off between quantity and quality, for example, between a high-quality, low-quantity strategy versus a low-quality, high-quantity strategy. No country has generated evidence related to this decision, but many countries have made implicit decisions within certain parts of their education and training systems. For example, Great Britain opted in the 1980s to replace low-volume, high-quality training with high-volume, low-quality training for both young workers (apprenticeship and Youth Training Scheme, respectively) and adult workers (Training Opportunities Scheme and Employment Training, respectively; see Chapter 4, Publicly sponsored training). The former choice compares unfavourably to the progressive development of apprenticeship in postwar Germany (Marsden and Ryan, 1991b).

12. We note an interesting problem as VET programmes become more integrated into a coherent system: the goals of personal development that dominate general or academic education would join the more employment-oriented goals of VET programmes, creating difficulties for evaluation. But such a fusing of goals might help prompt VET programmes to become more general – a shift that is underway in many countries through interest in integrating academic and vocational education (Achtenhagen and Grubb, 1999; Grubb, 1995a).

13. This is the Centre for Employment Training in San José. Some aspects of this programme – its combination of academic and vocational skills training, and its use of enterprises as part of the training – could be replicated by other programmes.

14. 'Lifelong learning' is often a slogan in search of content. However, a great deal of the writing about lifelong learning falls into either a pedagogical argument – that if individuals are educated to be autonomous learners, they will be able to learn on their own throughout their lives – or an institutional argument, that education and training institutions should be created in ways to maximize access to individuals

throughout their lives. The point we are making here is one version of this institutional argument. In the best of all worlds, of course, countries interested in lifelong learning would follow the recommendations of both the pedagogical and the institutional perspectives.
15. See in particular Psacharopolous and Woodhall (1985), Ch. 10, 'Intersectoral Links'.

6

From evaluation to policy

The treatment of evaluation evidence in policy-making

When we outlined the purposes of evaluation in Chapter 2, the first and most obvious application involved the use of evaluation evidence to formulate government policy, particularly to provide evidence about the VET programmes most worth undertaking compared to those that should be closed. The evaluations reviewed in Chapter 4 were supported largely by governments, or by foundations, donors like the World Bank, or inter-governmental agencies like the Organisation for Economic Co-operation and Development (OECD), all with intense interests in government policy or in using evaluation to shape their own policies.

But the rules and procedures governing evaluation and social science evidence – the concern with the validity of conclusions discussed in Chapter 3 – are different from the rules governing politics. Therefore an important question becomes how evaluation and other social science evidence are used in the policy process. If evaluation findings are never used, or if they are used inappropriately, then honesty might require us to abandon evaluation, and to recommend that governments forgo evaluation that they are not going to use in any desirable way. But if we can determine the ways that evaluation can be helpful, or has been effective, then we could at least recognize the limits of evaluation, and perhaps shape it in ways that might be more effective. To do this, we first examine some general considerations about the use of evaluation and other research, much of which suggests that evaluation has not been widely used in policy-making. We then develop several cases where it seems that evaluation has been more effective, and draw some conclusions from these brief case studies. Finally we outline how decisions might be made if evaluation evidence is lacking, or ignored, in order to argue once again for the value of evaluation as an antidote to politics as usual. This chapter is therefore concerned with plain talk about politics and policy-making itself.

Use and abuse of evaluation evidence

In the 1960s, in many advanced countries, a view developed that policy could be rationally planned to resolve social problems, relying on various kinds of evidence – 'hard data' – to sort out effective from ineffective solutions. The use of planning-programming-budgeting systems (PPBS) in American defence policy, the rise of cost-benefit analysis, the development of policy analysis as a rational approach to policy-making, and the requirement in various legislation to use social science evidence – for example, the requirement in the German Employment Creation Act of 1969 and the enactment of environmental impact statements and cost-benefit analysis in the American regulation – all reflected this view of social science evidence. But as the 1970s and 1980s wore on, it became clear that evidence was not being used according to this 'rationalist' perspective and, in addition, that social problems were persisting and even worsening, evidently resistant to the rational analysis that sought to solve them. In this process, there developed the view of evaluation described in Chapter 2, Evaluation as a mechanism of public debate about VET: as providing information to inform public debate, to provide the 'plain talk' about VET and other social programmes.

But of course this purpose of evaluation simply raises the further question: in what ways has such evidence been used to inform public debate and policy? In examining evidence from several advanced countries, a number of conclusions seem evident.[1]

First and most obviously, policy-makers often simply ignore evaluation evidence, particularly when its findings are contrary to a political or ideological position. The example of British training policy in Box 6.1 is illustrative: a Conservative government wedded to market-like mechanisms and quasi-private markets for training simply ignored evidence that others kinds of training worked. A similar example from the United States involves recent Congressional action in vocational education: while Congress had mandated a comprehensive analysis of its vocational education policy in 1990, it was so intent on consolidating various VET programmes in 1996 that it totally ignored the results of its own study. In this case a shift from a Democratic to a Republican Congress contributed to the practice, but the point is that policy-makers as a group do not necessarily pay attention to the evidence that they have requested.

Box 6.1   Evaluation and political choices

Adult training in Great Britain

Between 1972 and 1985 the British Government sponsored occupational training for adult workers under the Training Opportunities Programme (TOPS). TOPS delivered full-time training for occupational skills, using a long-standing network of public training centres (Skillcentres), serving primarily the unemployed and adult females returning to the labour force.

Between 1985 and 1988, four programmes were introduced rapidly, including the Job Training Scheme (JTS, a limited reshaping of TOPS), and culminating in Employment Training (ET), which replaced them all in 1988. Public training facilities were successively commercialized and privatized. Public training for adults was redirected to employer provision; to job-specific uncertified skills, learned through on-the-job training and work experience; to lower costs per trainee; and to serving the long-term unemployed. The direction of reform reflected the goals and methods favoured by the Thatcher Government.

Evaluation of TOPS had been confined to two essentially uninformative criteria: net cost to the public budget per participant removed from unemployment, and subsequent rates of participant employment. More sophisticated evaluation was launched only after the reforms of 1985-8 were well under way. A quasi-experimental evaluation of JTS (and by proxy, TOPS) was launched in that programme's last year (1987). The results were mostly favourable, particularly for females and for those who found work 'in trade'. The results were, however, released only later (Payne, 1990a, 1990b). The publication delay was widely attributed to official embarrassment at having jettisoned a successful programme, and having acted before an effective evaluation had been completed.

Quasi-experimental evaluation of ET has subsequently found that, unlike JTS, it did not improve the earning power of participants (Payne et al.,1996). There has, however, been no return to the more successful TOPS/JTS approach to adult training. Political considerations thus led to the scrapping of an effective public training service in favour of a less effective alternative, without either awaiting or responding to the evidence that the government itself had commissioned.

Sources: Disney et al. (1992); Payne (1990a, 1990b, 1994); Payne et al. (1996)

Second, when policy-makers have cited social science evidence, they have typically used evidence selectively, when it reinforces their own conceptions of the problem and their favoured solutions; they have tended to ignore contrary evidence, or evidence that would make them rethink their positions. In addition, certain topics with great political appeal have dominated, and other topics with less political importance have been neglected. Thus unemployment, economic and technological change, and the skills of the labour force (especially in the form of employer complaints) have been topics of enduring interest;[2] at other times and in certain countries welfare, immigration, and the poor state of the education system have been favoured topics. The topics emphasized by policy-makers for attention are selected for their political importance, for their ability to generate attention in the media and among voters, not for their importance in resolving empirical debates, or improving the quality of evidence.

In the selective use of evidence, policy-makers have avoided the complexities of theory and methodology. Instead, they have often used social science results in simplified ways, to tell almost commonsensical stories consistent with the particular ways in which they want to frame problems. The selective use of evidence, rather than expanding understanding, has sometimes constrained and limited interpretations by labelling problems and defining issues in particular ways; rather than a source of enlightenment, it might even be interpreted as a form of 'endarkenment' by eliminating certain issues from discussion (Wingens and Weymann, 1988). Thus the depiction of economic growth and competitiveness as issues to be blamed on education and training, the identification of unemployment as due to 'problem groups' with 'deficiencies' in their employment-related skills, and (in countries like the United States and the United Kingdom) the consistent laments about the decline of educational standards are ways in which issues are framed, precluding other interpretations. Another common example is the current discussion of skills in the labour force taking place in nearly every country: commission reports and government documents have cited a variety of social science evidence, as well as the persistent testimony of the business community, to identify a set of 'core' or 'key' skills required for a highly skilled labour force. This effort has therefore succeeded in creating a new political agenda on behalf of VET, though at a cost: the evidence that is contrary to the vision of a highly skilled labour force, for example, the evidence in many countries of the increasing bifurcation of the labour force, with many low-skilled jobs persisting, has been ignored, as have other policies (like macroeconomic policy, capital and investment policy) that might be necessary preconditions for VET to be effective.

Third, policy-makers may call for 'hard data' – presumably, quantitative results, including outcome evaluation of great sophistication – but they rarely rely on such 'hard data'. Instead, they rely on simplified versions of research findings, and simple numbers like benefit/cost ratios (see Box 6.2, on the Perry Pre-school Programme). Very often they rely on anecdotes, or individuals who personify the underlying problems; and they often use these to reinforce certain stereotypes – the uneducated job-seeker, the welfare mother without employment skills, the worker unable to keep up with changing technology.

In this habit, they are reinforced by journalists, whose methods of personalizing issues by concentrating on the experience of individuals – `story telling' – makes the issues more vivid in the public mind, but may also misconstrue the problem by concentrating on an atypical individual. The call for `hard facts' may express a wish for certain data to strengthen an existing position, but when `hard facts' are contrary to political positions they are generally ignored.

Box 6.2   Simplification of evidence

The Perry Pre-school and Head Start programmes, United States

The Perry Pre-school Project was a small, expensive, high-quality early childhood project developed in the mid-1960s with the help of many experts, intended to improve the school performance of low-income children. The programme was evaluated with highly experimental (random-assignment) methods. The evaluation, which has taken place in stages over several decades, included among its outcome measures children's performance in school, and later outcomes related to crime, pregnancy, and employment.

Consistently, the evaluations included cost-benefit analysis, and these results – with benefit-cost ratios varying from 3.6:1 up to 7:1 in different evaluations – were the basis of endless reports, newspaper articles, and other media events. Over time, the idea that early childhood programmes could have substantial benefits – and benefit-cost ratios of 7:1! – became embedded in the understanding of the public at large and policy-makers. When Ronald Reagan tried to cut Head Start in the early 1980s, the image of effective early childhood programmes effectively saved Head Start, and the aura generated by the Perry Pre-school has continued to strengthen the case of early childhood advocates.

The use of the Perry Pre-school evaluation has come at some cost. While the Perry Pre-school was a high-quality programme, the importance of quality (and therefore high expenditures) did not influence policy-makers as much as the simpler evidence about benefit-cost ratios, and many publicly funded early childhood programmes (including Head Start) continue to be of low quality. Evidence about the Perry Pre-school was applied to Head Start, a much larger programme with much lower expenditures and uneven quality, even though such an application certainly violated the usual rules of evidence. And the limited scope of the evaluation, involving only 123 children, was ignored. However, advocates have had no incentive to contradict the use of the Perry Pre-school to support early childhood programmes, and so these 'technical' problems with the use of evaluation evidence have been largely ignored.

Source: Schweinhart, Barnes and Weikart (1993)

Despite the generalizations about the cases where evaluation has not been used, in a small number of cases it appears that evaluation results have made some difference to policy debates. One of these involves the Perry Pre-school Project in the United States, described in Box 6.2, where the effects of a high-quality, high-cost pre-school programme could be summarized in one powerful statistic – the benefit-cost ratio – and where the constant repetition of these evaluation results created a new image in public discussion of early childhood programmes as efficient as well as equitable.

A second example from the United States involves the evaluation of youth programmes. After many years of consistently negative evaluations of re- medial training programmes for youth, Congress in the mid-1990s began to try to eliminate funding for such programmes on the grounds of their ineffective- ness. In this case, political considerations prevailed, because such programmes are useful for keeping teenagers out of trouble during the summer, but the point is that consistent evaluation results over relatively long periods of time almost succeeded in changing political sentiment.

A third example suggests that sustained attention from researchers some- times expands the issues that governments address. A great deal of research on the informal sector in developing countries (see Chapter 7, Special issues in developing and transitional countries) has succeeded in bringing this phe- nomenon to the attention of governments and international aid agencies, and now it has become possible to consider loans and training appropriate to the informal sector, when such policies had not previously been considered.

What are the implications for evaluation of these results, common across many advanced countries? If policy-makers consistently ignore evaluation evi- dence, or use it selectively, or simplify it to support political positions, does evaluation do any good? Should it be undertaken at all? Or – *how* should it be carried out to have maximum impact?

One obvious conclusion is that evaluation needs to be carried out consis- tently, over longer periods of time, to have any effect. An evaluation of a sin- gle programme, no matter how carefully done, is not likely to influence policy. However, an evaluation *agenda*, carried out consistently over a decade or more, may have some influence by slowly changing the ways that pol- icy-makers and citizens view VET programmes. This is also a way for a coun- try to develop expertise in evaluation, as we will clarify in Recommendation 7 in Chapter 8. And of course, only a consistent evaluation programme can get VET programmes themselves to begin thinking in terms of effectiveness.

A second clear recommendation is that evaluations should be carried out in such ways that policy-makers can make use of the results. No matter how much policy-makers may call for 'hard data', they will almost never use it. Therefore evaluations should take care to generate the kind of qualitative information – including the stories and anecdotes that policy-makers often prefer – *in addition to* any 'hard data' that they collect. This has the additional result of generating new *kinds* of evidence, including evidence that may provide better information about improving the quality of programmes. A good example is the New Chance evaluation described in Boxes 3.6 and 3.12.

A third and common recommendation is that evaluators and researchers must be able to communicate with policy-makers. This means that the details of method and theory, while critical to generating valid results, are not important in policy forums. What is important is the translation of results into a coherent 'story' or way of framing the problem and its solution. If evaluators themselves do not participate in such framing, then policy-makers will do so in ways that reinforce their own political and ideological positions.

Fourth, evaluation should probably be avoided when decisions will be made on purely ideological or political grounds, for under these conditions it is simply useless – at least in policy-making. One can argue that evaluation in this case could still contribute to public debate by informing those interested more in effectiveness than political consequences. Even an intransigent, ideologically driven government might, in the presence of democratic institutions, be induced by electoral considerations to take the results of evaluation into account if the electorate is made aware of the evidence. Otherwise, this is, in part, a recommendation to governments to be honest about their intentions: they should invest in evaluation only when there is a good chance that their decisions will depend on the kind of empirical evidence that evaluation can generate.

Finally, the use of evaluation in the political process should probably be considered in planning evaluations. If, for example, evaluations will be used by a tripartite body, then some consensus within that body about the purposes of evaluation, and which outcomes and intermediate processes should be investigated, might help to have the results accepted. If those policy-makers who will act upon the results of evaluations comprise a relatively stable group, then early discussions about the nature of evaluation should be helpful. If, on the other hand, the group of policy-makers is quite unstable, then it is hard to imagine how evaluations ordered by one group could be appropriately used by a very different group. Under these conditions, other purposes of evaluation, for example, helping programmes improve their quality, or helping individuals learn more about quality, should probably displace the attempt to influence policy.

Alternative grounds for decisions

What happens when evaluation is missing or flawed (for any of the reasons examined in Chapter 5), or likely to be ignored by the political process? What are the other bases for making decisions about VET programmes – other than the obvious political mechanisms? There are, we think, at least two other help-ful ways of thinking about VET programmes, ways that might help to develop more effective programmes over time – one involving the logic of VET programmes themselves, the other concentrating on the logic of market fail-ure. Otherwise, however, decisions are likely to be made by politics as usual, with certain predictable effects for VET.

The logic of VET programmes, or human capital revisited

One way to make decisions, if evaluation evidence about outcomes is missing or weak, is to return to the stages outlined in Chapter 1, Why should VET work? If a programme does not meet the conditions required in earlier stages – the implementation of a programme with specific characteristics related to subsequent employment (Stage 1), the development of a teaching programme to convey those competencies required in employment (Stage 2), and the alter-ation of economic behaviour (Stage 3) – then it cannot be particularly effective. Thus one approach, in the absence of information about outcomes, is to be careful about these structural features of VET programmes.

This perspective leads to many different kinds of recommendations, essentially aimed at improving the quality of VET programmes: making sure that programmes target appropriate occupations; hiring instructors with the right experience and occupation-specific knowledge, as well as facility with different teaching methods; making sure that the competencies conveyed in the programme are job-related, up-to-date, and appropriately broad; and many other details of enhancing quality. Indeed, when educators and train-ers concentrate on VET programmes, they usually emphasize various aspects of these three stages, rather than the outcomes at Stage 4 associated with con-ventional evaluations.

Market failure

Another way of assessing the case for government intervention in VET, espe-cially in advanced economies with well-developed markets, is to consider whether and how markets fail to allocate resources appropriately. The pre-sumption is that government need not intervene where markets are working adequately. In the case of VET, numerous observers have noted that education and training are subject to various types of market failure, with potentially important implications for an economy's growth path. A key source of failure is the 'poaching' externality: employers who pay for training fear the loss of their skilled workers to other employers and therefore cut back their training efforts. Moreover, individuals who would otherwise have sponsored their own training can be prevented by their inability to borrow against the human capital which they would like to acquire; they can be discouraged by being more risk-averse than is socially desirable; they may find that the employer provides less training than anticipated; or they may just be ignorant of their own best interests. The consumers of VET – both potential trainees and employers – may be uninformed, and providers of training may not respond to price-like incentives (Finkelstein and Grubb, 1998). Finally, the private returns to training may diverge from the public ones as a result of income taxation and distorted pay structures (eg Lucas, 1988; Stern and Ritzen, 1991; Ryan, 1994; Booth and Snower, 1996).

The implication for public policy is then a *prima facie* case for intervention – as long as the 'government failure' associated, for example, with bureaucratic inertia and political interference would not cause still more inefficiency than the market failure itself. The case for intervention is particularly strong in two areas. The first is the educational end of the VET spectrum, where the youthfulness, inexperience and lack of assets that characterize many potential participants make their decisions prospectively less attractive from the standpoint of both efficiency and equity. The second is the more transferable end of the spectrum of in-service training, where employers are least willing to provide and finance desirable amounts of training.

Arguments based on market failure can in principle step into the vacuum when evaluation evidence is not available and complement it usefully even when it is, given the intrinsic limits of evaluation evidence. At the same time, political factors are no less of a threat to the integrity of public training decisions when it comes to the use of market failure arguments than they are for the use of evaluation evidence. An example of the potential contribution and abuse of market failure arguments in public training decisions is provided in Box 6.3.

Box 6.3   Market failure: use and abuse

Public training policy (United Kingdom)

Although formal evaluation methods have recently come into official use in the United Kingdom, they have provided only scanty evidence at a time of repeated innovation in programme design. A new, more widely applicable, evaluation criterion has consequently been adopted for proposed public programmes. The finance department (HM Treasury) requires that ministerial proposals be shown relevant to some market failure, preferably an economic externality.

Requiring that proposals for public intervention address a defect in the market economy makes sense, particularly when more direct evidence is not available, and particularly when policy favours economic deregulation. However, public expenditure decisions are made primarily on political grounds and political factors can be seen in two attributes of British policy research. First, both the spending and the finance ministries have deployed their economic expertise, the former to justify theoretically their proposals, the latter to explode the former's justifications (given the political priority attached to cutting public expenditure). Second, academic economists have responded to the incentive to elaborate theories of market failure. The 'theory' contributors to a recent influential volume on the economics of training (Booth and Snower, 1996, Part I) treat market failure as pervasive and externalities as its only source. The source of the externalities with which public policy must grapple is located variously in monopsony power, credit constraints, labour market matching, product innovation and market segmentation. Some contributions advance economic knowledge significantly, others not at all.

Sources: as Box 3.2, above; Keep (1991), Marquand (1994)

Politics as usual

Evaluation can be interpreted as one way to develop empirical evidence that can then serve as the basis for non-political arguments about how VET programmes should be changed – expanded, eliminated, or reformed as the case may be. Similarly, focusing on the structural conditions necessary to enhance quality is a way of suggesting changes that is not necessarily simply a reflection of politics. And market failure arguments, though they are intensely value-laden, represent also an effort to move away from the naked exercise of interest group politics and to develop more principled arguments about when governments should – and should not – support VET programmes.

When these non-political bases for making decisions fail, then public decisions are made on political grounds. Of course, the nature of politics varies from country to country: modern liberal democracies usually operate with some version of interest group politics, sometimes moderated by a more collective or social democratic culture. Other countries struggling to enhance their growth are ruled by dictatorships, theocracies, a ruling elite or monarchy, one party 'democracies', or other non-democratic arrangements. Thus it is impossible to say anything general about the directions that political decisions about VET programmes will take: they will vary as much as political arrangements do.

However, our concern is that political decisions about VET programmes are likely to undermine the effectiveness of these programmes. In particular, purely political decisions are likely to lead to the following problems.

First, political decisions are often short-run decisions, aimed at gaining political advantage, or support from some block of voters, or legitimacy from some internal or external group (like an international funding agency) over the short run. The long-run perspectives that are necessary for effective VET programmes – the need to develop skills that can enable individuals to find and keep employment, to advance over time, to continue to improve productivity as technologies and work organization change – are too easily undermined by short-term political goals, such as enrolling large numbers of individuals quickly, or getting large numbers out of unemployment or off welfare rolls. Similarly, the stability and long-term perspectives required for good evaluation of VET programmes – the ability to measure benefits over the long run, the need for a stable evaluation effort – cannot be sustained where governments change their priorities frequently, eg in response to electoral cycles or to the career ambitions of individual ministers of education and employment.

Second, the breadth of VET is also likely to be undermined by purely political decisions. Many observers have concluded that narrow, job-specific forms of VET are inappropriate, particularly in an economic world where jobs and technology change quickly. The efforts in many advanced countries to integrate academic and vocational education, to develop broader forms of vocational education, or (from the point of view of the World Bank) to promote broader 'academic' education over narrow 'vocational' education are all examples of the growing aversion to narrow programmes. But broader and more integrated VET programmes lead to benefits only in the longer run, and their consequences in production – flexibility, the ability to anticipate and solve problems, the ability to perform as jobs become more complex or as individuals advance – are not immediately visible, and may not be supported by employers concerned with the current labour force. Again, a present-oriented policy, or one responsive to present-oriented employers, is likely to ignore the possibilities for broader programmes.

Third, the quality of VET programmes is another issue that is not well considered by purely political decisions. There is rarely a political constituency for high-quality programmes. The political considerations of announcing decisive action are better served by increasing programmes than by enhancing their quality: headlines shouting 'Job Programmes to Expand!' are more powerful than headlines announcing 'Programme Quality to Improve!'. And even those who operate education and training programmes are often more concerned about expanding the size of programmes than about enhancing their quality, particularly under funding mechanisms where revenues are increased by growing enrolments rather than any measures of quality.

Fourth, equity issues are often given little attention in conventional politics. Particularly with the decline of the Welfare State in many developed countries, the notion of correcting inequalities through government action has become less powerful than in the past. To be sure, remedial education and training programmes remain more attractive policies in many countries than do simple grants or welfare systems, but the substitution of cheaper, quicker programmes in place of longer-term, higher-quality programmes – at least for the poor and unemployed who lack political power – is always likely. So we can see public education and training systems in countries like the United States and the United Kingdom, where the highest subsidies are reserved for the children of the middle class who attend public universities, middling subsidies go to those individuals who attend lower-cost community colleges or further education colleges, and the smallest subsidies of all are reserved for those in short-term job training programmes and adult education, who in many ways have the greatest needs for education and related support services. Programmes for the poor and unemployed are not completely neglected in these countries, then, but their funding is much less generous than the funding for middle-income and employed constituencies.

Fifth, system-building is also a problem in purely political decisions. In many advanced countries, it has been tempting to develop new programmes to serve new constituencies rather than to consolidate and rationalize old programmes: legislators get their names on new programmes, the development of new programmes satisfies the political appetite for novelty, and new programme operators and trainees become political advocates. In the United States, therefore, VET programmes have typically proliferated; then, periodically, Congress has realized that it has created a quagmire of overlapping programmes and has tried to consolidate them. In the United Kingdom under Conservative governments, programmes proliferated and then were abandoned and replaced with new ones before their effects were clear, in a desperate attempt to seem forward-looking (see Box 6.1, above). Once different VET programmes are created, then their operators and clients become advocates for maintaining them as they are, so co-ordinating them in more rational 'systems' becomes difficult. And so VET in many countries has become an agglomeration of unrelated programmes, rather than a coherent system.

Sixth, conventional political processes are also poorly suited to making trade-offs among different types of VET programmes. For example, should a country invest in reforming its pre-employment education system, or in providing remedial training? Should it concentrate resources on upgrade training, or on broader pre-employment education that makes upgrade training less difficult in the future? Should it emphasize retraining for individuals who have already proved themselves in the labour force, or remedial training for those with weaker labour force experience and possibly complex barriers to employment? These kinds of questions can be decided politically, of course; and countries have come to some decision about them, usually implicitly, without overt debate. But often political forums are poorly suited to these debates; for example, the separation in most countries of education ministries and of labour ministries responsible for training precludes careful consideration of VET as a whole.[3] And questions about trade-offs, while partly value-laden and therefore political, also depend on the relative effectiveness of different VET programmes, and therefore cannot be carefully considered without evaluation evidence.

Finally, on an even larger scale, conventional political process are poorly suited to making decisions among different areas of policy. Should unemployment be reduced through training programmes or through macroeconomic policy? Should low-income workers be supported through training, loan programmes, health and nutrition programmes, or through some skilful combination of the three? In most countries, the political arenas for deciding macroeconomic policy, investment and loan policies, health and nutrition policies and different aspects of VET policy are scattered in independent ministries, independent legislative committees, and often in different governmental and non-governmental agencies (including, for developing countries, foreign donors). There is no central political arena for making decisions about these trade-offs. And, like the trade-offs among VET programmes, these trade-offs among different policy areas depend on questions of effectiveness, and on the potential complementarity among different policy, for example, the possible complementarity between training and other full employment policies.

So we conclude that the effective development of VET policies requires some independence from political processes. Such protection is necessary to achieve the national goals articulated by the same political process: in country after country, national commissions and legislatures have declared the importance of improving education and training to enhance the country's growth, productivity, competitiveness, standard of living, and progress out of poverty, and yet VET policies that might help achieve these goals are likely to be undermined by politics as usual. This, then, is the role of evaluation, properly conducted: over the long run it can provide the information, the perspectives, the ways of understanding the possibilities and limits of education and training that might allow such national dreams to be achieved.

Notes

1. This section draws on: an excellent review of German policy-making in labour market and education policy by Wingens and Weymann (1988); reviews of the American experience in Weiss (1977), Weiss (1979), Weiss (1989), Weiss and Bucuvalas (1980), Berman and Kennedy (1989), and a special issue of the *Journal of Policy Analysis and Management* (Lynn, 1989); and a review that covers both American and British experiences by Heller (1986).
2. In Wingens and Weymann's (1988) analysis of the German experience, these three issues alone accounted for about one-third of all references to social science evidence.
3. In theory, merging departments of education and labour, as England and Wales, and Australia have done recently, provides a forum in which this particular trade-off can be discussed. In practice, however, two different organizations and cultures within a single agency tend to retain their separate identities, and so the benefits take time to accrue.

7

International developments and their implications for evaluation

Education and training around the world are enormously varied, of course, and generalizations are difficult to make. Still, several developments are now taking place in many countries with substantial implications for VET, and thus for the evaluation of VET.[1] Some of these create certain conceptual and technical difficulties in carrying out evaluation, and others threaten to undermine the evaluation enterprise itself. As policy-makers think about the role of education and training, it is worth keeping these trends in mind in order to prevent carrying out the wrong kinds of evaluations, or undermining evaluation in ways that are later seen to be short-sighted.

In the vast range of developed, transitional and developing countries, there are still surprising similarities in the issues countries face. The specific forms they take may vary somewhat, and the vocabulary to describe them differs from country to country. For example, work-based learning exists in advanced countries as formal apprenticeships in the German dual system, as co-operative education and internships in other countries, and as school-based enterprises; in developing countries it appears as traditional, informal apprenticeships, as efforts to establish education-with-production, and sometimes as training linked to public sector enterprises but some of the same problems emerge wherever work-based learning takes place, despite the variation in vocabulary, intensity and formalization. Throughout this chapter, therefore, we will try to discuss the similarities among countries, though we return in the last section in this chapter to some special problems in transitional and developing countries.

The declining role of the state

In many countries, belief in the state as the solution to all social problems is weakening. The programmes of the Welfare State – transfer programmes and regulations – are being reduced, if not dismantled, and the idea that a social problem automatically requires a governmental solution is being replaced by a greater belief in individual solutions and market mechanisms. This has been happening both in developed countries, including European countries with strong state traditions, and in many transitional and developing countries moving towards market-oriented economies. To some extent VET programmes have been spared cuts as government funding declines because they are seen as critical *preconditions* for market-oriented economies and for economic growth. Nonetheless, it is certainly more difficult to find government revenue, particularly for retraining and remedial training, and the efforts to support upgrade training in firms, which might be politically popular even in countries where employers are pressing to reduce the size of the state, have not been particularly successful in any country.

Reductions in state spending have two contradictory effects on VET evaluation. On the one hand, it becomes more important for governments to spend their resources wisely. This sometimes emerges as a demand for evidence – 'hard data' – to prove that VET programmes are effective, thereby increasing the demand for standard outcome evaluation. The more important and difficult issues, however, are making VET investments that have long-run effects, and examining the trade-offs between different types of VET programmes and among VET and complementary policies (like those regarding investment). Here standard outcome evaluation is generally inadequate, because of its short-term focus and emphasis on evaluating one programme at a time. This implies that governments need to orient their evaluations to longer-run issues and to the trade-offs that they will inevitably face if their budgets continue to decline.

On the other hand, of course, reduced government spending might mean that less evaluation is carried out, rather than more. Evaluation is usually the easiest and politically most expedient part of a programme to cut: direct services are not involved, no political constituency will complain, and evaluation often seems useless to policy-makers in any event.

We have no general solution to this dilemma. The standard recommendation in this situation would be to 'work smarter' – that is, to carry out less evaluation, but of a higher quality. But this in turn requires some judgement about what evaluation is most necessary, and in turn that requires that a country have a clear set of priories for VET, or a coherent process or framework for deciding what those priorities will be in the coming years. In the absence of such a policy, we suspect that countries will continue – as many of them already have – to undertake reduced evaluations of limited usefulness, and then they will find themselves without the evidence on which to make critical judgements about directions for public spending. Once again, as we have argued throughout, evaluation and policy are tightly linked: evaluation can contribute to policy-making only if there are clear priorities and plans, and in turn coherent policies require evaluation of particular kinds – rather than random and inconsistent efforts that can make little difference to the political process.

Decentralization to subnational governments

Many countries have decentralized policy-making, and often the funding of programmes, to subnational governments like provinces, states, or even cities and towns. Sometimes this policy is part of an overall reduction in the central state; sometimes it represents an effort to shift costs to a different level of government; and sometimes it reflects a belief that the central government cannot provide adequate solutions to local problems. Decentralization of VET creates a series of interesting questions about the variation in programmes that typically takes place and about the equity effects (particularly when regions or states vary in their abilities to support VET). Often, regional variation can create 'natural experiments', where the differences in VET programmes from region to region can provide real information about more and less effective practices. And of course decentralization raises empirical questions about decentralization itself. Is it true that state or provincial governments can provide more effective programmes better suited to local conditions, or is this an ideological position with no basis in reality? Can a country trying to establish a *national* VET policy, in order to compete more effectively in a global economy, accomplish this through *local* decisions?

Unfortunately, decentralization typically creates serious problems for evaluation, because subnational governments rarely have the capacity to evaluate their own programmes; economies of scale imply that evaluation efforts are probably best left to a central government. Furthermore, the most important questions about decentralization itself – particularly the questions about differences from region to region – are unlikely to be posed by subnational governments concerned only with their own well-being. If decentralization rests on empirical claims, rather then being an ideological and political decision, then evaluation should continue to be carried out by the central government. Otherwise, it will be neglected and will fail to ask the right questions, undermining its role in providing plain talk.

The lure of market mechanisms

One consequence of the growing distrust of government is the effort in many countries to use market-like mechanisms to provide services, such as vouchers or tax credits to support VET. The arguments on behalf of market-like mechanisms are that they allow consumer choice, stimulate greater efficiency and effectiveness by forcing providers to be market-oriented, and reduce government bureaucracies and therefore costs. They are sometimes proposed as ways of circumventing providers of education and training that are incapable of reform, thereby contributing to greater effectiveness. Of course, there are also ideological grounds for using market-like mechanisms, and they have been especially popular with conservative governments.

In our interpretation of the available evidence, market-like mechanisms have not worked especially well, except under certain conditions. When they have been used for remedial training, the individuals have usually been too poorly informed about the options available to make wise decisions. When tax credits have been used to increase firm-based training, most employers do not appear to increase training by much, and most of the subsidy goes to training that would have taken place anyway. Where private vocational institutions have been used for pre-employment training, there have been substantial problems with low quality and fraud. The only area of VET where voucher mechanisms have worked well has been in the funding of post-secondary education, where the Australian and the American systems of grants and loans have expanded access to low-income students, 'consumers' are relatively sophisticated, the 'product' is well understood, and it is possible that choice mechanisms constrained by mechanisms of quality control, like the individual referral methods described by Barnow and King (1996), might be effective. But the implication is that governments should be cautious when considering market-like mechanisms, and ask whether the conditions necessary for markets to function efficiently and equitably are met.

The use of market-like mechanisms generates some obvious questions and certain technical problems for evaluation. In addition to the conventional questions about outcome effectiveness and cost,[2] questions arise about the existence of choices (a special problem in rural areas), about the choice process and the adequacy of information, and about the responsiveness over time of VET providers to the incentives created by vouchers. While the number of evaluation questions increases, evaluation may become more difficult because individuals receive VET in many different institutions and so the problem of figuring out what they learn (ie Stage 2) is made much more difficult. But if market-like mechanisms are to be used to enhance the effectiveness of VET, rather than simply for ideological reasons, it is crucial to answer these kinds of questions.

High-performance work, key skills, and broader conceptions of VET

One of the common dreams about VET is that it can create the kind of highly skilled, flexible labour force that is widely regarded as necessary for work in high-performance firms – those firms that enhance productivity by having flatter hierarchies, higher-quality (and often customized) production, and greater flexibility in their operations as demand waxes and wanes. In turn, this has led many countries to articulate 'key' or 'core' skills necessary for high-performance work – like problem-solving or trouble-shooting, the ability to communicate effectively with others and to work in teams, the capacity to perform independently even under difficult and ambiguous working conditions, and the like. And because a great deal of traditional VET has emphasized the technical requirements of narrowly defined jobs, this has led to efforts to upgrade the quality of vocational education by incorporating key skills, or to integrate vocational and general education, or – particularly in developing and transition countries – to create 'diversified' schools combining both vocational and academic skill training. In many ways, this is a current manifestation of a much older debate, about how general or specific preparation for employment should be.

The efforts to create broader and more integrated forms of VET pose obvious evaluation problems, of whether the newer forms are more effective than older, more traditional, and more specific forms of VET. However, the question of effectiveness becomes a difficult one, because the purpose of integrated programmes is to give individuals skills for enhanced employment over the long run – and therefore longer-run evaluation is necessary in place of conventional short-run efforts.

Furthermore, the issue of what constitutes a broad and integrated programme is a difficult one, to which there are several dimensions. One is the balance of academic and vocational skills; another is the breadth of skills, and whether they are designed for a narrowly defined occupation or a broader range of related occupations; and the third and most difficult is whether the teaching of both academic and vocational subjects is changed – whether the teaching is effectively integrated, or whether instead both areas are taught in conventional ways with no attempt to integrate the two. Many claims to create broader and integrated programmes have failed to change practices at all; many have taken conventional vocational programmes and added a bit of standard didactic academic teaching, now labelled 'key' or 'core' skills – and such programmes should not be taken as evidence of what integration can do. Thus evaluating an integrated or diversified programme requires much more careful attention to the process of teaching and learning in Stage 2, to determine what is actually taught within a programme and whether it lives up to the claims of being integrated, than most evaluations.[3]

The search for work-based learning

Many countries have recently tried to strengthen work-based approaches within their VET systems, partly because of the strong reputation of the German dual system and partly because school-based VET has always been criticized for being outdated and inconsistent with the demands of real work. Work-based learning has taken the form of apprenticeship programmes, co-operative education, school-based enterprises, and work experience in advanced countries; in developing countries, there are parallel efforts to promote traditional apprenticeships, education-with-production or 'learning by doing'. These efforts vary in their duration, breadth, and extent of formalization, but they are all characterized by the view that work is a better setting for certain forms of VET than school-like settings can be.

The creation of work-based learning presents some special problems for evaluation. A basic one is whether there is any learning going on, or whether – as has been true for many forms of apprenticeship – learning on the job is minimal compared to production, with apprentices providing routine labour at low cost and learning relatively little. (This charge has been made even against parts of the much-praised German dual system, for example.) Therefore some attention to the content of the work-based component – in effect, to the teaching/learning process of Stage 2 – is necessary. The same questions that one would ask of a school-based programme – whether its content is job-specific or broader, whether more general or 'academic' foundations of work-related competencies are incorporated, whether there is any effort to provide the 'higher-order skills' that employers have called for, whether 'academic' or theoretical content is integrated with 'vocational' or practical skills – need to be asked of work-based learning as well, in order to understand why such a programme might succeed or fail. Then, the long-run effects of work-based learning are crucial. If a work-based programme is narrowly devised, then a trainee is likely to have inadequate skills as work changes, and long-run employment experiences may be poor; if, on the other hand, it provides the deeper understanding of work processes that its proponents claim, long-run effects should be positive. But these differences will not be revealed by conventional short-term evaluations.

The search for work-based learning provides an excellent example of the dreams that have been spun for particular VET programmes. Here is an area where plain talk is particularly necessary, both because it has proved difficult to implement work-based programmes in countries without supportive institutions (including stable tripartite discussion and agreements) and because so few administrators and policy-makers have wrestled with the issue of what can be learned in work placements. Even in Germany, there is very little understanding of what takes place in the work-based component of the dual system, and there is little integration with the school-based component (Achtenhagen and Grubb, 1999). Work-based learning certainly has much to offer, but precisely what it *does* provide trainees is a subject that only careful evaluation can determine.

Continued concern for the poor and underemployed

Most countries, developed and developing alike, are concerned about their worst-off members – the poor, the unemployed and underemployed. Particularly in market-oriented societies, VET is an attractive alternative to social welfare payments, since it promises to create wealth rather than to redistribute it, and so remedial training programmes of great variety have been developed, reformed, and tried again and again in many guises. Even though state budgets are declining, we doubt that training-related efforts on behalf of the poor will cease; indeed, with the decline of the Welfare State in many countries, training is likely to be substituted for social welfare approaches.

Remedial training programmes have been among the most widely evaluated programmes, and so more is known about their effects than about most other forms of VET. Unfortunately, this form of training has led to many of the most discouraging evaluations, particularly in countries (like the United States and the United Kingdom) that have developed short, low-quality programmes, or have substituted job search assistance for any real training; as we saw in Chapter 4, Publicly sponsored training, the more substantial programmes in Germany and Scandinavia respond to the fact that more substantial barriers to employment among the poor require more substantial counter-measures. Furthermore, many remedial training programmes are poorly linked to other institutions, especially the conventional education system; they contribute to the fragmentation rather than the coherence of VET.

Based on these relatively consistent results, countries that want to help the poor through training need to be prepared to make substantial efforts, rather than engaging in symbolic and ineffective measures. Evaluation can be helpful in determining where specific programmes are inadequate, or – with sufficient understanding of how programmes work – what aspects need to be reformed. But they cannot avoid the need for hard choices, and countries that ignore the evidence about remedial programmes, or that develop measures that make their efforts look better than they are, will in the end find that they have spent a great deal of money on ineffective programmes – money that might have been used in a different way to help the poor.

Special issues in developing and transitional countries

The education and problems in developing and transitional countries may seem a world away from those in developed countries. But many of the issues are remarkably similar, although a few (particularly the informal sector in developing countries) are quite distinct. Therefore many of the evaluation issues are the same, and there is much to learn from the results in developed countries – thankfully so, because there has been much less evaluation of any kind in transitional and developing countries except on the issue of academic versus vocational pre-employment education. In this section we offer some tentative observations about the major issues and about the potential role of evaluation in developing and transitional countries – tentative because it is impossible to make many generalizations about such a vast array of experiences, and because we are far from being experts in this area.[4]

We note that, particularly in developing and transitional countries, the orthodox view of evaluation that calls for the most methodologically rigorous approaches is particularly inappropriate. Such countries often do not have the resources or the technical expertise to develop the data systems necessary for keeping track of services and students, for monitoring short- and long-run outcomes, for accounting for costs, or for carrying out sophisticated evaluations; many of them are quite small, so the economies of scale that allow a great deal of evaluation in countries like the United States are simply not present. (These are also problems for subnational governments in developed countries, as discussed in the section, Decentralization to subnational governments, above.) Under these conditions, using a variety of evaluation methods constitutes, as we have recommended, the only sensible strategy.[5]

A small number of issues have dominated the international writing about VET in developing and transitional societies, as well as the efforts of countries themselves and of international agencies to formulate effective VET policies. These are as follows.

Pre-employment education

One of the most wide-ranging discussions has involved whether pre-employment education should be academic or vocational, or some mixture (often referred to as diversified education, in the language of the World Bank, or integrated instruction). Of course, this issue is just as contentious in developed countries as it is elsewhere in the world: the English-speaking countries are all wrestling with different forms of integrated schooling, and even the much-praised German dual system is being threatened by more students wanting to continue in academic rather than vocational tracks. The balance between academic and vocational content is a question that every schooling system even remotely concerned with occupational preparation must confront.

On this question, an orthodoxy seems to have emerged: based on reviews of evidence (eg Psacharopoulos, 1987; Psacharopoulos and Woodhall, 1985), the World Bank has apparently concluded that academic education is most appropriate at primary and lower secondary levels, and that neither conventional full-time vocational education nor diversified forms of education are worth their extra costs (World Bank, 1995). However, the evidence is not as clear and uniform as some of the literature suggests (Bennell, 1998): the results depend on the methodologies used, the nature and quality of the data available, and the countries studied, with some evidence that many of the most negative conclusions about vocational education come from sub-Saharan African countries where vocational education has been poorly implemented, with especially high costs.

Furthermore, much of this research simply analyses the data available from different schooling systems, without asking very carefully whether a vocational programme is broad or specific, whether a diversified programme integrates the issues in any way, or how any of these programmes are linked to or detached from employers.[6] But evaluations of academic versus vocational versus diversified systems of education need to enquire carefully about the implementation of these programmes, about the details of their content and teaching, and about their links to employers and the labour market generally before drawing any conclusions about their value in enhancing employment and earnings. Such investigations need not be particularly extensive or expensive, though they will typically require individuals with skills different from the economists and statisticians who have generated most of the existing evidence about the academic–vocational controversy. Furthermore, as countries struggle with broader forms of vocational education – like the English-speaking countries, with their efforts to develop broader and more integrated vocational education, and China, with its new emphasis on vocational schools that still maintain a great deal of academic instruction – the appropriate methods of evaluating academic versus vocational approaches is an issue that virtually all countries confront.

Supply-driven versus demand-driven VET

Another consistent issue has been the tendency in developing and transitional countries to have public-supported VET institutions rather than employers determine the content and methods of VET, with frequent complaints from employers that the resulting training is irrelevant to their actual needs. This is, of course, a frequent complaint in developed countries too, particularly in countries with school-based systems of VET, where a common critique is that schools become out of touch with the skills required in production and cannot possibly be up-to-date in equipment and production methods. Part of the enthusiasm for work-based learning (see Chapter 5, Evaluating VET programmes alone) stems precisely from the contention that employer-based systems must by their nature be demand-driven.

Evaluation can be helpful in clarifying whether or not VET systems are supply-driven. One approach has been to determine what fraction of a programme's graduates find related employment, and to document the earnings differences between those with and those without training-related employment (eg Chung, 1990, for China; Grubb, 1997, for the United States). The finding that only a small fraction of graduates moves into training-related employment is usually taken as a sign of supply-driven VET; when combined with evidence that the returns to unrelated employment are low, the implication is that VET is both job-specific and poorly articulated with such specific jobs. But a different evaluation method would look more closely at the process by which employers hire, what sources of labour supply they prefer, and what their attitudes towards public VET systems are. This approach might provide information about how to make VET institutions more demand-oriented, rather than calling either for a work-based system – an approach which is simply unworkable in many countries – or in shifting to voucher-like mechanisms, with the special problems pointed out in the section, The lure of market mechanisms, above. That is, a closer examination of Stage 3 of the process of human capital development would provide developed, transitional, and developing countries alike a better sense of how to reform their VET institutions.

In addition, evaluation also creates both the information and the incentives to force suppliers of VET to be more responsive to the market (de Moura Castro and Andrade, 1989), particularly if it becomes clear that certain providers are failing to place their students in appropriate jobs. For this purpose, even non-experimental gross outcome measures may be useful, although they are poor measures of effectiveness in the more fundamental sense.

Implementation problems

An enduring issue in developing countries is that, when governments and donor agencies initiate training programmes, they are often not appropriately implemented. Indeed, USAID's review of 16 years of funding VET projects concluded that, while diverse kinds of programmes could all yield acceptably high rates of return under appropriate conditions, the most serious barrier to all of them was the difficulty of implementation, particularly when VET programmes were complex and the context of the programmes – economic conditions, political and cultural factors – was unsupportive

(Herschbach, Hays and Evans, 1992). This finding simply underlines the need for process evaluations, concerned with the initial implementation of human capital programmes.

However, implementation studies also need to recognize the difference between the 'programme' approach outlined above, and a more 'systems' approach. For any one VET programme, the reasons for its failure to be implemented may be idiosyncratic, for example, the incompetence of a particular director, turnover in project monitors, or unforeseen calamities ranging from the unavailability of space to wars and famines. But the 'system' question for any particular country is whether there are *systematic* problems that preclude successful implementation – conditions hostile to VET programmes that are unlikely to be any different for the next VET programme down the line. One 'solution', of course, is simply for countries and donors not to support VET where such conditions undermine effectiveness. The alternative, system-building approach is to examine what must be done to improve economic, political, and cultural conditions for another generation of VET programmes. Whether this is possible or not may depend on local conditions, of course, but at least evaluation can provide the evidence to see what the task might be.

Encouraging private sector training

Still another persistent theme in developing and transitional countries – as in many developed countries with the dual system – is the need to promote upgrade training by employers of their workers. In part, this view responds to complaints that school-based and publicly provided VET is too supply driven, and that firm-based training resolves the problem of demand; in part, this policy can draw upon evaluations of firm-based training that, as reviewed in Chapter 3, Programme effects, are more positive than the results for many other VET programmes. Again, this issue is relatively similar to the problem in developed countries – at least those without a dual system – of increasing employer training particularly because market failures are likely to lead employers to under-provide training (Lynch, 1994; Stern and Ritzen, 1991).

Conventional evaluation has been helpful in clarifying the value of firm-based training, as pointed out in Chapter 3, Programme effects. However, in shifting to the policy issue of how a government might enhance private training, there are two additional questions to confront. One is the question of whether a particular type of government programme, for example, a programme of grants from a training fund, or a tax expenditure of some kind, increases the amount of training provided, rather than supporting those firms that would have provided training anyway. In both developed and developing countries, government programmes designed to enhance firm-based training have had decidedly mixed records (Bennell, 1996). For this question, evaluation evidence would be useful to see whether similar programmes elsewhere – in other regions of a country, or even other countries – have been effective.

The other question is whether public support for private-sector training is justified – a more normative question for which empirical evidence is not especially relevant.[7] In effect, the generally positive results for private sector training (see Chapter 4) have often generated enthusiasm for government support that ignore these normative problems.

Promoting work-based learning, education-with-production, and traditional apprenticeships

Another consistent enthusiasm, in developing countries especially, is the promotion of work-based learning in the form of traditional apprenticeships and in education-with-production (or learning-by-doing) programmes that combine production for the market with learning on the job. Sometimes these efforts try to enhance traditional apprenticeships, for example by introducing literacy, basic business practices, and the basic science (electricity, for example) underlying non-traditional occupations. These forms of VET have their counterparts in advanced countries in more formalized apprenticeships and in school-based enterprises (Stern *et al.*, 1994), so here too the efforts are quite similar across a variety of countries, though they vary substantially in their formality, content, and intensity.

As pointed out in the section, The search for work-based learning, above, all forms of work-based learning generate questions about how much education and training is going on alongside production, and this can typically be learned only by observing the process itself and seeing how (if at all) behaviour on the job changes as the result of the period of learning or apprenticeship. Long-run outcome measures are also important, to distinguish forms of work-based learning that prepare individuals more generally for a variety of tasks and employment from those that train individuals for specific and routinized production tasks. Particularly in dealing with traditional apprenticeships, and some education-with-production programmes that are based in traditional work patterns, relatively informal evaluation approaches (including follow-up studies) may be the only ones possible, both because sophisticated methods are too expensive and because they may generate false results when individuals are distrustful of government and formality. However, the area of work-based learning is one in special need of plain talk: there has been so much myth-making around work-based learning, both in advanced and transitional countries emulating the German dual system and in developing countries with their locally developed methods, that more evidence is needed to help clarify when this approach is useful and when (like school-based learning) it becomes narrow, didactic, and irrelevant to most future employment.

Providing training to the informal sector

Developing and transitional countries differ substantially from developed countries in the size of the informal sector – the variety of small-scale producers, small retailers, and providers of personal services that operate without any government notice or record-keeping, with enormous turnover, in chaotic and shifting markets without much regulation. There have been extensive debates about the informal sector – about its definition, size, and productivity – without much consensus except on the fact that it is very large in many countries and that improving its productivity would enhance both the livelihood of people depending on this kind of production and the overall productivity of many developing countries.[8]

Very often, training has been proposed for the informal sector, particularly in the areas of basic business practices, literacy to enhance the ability to obtain information and participate in literate society, health and safety considerations to reduce food contamination and appalling accident rates, and sometimes specific technical skills like carpentry or machining. (We note that, different though the informal sector may be from formalized employment in large firms in developed countries, the influence of training still follows the conceptual stages of human capital development outlined in Chapter 1, Why should VET work?) Whether training alone is sufficient, or whether it should be provided as part of a larger package of services (including small loans, marketing advice, perhaps the creation of co-operatives) does not seem to be resolved: more comprehensive services are more difficult to provide but sometimes more effective (Bennell, 1996; Middleton, Ziderman and Van Adams, 1993). Training for the informal sector must have all the characteristics of education-with-production, since it is impossible to stop production to engage in training; thus all the problems of work-based learning – the difficulty of disentangling training from production, the problem of identifying whether any learning is taking place – apply to training in the informal sector.

An enduring difficulty is how to provide training (and related services) to individuals working in the informal sector; there is some consensus that this must be done in informal ways, as different from formal schooling as possible, for individuals who are distrustful of authority and formal organizations. Indeed, the very notion of providing training, or any other service, is controversial: one perspective is that the informal sector should be left alone, and that any kind of intervention represents a kind of formalization that is intrinsically impossible.

By extension, evaluation methods involving informal sector activities must be informal too. A great deal of valuable information has been gathered by quite informal interview and questionnaire methods (eg the studies in Fluitman, 1989). Other informal methods could be developed in addition. For example, just as some training programmes have hired mentors and counsellors from the communities they serve, they could also hire informant/researchers from communities within the informal sector, to follow up individuals over time. Alternatively, part of the training for informal-sector producers could include record-keeping and diaries, as a way both to teach literacy and to have the participants describe their participation in different productive activities over time.

Still another possibility would be to work through the non-governmental organizations (NGOs) that often provide support to the informal sector, and that develop information and expertise about local operations but without making that information available to others; some observers (eg King, 1989) have proposed linking researchers and NGOs so that their experience can be more systematic and public. Overall, then, the informal sector is an area where the broader array of evaluation methods we have consistently proposed is necessary: an orthodox analysis of earnings within the informal sector, comparing groups with and without training in a highly or quasi-experimental design, is difficult to imagine.

In addition, the informal sector creates special difficulties for evaluation because of the inter-relatedness of its components. What may be crucial, for the livelihood and stability of a single producer, is the combination of capital (a simple machine, or truck), training (to know how to operate that machine), and access to a market; if any of these three (or six, or 39) elements fail, the producer may not survive. It is therefore difficult to disentangle the contribution of training alone, as conventional evaluation does. Again, other techniques – case studies in particular – and a broader range of questions about what makes someone in the informal sector successful are necessary if evaluation is to succeed.

The real role for evaluation in the informal sector is not, it seems to us, to carry out many evaluations of projects designed to improve the sector's productivity; the conditions for doing so are simply too difficult. It is instead to contribute to public debate about training and the informal sector, by having all those concerned about the informal sector – policy-makers, donor agencies, NGOs, researchers and evaluators alike – mindful of the questions about effectiveness that evaluation poses, so that they can search for the appropriate evidence wherever they might find it, and use the information they thereby develop to contribute to further understanding of what kinds of VET might be most effective in this enormous but elusive area of economic activity.

Developing systems and policies

Finally, we come back to a question that has vexed us throughout this report: the role of evaluation in helping create systems of institutions and national policies about VET, rather than simply passing judgement on individual programmes. (This is, of course, a problem that is just as serious in developed countries as in transitional or developing countries, since it is always easier to create individual VET programmes, or to experiment with a series of VET 'innovations', than it has been to create coherent systems.) Conventional evaluation certainly can provide the 'right' answer to the conventional evaluation question, of whether a particular VET programme dreamed up by an NGO, or an international donor, or a reform-minded government, improves outcomes defined in any number of ways. But this does not seem to be the right question, and evaluation does not seem to give a very useful answer – unless 'programme' evaluation is modified to pose the additional questions outlined as part of 'systems' evaluation in Chapter 5, 'Programme' versus 'systems' evaluation. Then it would be possible to see whether a particular programme could be the basis for a more extensive and more enduring system of VET, a system compatible with existing institutions and capable of reaching larger numbers of individuals.

In addition, just as a system-oriented form of evaluation could lead to a more coherent VET policy, we suspect that only with efforts to develop a coherent policy can substantive evaluation thrive. If a country is trying to develop a coherent policy – that is, some sense of what kinds of VET programmes should be given greatest priority, in what kinds of institutions, with what visions of human capital development underlying them – then it can engage in experiment and evaluation with some clear goal in mind. If not, and if, as is often the case for transitional countries, a country wants every kind of VET programme, or wants to emulate Germany because the dual system is thought to be the best in the world, then there is no real place for evaluation since the empirical questions, the trade-offs, and the comparisons for which evaluation is best suited are missing. Incoherent policy leads to 'programme' evaluations of free-standing programmes that are ultimately not used in policy-making; but the effort to develop coherent policy generates evaluations whose answers can play an important role in further developing that policy. Coherent policy and coherent evaluation reinforce one another, and this is as true for developing and transitional economies as it is in developed countries.

Notes

1. See also the analysis of trends by Caillods (1994).
2. If voucher mechanisms include high administrative costs, or costs of providing information so that 'consumers' can be well informed, then costs of the vouchers themselves may understate the total costs considerably.
3. As an example of neglecting the teaching/learning process, the evaluations of diversified programmes in Columbia and the United Republic of Tanzania by

Psacharopolous and Loxley (1985) conceptualized 'diversified' programmes in terms of the fraction of time spent on vocational and academic content. But this ignores the breadth of these programmes and the integration of teaching, and it is impossible to tell from the published record what approaches to teaching are present in these schools. In addition, they measure the employment effects of diversified schools one and (for Colombia only) three years after graduation, and find no advantages compared to conventional vocational schools. But, quite apart from the short-run nature of the outcome measures, this is not necessarily a test of what an integrated or diversified programme could accomplish, in the absence of better information about what the teaching looks like.

4. The review of studies by Middleton, Ziderman and Van Adams (1993) is particularly helpful. See also the country studies put together by the World Bank and the ILO (Gill, Fluitman and Dar, 1997).

5. See also the similar comments by Blaschke and Nagel (1995).

6. For a similar critique, acknowledging the diversity of what is usually lumped together as vocational education, see Dougherty (1989), Section 7. For the variety of practices in the United States alone, see Grubb (1995a).

7. This question is not usually raised in advanced countries that have tried to subsidize private-sector training. In the United States, California has the largest of a series of such programmes funded by states to promote economic development, but neither it nor any other states have asked themselves what kinds of private training merit public support. At the request of California's programme, Grubb *et al.* (1993) developed a series of criteria to justify public funding of private training, some of which correct market failures, a few of which are macroeconomic arguments about export promotion and import substitution, and a few of which are equity-related. By implication, however, the vast amount of private sector training which does not fit into one of these three categories should not be publicly subsidized

8. On the informal sector, see Fluitman (1989), especially King (1989); Middleton, Ziderman and Van Adams (1993), especially Ch. 6 and 8; McGrath and King *et al.* (1995); Birks *et al.* (1994).

8

Conclusions and recommendations

Towards a pragmatic perspective on
evaluating VET

The literature on evaluation has often taken its lead from the most sophisticated practices in the most advanced economies, for example, from the random-assignment studies of employment outcomes, with their particular
claims to validity, that are now routinely carried out in the United States, with
its relatively long history of evaluating job training. Thus one often encounters
recommendations that countries ought to evaluate their education and training programmes 'rigorously', as a way of making policy decisions – a statement
that also assumes that evaluation results will be directly used in public policy.
Among evaluation specialists and those who worry about methodology, this
view has become almost an orthodoxy: evaluation methods other than experimental designs are often treated as if they are failures, providing no useful
information at all, and evaluation is undertaken with the faith that results will
be directly incorporated into public decisions.

This position has much to recommend it, and it may be possible for countries to develop their evaluation efforts over time to the point where the most
sophisticated evaluations are possible, and even routinely used to inform
policy. But for many purposes, the orthodoxy is quite useless because many
countries lack both the resources and the expertise to fund sophisticated
evaluations, and because in fact evaluation is virtually never used to make
political decisions directly, as pointed out in Chapter 5. And under some conditions, the orthodox approach gives misleading or incomplete answers, as
indicated in Chapters 3 and 4 – in particular, given the frequency of negative
evaluations of remedial training programmes, it fails to give much sense of

why VET programmes might not work. So the orthodoxy is often impossible, and where it is possible it is often incomplete.

Instead, we recommend a greater variety of approaches to evaluating VET programmes, a greater variety of outcome measures, greater judgement about which problems in a VET programme might be worth investigating, and a different understanding of how evaluation results might be used. Our recommendations provide a more pragmatic approach to evaluation, one that might be useful in a greater number of settings and countries, and for a greater variety of purposes. Lying behind our recommendations are two central concerns: that evaluation generate new and better information about VET programmes, and that it be used to enhance understanding of how these programmes operate and what they can accomplish. In these concerns, the best should not be the enemy of the useful.

Recommendation 1

Evaluations of VET programmes should never lose sight of labour market outcomes, but in addition they should be more concerned than they have been by the processes leading to these results

Given the frequency of negative results, particularly for remedial training programmes and youth programmes, and the common finding of small effects, the real question is not whether programmes work but why they so often fail and how they *might* work. For these questions, more information about the sequence identified in Chapter 1, Why should VET work? – particularly Stages 1–3 – is necessary, and this can often be obtained only through 'process' evaluations or implementation studies, closer examination of teaching and learning mechanisms, and more careful understanding of how a programme fits into local labour markets. In particular, when evaluations are viewed as means for improving programmes, for informing potential participants, or for advancing public debate about VET, such qualitative approaches may provide more useful information than standard outcome evaluations. We also note that certain kinds of qualitative evaluation are relatively low cost, and do not require the kinds of statistical data that many countries find impossible to collect; they are therefore more likely to be viable in developing countries.

A greater understanding of the process by which a VET programme works requires more detailed knowledge of the institutions involved in the process – about the details of a particular educational institution or training programme, or local labour market including the intermediaries (trade unions, employer associations, local customs, local price-setting mechanisms) that can affect who is hired and who is not. The amplified human capital model outlined in Chapter 1, Why should VET work? pretends to a certain kind of universality, but its application for any particular VET programme requires an understanding of the institutional details.

Recommendation 2

The analysis of VET programmes should try to use a variety of evaluation methods, since each of them is imperfect and incomplete

While there has been a tendency to call only for the most sophisticated – ideally, highly experimental and quasi-experimental – outcome-oriented evaluations, these are not always useful. Often, particularly when results are negative, they provide few clues about what changes or further experiments are appropriate; they often provide no information about the implementation or the nature of the programme, and therefore cannot distinguish between slapdash efforts and well-designed programmes with dedicated teachers; they can be understood by only a small number of people; and the 'hard data' they generate are rarely used in political deliberations. They need to be complemented with other forms of evaluation in order to interpret the results. Of course, the costs of evaluation are important to keep in mind, and using a variety of methods may inflate costs unreasonably; but more sophisticated methods are also more expensive and at the margin it may be more informative to devote resources to different and complementary methods (especially qualitative approaches) than to increase the precision of the most sophisticated quantitative approaches.

Moreover, although weakly experimental forms of outcome evaluation, such as before/after and international comparisons, have often been dismissed on the ground that the comparisons are distorted by other influences, they can provide information that is relatively accessible, particularly in developing countries or countries without much expertise in evaluation, and their results can be more readily understood by a variety of policy participants. While the results may have biases, they may be able to provide an indication of the range in which benefits lie. For example, weakly experimental evaluations often prove more favourable than do more experimental ones, if only because the former cannot rule out positive selection and self-selection. They may then still be able to set an upper bound for outcomes, and indicate the need for redesign if effects are small. Such results are more useful than no results at all, and potentially more useful than information about outcomes or implementation only. They can be valuable as the basis for public discussion (see Recommendation 6) and the further development of evaluation methods (see Recommendation 7) even if they do not provide definitive answers for a particular programme.

We conclude, then, that an improved understanding of VET programmes requires a variety of evaluation methods, not an emphasis solely on the most sophisticated methods. Ideally, different methods would be used to investigate all the stages outlined in Chapter 1, Why should VET work? – a process evaluation would examine the implementation stage, a study of content, pedagogy and learning outcomes would document the competencies learned, interviews and observations would examine behavioural changes in economic life, and finally various kinds of outcome measures would examine final economic effects. For particular programmes, it might be appropriate to concentrate on only one or two of these, but our point is that the different methods generally complement rather than substitute for one another, and the incompleteness of each argues for using multiple measures.

The recommendation to use multiple methods of evaluation is particularly important in transitional and developing countries, where orthodox recommendations to carry out sophisticated evaluations lie somewhere between useless and destructive. In the first place, such countries lack the resources, the expertise, and the data to carry out sophisticated evaluations, and so the orthodox recommendation simply guarantees that no evaluation will take place. But, more dangerously, some of the training that occurs – particularly in the informal sector – is itself so informal, so intertwined with production, and so dependent on individuals distrustful of government bureaucracy and regulation that conventional data gathering and questionnaire completion might destroy the very programmes they are supposed to evaluate. Only careful observation and interview methods can be used to evaluate these fragile efforts, reinforcing our point about the need for carefully chosen, multiple approaches to evaluation.

Recommendation 3

VET evaluations should consider a broader range of outcome measures, in preference to a narrower range

In some cases, of course, VET programmes are intended solely to enhance the employment of trainees, and employment outcomes may be the only effects of interest. However, even in these cases intermediate outcomes, eg how much individuals learn or what credentials they earn (at Stage 2), may be important clues to the reasons why a programme works or doesn't, as well as goals in their own right. Other employment-related outcomes – the occupations individuals enter, for example – may provide information about long-run effects. Particularly with more broadly designed VET programmes, whose benefits are likely to affect productivity not measured by individual wages, some attempt to ascertain the effects of programmes on co-workers and overall productivity – even if only through interviews with employers, uncertain though they may be – is worthwhile. This is particularly the case in developing countries, where effects on productivity are especially important and difficult to measure by individual wages.

Particularly in countries with substantial unemployment, including most developing countries, a critical issue in all VET programmes is the displacement effect – the tendency for VET programmes to have their trainees employed at the expense of other individuals who are consequently unemployed. While displacement effects are notoriously difficult to measure, and have rarely been estimated for developed economies, some effort to do so (through employer interviews, for example) should be part of any sustained evaluation project. It is possible, in some economies, that VET programmes have their greatest influence not by increasing overall employment, but by substituting more productive individuals for less productive ones; in other cases, an expansion of the supply of skilled workers might increase output and employment. Any attempt to provide additional information about which of these effects is present would help inform subsequent policies. For example, evidence on the difference between occupations from which participants departed and those into which they move is potentially informative about the extent of displacement.

While most evaluations have concentrated on earnings and employment measures, other outcomes have sometimes been investigated, for remedial training (including measures like criminal activity and pregnancy), for employer training (including measures like productivity), and retraining (including measures like self-confidence and independence). Depending on the purposes of a particular programme, such wider outcomes should be included in other evaluations.

In addition, various outcomes related to health and safety conditions are potentially important and may be open to measurement. Because many VET instructors spend considerable time on the basic safety issues in using tools, operating machines, and coping with other job-specific safety concerns, an obvious question is whether this kind of explicit instruction has any effect on learning or on behaviour on the job (measured by accident rates, for example). Particularly in developing countries, where accident rates are often high and health issues particularly serious (and difficult to treat), the inclusion of health effects would capture a potential dimension of VET programmes that is now widely neglected. In turn, the inclusion of health effects in evaluations might make VET programmes more aware of the importance of such outcomes.

Recommendation 4

Evaluations should consider long-run as well as short-run effects of VET programmes

As we saw in Chapter 3, Outcome measures, short-run measures of effects may be misleading. They may be positive when long-run effects fade; conversely, the short-run effects of broader programmes may be negative (as individuals reduce their employment to attending school), while the longer-run effects are positive. To avoid the misleading conclusions that have sometimes been drawn from short-run outcomes, VET evaluations ought to incorporate long-run as well as short-run effects among the outcomes measured.

There are often legitimate needs for short-run measures, especially for managerial purposes; and some programmes established for short-run purposes need not wait for long-run outcomes. More pragmatically, the measurement of outcomes over long periods of time increases the complexity and expense of evaluations, and so other measures – like the occupation trainees enter, or the stability of employment in the sectors and occupations they enter – may be second-best but unavoidable proxies. In other cases, it may be impossible to collect long-run information for all programmes, but a subset of programmes (or trainees) could be followed for longer periods of time to determine the long-run consequences of short-term measures.

The effort to determine long-run effects is particularly important because of the incentives it provides in programme design. Long-run measures would cause programmes to concentrate more on teaching those abilities that serve individuals well in the long run – rather than aiming for short-run job placements, as has often been the case. In particular, the emphasis in many remedial and retraining programmes and in some national policies on job search assistance – which can only be effective if individuals already have the fundamental abilities necessary for jobs, and if ignorance about job opportunities and about job-finding procedures explains unemployment – could be corrected if there were more attention to long-run effects. Collecting information about long-run effects would also provide a necessary corrective to the tendency for the political process itself to think in short-run terms.

A concern with long-run effects implies that evaluations of VET programmes, and VET policy in general, should understand the division between *education* and *training* – including the institutional differences that vary from country to country – but may need to soften or eliminate the distinction. Some types of pre-employment and remedial training have had only short-run effects on employment and earnings, while enduring effects have come largely from education programmes leading to well-established credentials. The implication is that either training programmes need to change their goals or overall policy should aim to enrol individuals in education rather than short-term training – or facilitate the transition from 'training' to 'education'. In any case, evaluations need to be designed so that comparisons are possible between education and training programmes, in order that the trade-offs between the two can be reasonably discussed.

Recommendation 5

Evaluations of VET programmes should be concerned not only with their efficiency-related outcomes, but also with their effects on equity

Most evaluations are efficiency-related, concentrating on effects for participants and sometimes on net benefits to the economy as a whole (see Chapter 3, Cost-benefit analyses). The equity objectives that could also inform most public programmes are widely ignored. Equity-related effects can be brought into the picture in two ways. The first documents variation in outcomes amongst participants *within* the relevant programme; the second documents outcomes for participants *as a whole*, relative to non-participants. The former, or within-programme equity, depends on whether more disadvantaged participants receive more help than do others. The second, or programme-wide equity, depends on whether participants as a whole receive help from the rest of society, a test applicable to remedial programmes in particular.

Within-programme equity can be studied by collecting information on outcomes separately for sub-populations of particular interest – like women, youth, the long-term unemployed, or members of minority groups – and seeing if the benefits are greater for the less advantaged clients, whether, for example, the most disadvantaged benefit more from remedial training, or if well-educated workers benefit more from firm-based upgrade training. Implementation evidence is also relevant, concerning the presence of either positive selection ('creaming') by programme administrators or *self*-selection by participants, as when only more motivated individuals show up.

Programme-wide equity is examined by reporting separately net gains to participants, including the gains during participation in the programme that are typically excluded in academic research but excluding the net gains to non-participants that enter into cost-benefit analysis. It is also of interest to know whether a programme that produces no downstream benefits for participants does at least make them better off while taking part than they would otherwise have been – in which case it can at least claim some success, on grounds of equity.

Evaluation needs to confront a special difficulty in the concern with equity. Very often, the effort to enhance equity has led countries to develop remedial training programmes; but evaluations reveal that these are among the least effective of all VET programmes. Sometimes, policy-makers have used this evidence to reduce such programmes, effectively abandoning the equity goal as hopeless; at other times, such findings have caused advocates to search for improved remedial programmes. In still other cases, analysts have recommended that remedial efforts be diminished in favour of strengthening pre-employment education that, if it were effective enough, would prevent the need for remedial training. Evaluation by itself cannot, of course, determine which of these paths a country takes, but it can provide the information by which a country discusses the full range of alternatives – which in turn requires information not only about a specific remedial VET programme, but about the plausible alternatives.

Recommendation 6

Although publicly sponsored training appears to succeed less often than does privately sponsored training, governments should approach with caution any harnessing of private provision to public goals

Private training does have the advantage of a clear link to market demands. At the same time, a market economy is expected to produce too little training amongst employers and workers alike. Moreover, public programmes often have equity goals that fall outside standard evaluation criteria and employers have less reason to subscribe to those goals than to efficiency-related ones. Furthermore, the training provided by employers is likely to be narrowly job specific, suiting more the interests of employers than those of trainees and the wider economy. Finally, in the absence of effective quality control, some employers may avoid training altogether in favour of the exploitation of trainee labour.

Recommendation 7

Countries and international agencies should seek to incorporate evaluation into tripartite discussions and other political forums, recognizing that the use of evaluation evidence depends on political factors

The consistent finding that evaluation results are not often directly used to make public decisions – that they are more likely to be ignored, used selectively to strengthen existing political positions, or used in highly simplified forms to label or frame problems in particular ways – means that the political use of evaluation should be considered from the outset. If, as has been true in the vast majority of cases, evaluation is only one of several factors in public decisions, then evaluators should recognize that they can be most useful in providing information for principled debates about the direction of VET. As a possible counterweight to more conventional political decisions, such evidence is more likely to be useful if it can be understood by policy-makers, and if policy-makers have understood and accepted the need for evaluation. Therefore having evaluation discussed and designed in the stages of formulating and implementing policy – rather than leaving it to the last stage of developing VET programmes (in the conventional cycle of planning, implementation, and evaluation) – would enhance its value.[1]

It also seem evident that evaluation of education and training should be discussed in *tripartite* forums, rather than any other political forums. The education and training programmes discussed include those aimed at potential and current workers (pre-employment, remedial, and retraining), as well as upgrade training sponsored by employers. The benefits accrue to both workers and employers, and sometimes – as in discussions about the specificity and breadth of programmes – the balance between the two is at issue. The ways VET is provided – whether it is largely carried out in school-like settings independent of production, within work settings (in on-the-job training), or in some combination of the two (in the German dual system, for example) – is often the subject of lively debate. It is hard to imagine effective discussion of these aspects of VET – and therefore of aspects of evaluation which inform such debate – that fails to include both trade unions and employers. And public funding is virtually always involved in these discussions – sometimes with good reason and sometimes, as illustrated in Chapter 7, The search for work-based learning, with little more than political justification – and so government representation is necessary. Indeed, in countries with strong evaluation but weak forms of tripartite discussion – the United States is the obvious example – certain issues have been almost impossible to raise and resolve: efforts to increase work-based learning have foundered on the lack of employer participation, efforts to correct the weaknesses of remedial training have lacked any voice from trade unions. 'Discussions' about VET may even be simply internal debates within government, driven either by ideology or by suppliers of training without acknowledging the interests of workers and employers. The strong evaluation tradition in that country would be much more useful were there strong tripartite forums in which to discuss the results.

Recommendation 8

Countries and international agencies should view the evaluation enterprise as a long-term activity, one that requires stability and longevity to become more influential and more sophisticated over time

The evaluation of individual programmes has rarely had much impact. Instead, as argued in Chapter 6, Use and abuse of evaluation evidence, evaluation has been most influential when it has generated a relatively consistent set of results, over longer periods of time, so that it was able to change the conception of what social programmes can do. The obvious implication is that requiring evaluation for VET programmes on a random basis – with one programme evaluated for a short while and then abandoned as political interest moves elsewhere – is likely to be quite useless in influencing policy. Instead, countries and international agencies should establish evaluation *agendas* that they pursue over longer periods of time, allowing results to accumulate and issues to become better understood and elaborated. A longer-term commitment to evaluation may also help change the orientation of VET providers – from a concern to ensure their own longevity (the problem in supplier-driven VET systems) to a concern for outcomes.

In addition, a commitment to a long-run evaluation agenda is probably the only way to enhance the sophistication of evaluation over time – that is, to shift from the relatively inexpensive, unsophisticated methods described in Chapter 3, The challenge of comparison, towards more sophisticated methods. This is, after all, the trajectory that the United States has followed. Manpower programmes in the 1960s were evaluated using relatively simple methods, including descriptive statistics without comparison groups. During the 1970s the use of quasi-experimental methods with control groups became more common, and their limitations were increasingly understood and debated during the 1980s. Fully experimental methods then began to be used in the mid-1980s, and the methodology of doing them has improved considerably since then – with greater detail about programme content, more analysis of different kinds of services and results for different populations, (occasionally) greater use of supporting qualitative evaluation, and the application of experimental methods to education programmes outside the realm of 'training'. This is a *developmental* process, in which early results are used not only to assess programmes but also to advance the sophistication of evaluation itself. And in the process, a country can develop the expertise and the research organizations that can carry out evaluations of increasing levels of sophistication.[2]

The recommendation to think of evaluation as a long-run agenda is consistent with an interest in building *systems* within countries, rather than isolated *programmes*. What is important, especially within developing countries, is not to fund a single effective programme that reaches a few individuals, but rather to develop education and training systems that reach an entire population. So, too, what is important is not that one or two programmes are carefully evaluated while the broad range of VET is left unexamined, but rather that the deeper practices underlying evaluation – the concern with effectiveness, the weighing of alternative ways of accomplishing goals, the commitment to continuous improvement – become embedded within all programmes. This requires institution- and system-building over a period of time, not random and discontinuous efforts.

Recommendation 9

Rather than continuing with conventional 'programme' evaluation, countries should incorporate 'systems' perspectives into evaluation

As argued in Chapter 5, 'Programmes' versus 'systems' evaluation, conventional approaches to evaluation reinforce the tendency to think of programmes as independent, free-standing efforts that succeed or fail on their own. In our view – and indeed, in the view of most observers – countries need coherent, comprehensive, and transparent systems of VET programmes, not independent projects that benefit only a few people here and there. Creating such systems may be difficult and expensive, of course, but for evaluation the problem is relatively simple: it is not difficult, and certainly not expensive, to add a few questions to standard evaluations in order to orient the results towards a systems perspective. By asking these questions – about links to other programmes, replicability, consistency with established institutions, and the like – any evaluation can provide the information necessary to see whether a specific programme can contribute to system-building. Whether governments (or employers) can act on that information is, as always, a separate issue, but at least the issues of systems-building will become clearer over time.

In the end, the promises of VET for enhancing employment, growth, and international competitiveness – the dreams that most countries start with – cannot be realised without plain talk. Deception about the effectiveness of a VET programme may be useful in the short run, to make government officials or programme operators look good. But in the end, such efforts contribute only to undermining the dreams of a country, both because it has spent its resources to no end and because education and training themselves become devalued when they fail to deliver their promises. The only solution, then, is to be as careful as possible in assessing what programmes can do, and then in building more effective programmes and systems from that empirical evidence. Thus evaluation, as a particular form of plain talk, will contribute to advancing these dreams rather than deflating them.

Notes

1. This recommendation is consistent with the recommendation of 'participatory' evaluation that has become particularly popular in the United States and Canada, especially for community-based programmes like literacy efforts; see, for example, Askov, Hoops and Alamprese (1997) and the workbooks developed by ABC Canada. The idea is simply that all stakeholders – those with an interest in the programme – should participate in formulating as well as reviewing evaluation. The case for the democratization of policy evaluation has also been argued by Campen (1986).

2. In the United States, many evaluations of remedial training programmes are carried out by a small number of research firms – like the Manpower Demonstration Research Corporation, Mathematica Policy Research, and Abt Associates – that have developed highly concentrated expertise in evaluation and strong reputations for careful and impartial analysis. For the evaluation of large-scale and complex programmes, governments routinely turn to such organizations, augmented by specialized expertise in universities. (Most universities do not have the capacity to carry out large-scale evaluations, though they often carry out smaller-scale efforts.) The development of such concentrated expertise has required a long period of relatively stable investment in evaluation, and can be viewed as a part of building an overall evaluation system.

References

Aaron, H (1978) *Politics and the Professors: The Great Society in perspective,* Brookings Institution, Washington, DC

Achtenhagen, F and Grubb, WN (1999) Vocational and occupational education: pedagogical complexity, institutional diversity. Forthcoming in *Handbook of Research on Teaching,* 4th edn, ed V Richardson, American Educational Research Association, Washington, DC

Ackum, S (1991) Youth unemployment, labour market programmes and subsequent earnings, *Scandinavian Journal of Economics,* **95,** pp 531–43

Ackum Agell, S (1995) Swedish labour market programmes: efficiency and timing, *Swedish Economic Policy Review,* Spring, **2** (1), pp 65–98

Affichard, J (1981) Quels emplois après l'école: la valeur des titres scolaires depuis 1973, *Economie et Statistique,* June, **134,** pp 7–26

Affichard, J, Combes, M-C and Grelet, Y (1992) Apprentis et élèves des lycées professionnels: où sont les emplois stables?, *Formation Emploi,* April, **38,** pp 9–28

Alfthan, T and Jonzon, B (1994) *Retraining Adult Workers in Sweden,* Training Policy Study no 3, ILO, Geneva

Altonji, JG (1992) The effect of high school curriculum on education and labour market outcome, working paper 4142, National Bureau of Economic Research, Cambridge, MA

Ashenfelter, O and Card, D (1985) Using the longitudinal structure of earnings to estimate the effects of training programmes, *Review of Economics and Statistics,* **67,** pp 648–60

Ashenfelter, O and LaLonde, R (eds) (1996) *The Economics of Training,* vol I: *Theory and Measurement,* vol II: *Empirical Evidence,* Edward Elgar Publishing, Cheltenham

Askov, E, Hoops, J and Alamprese, J (1997) *Assessing the Value of Workforce Training,* National Alliance of Business, Washington, DC

Auer, P (1994) Further education and training for the employed: systems and outcomes, in *Labour Market Institutions in Europe,* ed G Schmid, London, M E Sharpe

Auer, P and Kruppe, T (1996) Monitoring of labour market policy in EU member states, in *International Handbook of Labour Market Policy and Evaluation*, ed G Schmid *et al.*, Edward Elgar Publishing, Cheltenham

Axelsson, R and Löfgren, K-G (1992) *Arbetsmarknadsutbildingens privat- och samhällsekonomiska effeckter*, EFA, Stockholm, cited in Alfthan and Jonzon (1994)

Baily, MN, Burtless, G and Litan, RE (1993) *Growth with Equity: Economic policymaking for the next century*, Brookings Institution, Washington, DC

Balsan, D, Hanchine, S and Werquin, P (1994) Analyse salariale des dispositifs d'aide à l'insertion des jeunes, *Formation Emploi*, **46**, pp 31–46

Balsan, D, Hanchine, S and Werquin, P (1996) Mobilité professionnelle initiale: éducation et expérience sur le marché du travail, *Economie et Statistique*, September, 299, pp 91–106

Barnow, B (1992) The effects of performance standards on state and local programs, in *Evaluating Welfare and Training Programs*, ed C Manski and I Garfinkel, Harvard University Press, Cambridge, MA

Barnow, B (1997) *Exploring the Relationship between Performance Management and Program Impact: A case study of the Job Training Partnership Act.* Institute for Policy Studies, Johns Hopkins University, Baltimore, MD

Barnow, BS, Cain, GC and Goldberger, AS (1980) Issues in the analysis of selectivity bias, in *Evaluation Studies Review Annual*, **5**, pp 43–59, ed E Stromsdorfer and G Farkas; reprinted in *Theory and Measurement*, ed O Ashenfelter and R Lalonde, Edward Elgar Publishing, Cheltenham

Barnow, B and King, C (1996) The baby and the bath water: lessons for the next employment and training programs, in *Of the Heart and Mind: Social policy essays in honor of Sar Levitan*, ed G Mangum, WE Upjohn Institute for Employment Research, Kalamazoo, MI

Barron, JM, Berger, MC and Black, DA (1997) How well do we measure training?, *Journal of Labour Economics*, July, **15** (3), pp 507–28

Barron, JM, Black, D and Lowenstein, M (1989) Job matching and on-the-job training, *Journal of Labour Economics*, January, **7** (1), pp 1–19

Bartel, AP (1994) Productivity gains from the implementation of employee training programmes, *Industrial Relations*, October, **33** (4), pp 411–25

Bartel, AP (1995) Training, wage growth and job performance: evidence from a company database, *Journal of Labour Economics*, July, **13** (3), pp 401–25

Bassi, LJ, Sims, M, Burridge, L and Betsey, C (1984) *Measuring the Effect of CETA on Youth and the Economically Disadvantaged*, Urban Institute, Washington, DC

Baudelot, C and Creusen J (undated) *Apprentissage Pas Mort*, Paris, LERSCO-CNRS

Becker, G (1975) *Human Capital: A theoretical and empirical analysis, with special reference to education*, 2nd edn, Columbia University Press, New York

Béduwé, C and Espinasse, J-M (1995) Production de diplômes et diffusion de compétences, *Les Cahiers du LIHRE* (Université de Toulouse), 1 September

Begg, IG, Blake, AP, Deakin, BM (1991) YTS and the labour market, *British Journal of Industrial Relations*, **29**, pp 223–36

Bellman, L and Jackman, R (1996) Aggregate impact analysis, in *International Handbook of Labour Market Policy and Evaluation*, ed G Schmid *et al.*, chapter 5, Edward Elgar Publishing, Cheltenham

Bennell, P (1996) Privatization, choice, and competition: the World Bank's reform agenda for vocational education and training in Sub-Saharan Africa, *Journal of International Development*, May–June, **8** (3), pp 467–87

Bennell, P (1998) General versus vocational secondary education in developing countries: a review of the rates of return evidence, forthcoming, *Journal of Development Studies.*

Berg, I (1970) *Education and Jobs: The great training robbery*, Praeger, New York

Berman, BF and Kennedy, M (1989) The politics of the National Assessment of chapter 1, *Journal of Policy Analysis and Management*, **8** (4), pp 613–40 .

Bierhof, H and Prais, SJ (1996) *From School to Productive Work: Britain and Switzerland compared*, CUP, Cambridge

Birks, S, Fluitman, F, Oudin, X and Sinclair, C (1994) *Skills Acquisition in Micro-Enterprises: Evidence from West Africa*, OECD, Paris

Bishop, J (1994) The impact of previous training on productivity and wages, in *Training and the Private Sector*, ed LM Lynch, chapter 6, University of Chicago Press, Chicago, IL

Bishop, J (1996) *What We Know about Employer-Provided Training: A review of the literature*, Working Paper 96-09, Centre for Advanced Studies in Human Resources, Cornell University, New York

Blalock, AB (ed) (1990) *Evaluating Social Programmes at the State and Local Level*, WE Upjohn Institute, Kalamazoo, MI

Blanchflower, D and Lynch, LM (1994) Training at work: a comparison of US and British youths, in *Training for the Private Sector*, ed LM Lynch, University of Chicago Press, Chicago, IL

Blaschke, D and Nagel, E (1995) Beschäftigungssituation von Teilnehmern an AFG-finanziert beruflicher Weiterbildung, *Mitteilungen aus der Arbeitsmarkt- und Berufsforschung*, **2**, pp 195–213

Bloom, H, Orr, L, Cave, G, Bell, S, Doolittle, F and Lin, W (1994) *The National JTPA Study: Overview, impacts, benefits and costs of Title II-A*, Abt Associates, Bethesda, MD

Bloom, H, Orr, L, Cave G, Bell, S, Doolittle, F, Lin, W and Bos, J (1997) The benefits and costs of JTPA Title II-A programmes: key findings from the National Job Training Partnership Study Act, *Journal of Human Resources*, summer, **32** (3), pp 549–76

Bloom, HS (1990) *Back to Work: Testing re-employment services for displaced workers*, WE Upjohn Institute, Kalamazoo, MI

Blundell, R, Dearden, L and Meghir, C (1996) *The Determinants and Effects of Work-Related Training in Britain*, Institute for Fiscal Studies, London

Boesal, D and McFarland, L (eds) (1994) *National Assessment of Vocational Education,* US Department of Education, Washington, DC

Böhm, U (1994) Vocational education and training in Germany: national and international dimensions, in *The International Encyclopedia of Education,* ed T Husén and TN Postlethwaite, 2nd edn, vol 11, pp. 6653–60, Pergamon, Oxford

Bonnal, L, Fougère, D and Sérandon, A (1995a) L'impact des dispositifs d'emploi sur le devenir des jeunes chômeurs: une évaluation économetrique sur données longitudinales, *Economie et Prévision,* **115,** pp 1–28

Bonnal, L, Fougère, D and Sérandon, A (1995b) Une modélisation du processus de recherche d'emploi en présence de mesures publiques pour les jeunes, *Revue Economique,* May, **46** (3), pp 537–48

Booth, A and Snower, D (eds) (1996) *Acquiring Skills: Market failures, their symptoms and policy responses,* Cambridge University Press, Cambridge

Brown, CV and Jackson, PM (1990) *Public Sector Economics,* 4th edn, Basil Blackwell, Oxford

Büchel, F and Helberger, C (1995) Bildungsnachfrage als Versicherungstrategie, *Mitteilungen aus der Arbeitsmarkt- und Berufsforschung;* **1/95,** pp 32–42

Büchel, VF and Pannenberg, M (1994) On-the-Job Training, innerbetriebliche Karrierepfade und Einkommensentwicklung, *Jahrbuch für Nationalökonomie und Statistik,* **213/3,** pp 278–91

Büchtemann, C, Schupp, J and Soloff, D (1993) De l'école au travail: une comparaison entre l'Allemagne et les Etats Unis, *Formation Emploi,* October; **44,** pp 37–51

Burghardt, J and Gordon, A (1990) *More Jobs and Higher Pay: How an integrated program compares with traditional programs,* Rockefeller Foundation, New York

Caceres Cruz, G (1997) Chile Joven Programme: an opportunity for vulnerable groups, unpublished manuscript, Employment and Labour Market Policies Branch, ILO, Geneva

Caillods, F (1994) Converging trends amidst diversity in vocational training systems, International Labour Review **133** (2), pp 241–58

Cameron, S and Heckman, J (1993) The non-equivalence of high school equivalents, *Journal of Labour Economics,* January; **11** (1), pp 1–27

Campbell, D and Stanley, J (1963) *Experimental and Quasi-experimental Designs for Research.* Rand-McNally, Chicago, IL

Campen, JT (1986) *Benefit, Cost and Beyond: The political economy of cost-benefit analysis,* Ballantine, Cambridge, MA

Card, D and Krueger, AB (1995) *Myth and Measurement: The new economics of the minimum wage,* Princeton University Press, Princeton, NJ

Carnoy, M and Fluitman, F (1995) *Training and the Employment Problem of Industrialised Countries,* Training Policy Study no 15, ILO, Geneva

CEC (1993) *COMETT II: Evaluations,* Office for Official Publications of the European Communities, Luxembourg

CEC (1996) *COMETT II: The final evaluation report,* Office for Official Publications of the European Communities, Brussels

Chevalier, L and Silberman, S (1988) Peut-on encore parler d'insertion pour les jeunes sans formation?, *Formation Emploi,* **23,** pp 74–78

Chung, J-P (1990) Educated misemployment: earnings effects of employment in unmatched fields of work, *Economics of Education Review,* **1** (4), pp 331–42

Combes, M-C (1988) La loi de 1987 sur l'apprentissage, *Formation Emploi,* April, **22,** pp 83–97

Cook, T and Campbell, D (1979) *Quasi-experimentation: Design and analysis issues for field settings,* Houghton Mifflin Co, Boston, MA

Corson, W, Decker, P, Gleason, P and Nicholson, W (1993) *International Trade and Worker Dislocation: Evaluation of the Trade Adjustment Assistance programme,* Mathematica Policy Research, Princeton, NJ

Cörvers, F (1997) Sector-specific intermediate and high skills and their impact on productivity and growth in manufacturing sectors of the European Union, paper presented to CEDEFOP conference on R&D in Vocational Training, Thessaloniki, July

Couch, KA (1992) New evidence on the long-term effects of training programmes, Journal of Labour Economics, **10,** pp 380–88

Couppié, T (1992) La rôle des aides publiques à la sortie de l'ecole, *CEREQ Bref,* October, **82,** pp 1–4

Crain, RL, Heebner, A and Si, Y-P (1992) *The Effectiveness of New York City's Career Magnet Schools: An evaluation of ninth grade performance using an experimental design,* National Center for Research on Vocational Education, Berkeley, CA

Crane, J and Ellwood, D (1984) *The Summer Youth Employment Programme: Private job supplement or substitute?,* working paper, Department of Economics, Harvard University, Cambridge, MA

Cutler, T (1992) Vocational training and British economic performance: a further instalment of the 'British Labour Problem', *Work, Employment and Society,* June, **6** (2), pp 161–83

Dar, A and Gill, IS (1995a) *Evaluations of Retraining Programs in OECD Countries: Implications for economies in transition,* report no. IDP-156, World Bank, Washington DC

Dar, A and Gill, IS (1995b) *Costs and Effectiveness of Retraining in Hungary,* report no IDP-155, World Bank, Washington, DC

DE (1989) *Training in Britain,* Employment Department, Sheffield

DE (1991) *YTS Progress Report 1988/89,* Department of Employment, Sheffield,

DE (1994) *Labour Market Quarterly Report,* August, Department of Employment, Sheffield

Deakin, BF and Pratten, CF (1987) Economic effects of YTS, *Employment Gazette,* **95,** pp 491–97

de Koonig, J (1994) Evaluating training at the company level, in *The Market for Training,* ed R McNabb. and K Whitfield, Avebury, Aldershot

De Moura Castro, C, Alfthan, T and Oliveira, JB (1990) *Technical Change: Skills and implications for basic learning,* discussion paper no 49, ILO, Geneva

De Moura Castro, C and Andrade, A (1989) *Who Should be Blamed When Training Does Not Respond to Demand?,* discussion paper no. 45, Training Policies Branch, ILO, Geneva

Dickinson, K, West, R, Kogan, D, Drury, D, Franks, M, Schlichtmann, L and Vencill, M (1988) *Evaluation of the Effects of JTPA Performance Standards on Clients, Services, and Costs, National Commission on Employment Policy,* Washington, DC

Disney, R, Bellman, L, Carruth, A, Franz, W, Jackman, R, Layard, R, Lehmann, H and Philpott, J (1992) *Helping the Unemployed: Active Labour Market Policies in Britain and Germany;* Anglo-German Foundation, London

Dolton, P (1993) *The Econometric Assessment of Training: A review,* working paper, Department of Economics, University of Newcastle upon Tyne, Newcastle

Dolton, P, Makepeace, G and Treble, J (1994a) The Youth Training Scheme and the school to work transition, *Oxford Economic Papers,* October; **46** (4), pp 629–59

Dolton, P, Makepeace, G and Treble, J (1994b) Public- and private-sector training of young people in Britain, in *Training and the Private Sector,* ed L Lynch, chapter 9, University of Chicago Press, Chicago, IL

Doolittle, F *et al.* (1993, August) *A Summary of the Design and Implementation of the National JTPA Study,* Manpower Demonstration Research Corporation, San Francisco, CA

Dougherty, C (1989, March) *The Cost-Effectiveness of National Training Systems in Developing Countries,* Population and Human Resources Department, WPS 171, World Bank, Washington, DC

Eckert, H (1995) L'accès à l'emploi des bacheliers professionnels, *Formation Emploi,* January, **49**, pp 69–89

Elbaum, M (1988) Stages, emplois et salaires d'embauche: l'insertion des jeunes à quel prix?, *Economie et Statistique,* June, **211**, pp 5–22

Elias, P, Hernaes, E and Baker, M (1994) Vocational education and training in Britain and Norway, in *Training and the Private Sector,* ed LM Lynch, chapter 10, University of Chicago Press, Chicago, IL

Erhel, C, Gautié, J, Gazier, B and Morel, S (1996) Job opportunities for the hard to place, in *International Handbook of Labour Market Policy and Evaluation,* ed G Schmid *et al.,* chapter 9, Edward Elgar Publishing, Cheltenham

Evaluation Unit (1997) *Guidelines for the Preparation of Independent Evaluations and ILO Programmes and Projects,* May, ILO, Geneva

Evans, G and Butler, J (1992) Expert models and feedback processes in developing competencies in industrial trade areas, *Australian Journal of TAFE Research and Development,* **8** (1), pp 13–32

Eyssartier, D and Gautié, J (1996) L'évaluation macro-economique de la politique de l'emploi en faveur des jeunes, *CEE Quatre Pages,* September, 17, Centre d'Etudes de l'Emploi Noisy-le-Grand

Fay, R (1996) *Enhancing the Effectiveness of Active Labour Market Policies: Evidence from programme evaluations in OECD countries*, Labour Market and Social Policy occasional paper no 18, OECD, Paris

Finkelstein, N and Grubb, WN (1998) Making sense of education and training markets: lessons from England, Paper presented at the American Educational Research Association. Berkeley: School of Education, University of California, Berkeley, CA

Fisher, R and Cordray, D (1996) *Job Training and Welfare Reform: SA policy-driven synthesis*, Russell Sage Foundation, New York

Fitzenberger, B and Prey, H (1995) Assessing the impact of training on employment: the case of East Germany, discussion paper no 23, CILE, University of Konstanz.

Fluitman, F (1989) *Training for Work in the Informal Sector*, ILO, Geneva

Forgeot, G (1997) Les salaires d'embauche des jeunes: l'influence du statut au premier emploi, *Economie et Statistique*, **304**, pp 95–107

Foudi, R, Stankiewicz, F and Trelcat, HM (1993) L'efficacité des stages de formation, le case des demandeurs d'emploi de basse qualification, *Formation Emploi*, **41**, pp 21–42

Fraker, T and Maynard, R (1987) The adequacy of comparison group designs for evaluations of employment-related programs, *Journal of Human Resources*, **2** (2), pp 194–227

Franz, W and Soskice, D (1995) The German apprenticeship system, in *Institutional Frameworks and Labour Market Performance*, ed F Buttler, W Franz, R Schettkat and D Soskice, Routledge, London

Freedman, S and Friedlander, D (1995) *The JOBS Evaluation: Early findings on program impacts in three sites*, Manpower Demonstration Research Corporation, New York

Freeman, C (1989) New technology and catching up, *European Journal of Development Research*, **1** (1), pp 85–99

Freeman, RB (1974) Occupational training in proprietary schools and technical institutes, Review of Economics and Statistics; **56**, pp 310–18

Friedlander, D (1988) *Subgroup Impacts and Performance Indicators for Selected Welfare Employment Programs*, MDRC, New York

Friedlander, D and Burtless, G (1995) *Five Years After: The long-term effects of welfare-to-work programs*, Russell Sage Foundation, New York

Friedlander, D, Greenberg, D and Robins, P (1997) Evaluating government training programs for the economically disadvantaged, *Journal of Economic Literature*, **35** (4), pp 1809–55

Friedlander, D and Robins, P (1995) Evaluating program evaluations: new evidence on commonly used nonexperimental methods, *American Economic Review*, **85** (4), pp 923–37

Gardner, H (1983) *Frames of Mind: The theory of multiple intelligences*, Basic Books, New York

Garonna, P and Ryan, P (1991) The regulation and deregulation of youth economic activity, in *The Problem of Youth*, ed P Ryan, P Garonna and RC Edwards, chapter 2, Macmillan, London

Gaude, J and Payne, J (1994) *Vocational Education and Training: Definitions, taxonomy, and measurement issues*, Occasional Paper no 10, Training Policies Branch, ILO, Geneva

Geraci, VJ (1984) *Short-term Indicators of Job Training Program Effects on Long-term Participant Earnings*. Project Working Paper 2, University of Texas, Center for Economic Research, Austin, TX

Gill, I, Fluitman, F and Dar, M (1997) *Skills and Change: Constraints and innovation in the reform of vocational education and training*. World Bank and ILO, Washington, DC and Geneva

Gospel, H (1995) The decline of apprenticeship training in Britain, *Industrial Relations Journal*, March 26 (1), pp 32–44

Goux, D and Maurin, E (1994) Education, expérience et salaire: tendances récentes et évolution de long terme, *Economie et Prévision*, 116, pp 155–78

Gramlich, E (1991) *Benefit-Cost Analysis of Government Programs*, Prentice-Hall, Englewood Cliffs, NJ

Grembowski, D and Blalock, A (1990) Evaluating program implementation. in *Evaluating Social Programs at the State and Local Level: The JTPA evaluation project design*, ed AB Blalock, Upjohn Institute, Kalamazoo, MI

Grossman, JB and Sipe, CL (1992) *Summer Training and Education Program (STEP): Report on long-term impacts*, Public/Private Ventures, Philadelphia, PA

Grubb, WN (ed) (1995a) *Education through Occupations in American High Schools*, vol 1: *Approaches to Integrating Academic and Vocational Education*. vol 2: *The Challenges of Implementing Curriculum Integration*, Teachers College Press, New York

Grubb, WN (1995b) *Evaluating Job Training Programs in the United States: Evidence and explanations*. Training Policy and Programme Development Branch, ILO, Geneva

Grubb, WN (1996a) *Learning to Work: The case for re-integrating job training and education*. Russell Sage Foundation, New York

Grubb, WN (1996b) *Working in the Middle: Strengthening education and training for the mid-skilled labour force*, Jossey-Bass, San Francisco, CA

Grubb, WN (1997) The returns to education and training in the sub-baccalaureate labor market, 1984–1990. *Economics of Education Review*, June, 16 (3), pp 231–46

Grubb, WN (April, 1999) *Learning and Earning in the Middle: The economic benefits of sub-baccalaureate education*. Occasional paper, the Community College Research Center, Teachers college, Columbia University

Grubb, WN and Associates (1999) *Honored but Invisible: An inside look at teaching in community colleges*, Routledge, New York and London

Grubb, WN, Badway, N, Bell, D, King, C, Herr, J, Prince, H, Kazis, R, Hicks, L and Taylor, J (1998) *Toward Order From Chaos: State efforts to reform workforce development 'systems'*, National Center for Research in Vocational Education, Berkeley, CA

Grubb, WN *et al.* (1993) *Choosing Wisely for California: Targeting the resources of the Employment Training Panel*, National Center for Research in Vocational Education and Center for Labor Research and Education, Berkeley, CA

Grubb, WN and Kalman, J (1994) Relearning to earn: the role of remediation in vocational education and job training, *American Journal of Education*, November; **103** (1), pp 54–93

Grubb, WN and McDonnell, L (1996) Combatting program fragmentation: Local systems of vocational education and job training, *Journal of Policy Analysis and Management*, Spring **15** (2), pp 252–70

Hanushek, EA (1986) The economics of schooling: production and efficiency in public schools, *Journal of Economic Literature*, September, **24**, pp 1141–77

Hanushek, EA (1992) Money might matter somewhere: a response to Hedges, Laine, and Greenwald, *Educational Researcher*, February; **23** (4), pp 5–8

Hanushek, EA *et al.* (1994) *Making schools work: Improving performance and controlling costs.* Brookings Institution, Washington, DC

Harhoff, D and Kane, TJ (1996) *Is the German Apprenticeship System a Panacea for the US Labour Market?*, discussion paper no 1311, Centre for Economic Policy Research, London

Heckman, JJ (1993) *The Case for Simple Estimators: Experimental evidence from the national JTPA Study*, Technical Report no 5, Harris School Job Training and Partnership Act (JTPA) Project, University of Chicago, Chicago, IL

Heckman, JJ and Hotz, VJ (1989) Choosing among alternative nonexperimental methods for estimating the impact of social programmes: The case of manpower training, *Journal of American Statistical Association*, December, **84** (408), pp 862–80

Heckman, JJ, Roselius, RL and Smith, JA (1994) US education and training policy: a re-evaluation of the underlying assumptions behind the 'new consensus', in *Labour Markets, Employment Policy and Job Creation*, ed LC Solmon and AR Levenson, Westview Press, Boulder, CO

Heckman, JJ and Smith, J (1996) Experimental and non-experimental evaluation, in *International Handbook of Labor Market Policy and Evaluation*, ed G Schmid *et al.*, chapter 2, Edward Elgar Publishing, Cheltenham

Heidegger, G and Rauner, F (1996, July) *Vocational Education in Need of Reform. Expert Opinion for the Ministry of Labour, Health, and Social Affairs of the Land North Rhine-Westphalia*, Institut Technik und Bildung, University of Bremen, Bremen

Helberger, C, Rendtel, U and Schwarze, J (1994) Labour market entry of young people analysed by a double threshold model, in *Labour Market Dynamics in Present Day Germany*, ed J Schwarze, F Buttler and GG Wagner, pp 142–64, Westview Press, Boulder, Colorado, CO

Heller, F (1986) *The Use and Abuse of Social Science,* Sage Publications, London

Herschbach, D, Hays, F and Evans, D (1992*) Vocational Education and Training: Review of Experience,* US Agency for International Development, Washington, DC

Hershey, A, Silverberg, M, Haimson, J, Hudis, P and Jackson, R (1998) *Expanding Options for Students: Report to Congress on the national evaluation of the school-to-work implementation,* Mathematica Policy Research, Princeton, NJ

HMI (1991) *Aspects of Vocational Education and Training in the Federal Republic of Germany,* HMSO, London

Hodkinson, P, Sparkes, A, and Hodkinson, H. (1996) *Triumphs and Tears: Young people, markets, and the transition from school to work,* David Fulton Publishers, London

Hofbauer, H and Dadzio, W (1984) Berufliche Weiterbildung für Arbeitslose, *Mitteilungen aus der Arbeitsmarkt- und Berufsforschung,* **2,** 183–200

Hofbauer, H and Dadzio, W (1987) Mittelfristige Wirkungen beruflichen Weiterbildung: die berufliche Situation von Teilnehmern zwei Jahre nach Beendigung der Maßnahme, *Mitteilungen aus der Arbeitsmarkt- und Berufsforschung,* **2,** 129–41

Hull, G (1993) Critical literacy and beyond: Lessons learned from students and workers in a vocational program and on the job. *Anthropology and Education Quarterly,* December; **24** (4), pp 373–96

Hull, G (1997) *Changing Work, Changing Workers: Critical perspectives on language, literacy, and skills,* State University of New York Press, Albany, NY

Hunting, G, Zymelman, M and Godfrey, M (1986) *Evaluating Vocational Training Programmes: A practical guide,* World Bank, Washington, DC

ILO (1998) *World Employment Report 1998–99: Employability in the global economy – how training matters,* ILO, Geneva

Jackman, R (1994) What can active labour market policy do?, *Swedish Economic Policy Review;* **1,** pp 221–57

Jeong, J (1995) The failure of recent state vocational training policies in Korea from a comparative perspective, *British Journal of Industrial Relations,* June, **33** (2), pp 237–52

Jessup, G (1991) *Outcomes,* Falmer Press, London

Jimenez, E, Kugler, B and Horn, R (1986) *An Economic Evaluation of a National Job Training System: Colombia's Servicio Nacional de Aprendizaje (SENA),* World Bank, Education and Training Department, Washington, DC

Johanson, R (1994) *Retraining adults in Germany,* Training Policy Study no 4, ILO, Geneva

Johnson, G (1979) The labour market displacement effect in the analysis of manpower training programmes, in *Evaluating Manpower Training Programmes: Research in labour economics,* ed F Bloch, Supplement 1, pp 227–57, Greenwich, CT, JAI Press; reprinted in Ashenfelter and LaLonde (1996)

Joint committee on Standards for Educational Evaluation (1994) *The Program Evaluation Standards: How to assess evaluations of educational programs,* 2nd edn, Sage Publications, Thousand Oaks, CA

Jones, I (1986) Apprentice training costs in British manufacturing establishments: some new evidence, *British Journal of Industrial Relations*, **24**, pp 333–62

Jones, I (1988) An evaluation of YTS, *Oxford Review of Economic Policy*, **4**, pp 54–71

Jonzon, B and Wise, LR (1989) Getting young people to work, *International Labour Review*, **128**, pp 337–56

Kang, S and Bishop, JT (1989) Vocational and academic education in high schools: complements or substitutes?, *Economics of Education Review*, **8**, pp 133–48

Kasperek, P and Koop. W (1991) Zur Wirksamkeit von Fortbildungs-und Umschulungsmaßnahmen, *Mitteilungen aus der Arbeitsmarkt- und Berufsforschung*, **2**, pp 317–32

Katz, LF and Summers, LH (1989) Industry rents: Evidence and implications, *Brookings Papers on Economic Activity*, **3**, pp 209–75

Keep, E (1991) The grass looked greener – some thoughts on the influence of comparative vocational training research on the UK policy debate, in *International Comparisons of Vocational Education and Training for Intermediate Skills*, ed P. Ryan, Falmer Press, London

Kemple, J, Friedlander, D and Fellerath, V (1995, April) *Florida's Project Independence: Benefits, costs, and two-year impacts of Florida's JOBS program*. Manpower Demonstration Research Corporation, New York

King, C (1988, July) *Cross-Cutting Management Issues in Human Resource Programs*, Research Report no 88-12, National Commission for Employment Policy, Washington, DC

King, C, Laweson, L and Olson, J (1995) *JTPA Success Stories in Texas: The who, how, and what of successful outcomes*, Center for the Study of Human Resources, University of Texas, Austin, TX

King, C, Lawson, L, Olson, J, Trott, C and Baj, J (1999) Training success stories for adults and out-of-school youth: A tale of two states, in *Improving the Odds: Increasing the effectiveness of publicly funded training*, ed B. Barnow and C. King, Urban Institute Press, Washington, DC

King, K (1989) Training for the urban informal sector in developing countries: Policy issues for practitioners, in *Training for Work in the Informal Sector*, ed F Fluitman, ILO, Geneva

Kirkpatrick, DL (1994) *Evaluating Training Programmes: The four levels*, Berrett-Koehler, San Francisco

Klerman, J and Karoly, L (1994) Young men and the transition to stable employment. *Monthly Labor Review*, August, **117** (8), pp 31–48

Kogan, D *et al*. (1989) *Improving the Quality of Training Under JTPA*, Berkeley Planning Associates and SRI International, for the US Department of Labor

Korpi, T (1994) *Escaping Unemployment: Studies in the individual consequences of unemployment and labour market policy*, Swedish Institute for Social Research, Stockholm University, Stockholm

Ladner, J (1995) *Tomorrow's Tomorrow: The black woman*, rev edn, University of Nebraska Press, Lincoln, NE

LaLonde, R (1986) Evaluating the econometric evaluations of training programmes with experimental data, *American Economic Review*, **76**, pp 604–20

LaLonde, R (1995) The promise of public sector-sponsored training programs, *Journal of Economic Perspectives*, Spring, **9** (2), pp 149–68

Layard, R and Glaister, S (1994) *Cost-Benefit Analysis*, 2nd edn, CUP, Cambridge

Lechner, von M (1995) *Effects of Continuing Off-the-Job Training in East Germany after Unification*, discussion paper no 95-27, Zentrum für Europäische Wirtschaftsforschung, Mannheim

Lee, D, Marsden, D, Rickman, P and Duncombe, J (1990) *Scheming for Youth: A study of YTS in the enterprise culture*, Milton Keynes, Open University Press

Leigh, DE (1994) *Retraining Displaced Workers: The US experience*, Training Policy Study no 1, ILO, Geneva

Lemaire, S (1993) Regards sur l'apprentissage, *Education et Formation*, April, **34**, pp 3–10.

Lengermann, P (1996) *How Long do the Benefits of Training Last? Evidence of long term effects across current and previous employers, education levels, test scores and occupations*, working paper no 96-18, Center for Advanced Human Resource Studies, Cornell University, New York

Levin, M and Ferman, B (1986) The political hand: Policy implementation and youth employment programs, *Journal of Policy Analysis and Management*, **5** (2), pp 311–25

Levitan, S and Johnston, B (1975) *The Job Corps: A social experiment that works*, Johns Hopkins Press, Baltimore, MD

Lhotel, H and Monaco, A (1993) Regards croisés sur l'apprentissage et les contrats de qualification, *Formation Emploi*, April, **42**, pp 33–45

Lindbeck, A and Snower, DJ (1990) Interindustry wage structure and the power of incumbent workers, in *Labour Relations and Economic Performance*, ed R Brunetta and C Dell'Arringa, pp 378–90, Macmillan, London

Lindley, RM (1996) The European Social Fund: a strategy for evaluation?, in *International Handbook of Labor Market Policy and Evaluation*, ed G Schmid *et al.*, Edward Elgar Publishing, Cheltenham

Long, DA, Mallar, CD and Thornton, CVD (1981) Evaluating the benefits and costs of the Job Corps, *Journal of Policy Analysis and Management*, **1** (1), pp 55–76

Lucas, RE (1988) On the mechanics of economic development, *Journal of Monetary Economics*, **22**, pp 3–22

Lynch, L (1992) Private sector training and the earnings of young workers, *American Economic Review*, March, **82** (1), pp 299–312

Lynch, L (1994) *Training and the Private Sector: International comparisons*, University of Chicago Press, for the National Bureau of Economic Research, Chicago, IL

Lynch, R (1997) *Designing Vocational and Technical Teacher Education for the 21st Century: Implications from the reform literature,* Information Series no. 368, ERIC Clearinghouse on Adult, Career, and Vocational Education, Center on Education and Training for Employment, Columbus, OH

Lynn, L (1989) Policy analysis in the bureaucracy: How new? How effective?, *Journal of Policy Analysis and Management,* **8** (3), pp 373–410

Magnac, T (1996) State dependence and heterogeneity in youth employment histories, Working Paper, INRA/CREST, Paris

Main, BM (1991) The effect of the Youth Training Scheme on employment probability, *Applied Economics,* **23** (2), pp 367–72

Main, BGM and Shelley, MA (1990) The effectiveness of the Youth Training Scheme as a manpower policy, *Econometrica,* November, **57** (228), pp 495–514

Majone, G (1989) *Evidence, Argument, and Persuasion in the Policy Process,* Yale University Press, New Haven, CT

Maldonado, C (1993) Building networks: An experiment to support small urban producers in Benin, *International Labour Review,* **132** (2), pp 245–64

Marquand, J (1994) Training policy and economic theory: A policy-maker's perspective, in *The Market for Training,* ed R McNabb and K Whitfield, Avebury, Aldershot

Marsden, DW and Ryan, P (1990) Institutional aspects of youth employment and training policy in Britain, *British Journal of Industrial Relations,* November, **28** (3), pp 351–70

Marsden, DW and Ryan, P (1991a) The structuring of youth pay and employment in six European economies, in *The Problem of Youth,* ed P Ryan, P Garonna and RC Edwards, chapter 3, Macmillan, London

Marsden, DW and Ryan, P (1991b) Initial training, labour market structure and public policy: intermediate skills in British and German industry, in *International Comparisons of Vocational Education and Training for Intermediate Skills,* ed P Ryan, Falmer, London

Martinson, K and Friedlander, D (1994) *GAIN: Basic education in a welfare-to-work program,* Manpower Demonstration Research Corporation, New York

Maynard, R (1984) The impact of supported work on youth, in *The National Supported Work Demonstration,* ed R Hollister, P Kempner and R Maynard, University of Wisconsin Press, Madison, WI

McGrath, S and King, K et al. (1995) *Education and Training for the Informal Sector,* vol. 1 and 2, Overseas Development Administration, London

McNabb, R and Ryan, P (1990) Segmented labour markets, in *Current Issues in Labour Economics,* ed D Sapsford and Z Tzannatos, pp 151–76, Macmillan, London

Meyer, B (1995) Lessons from US unemployment insurance experiments. *Journal of Economic Literature,* March, **33** (1), pp 91–131

Meyer, RH and Wise, D (1983) High school preparation and early labor force experience, in *The Youth Labour Market Problem,* ed RB Freeman and D Wise, University of Chicago Press, Chicago, IL

Middleton, J, Ziderman, A and Van Adams, A (1993) *Skills for Productivity: Vocational education and training in developing countries,* Oxford University Press, Oxford

Mincer, J (1974) *Schooling, Experience and Earnings,* NBER, New York

Ministère de l'Education Nationale (1995) *Les Apprentis en 1994–95: Des effectifs plus nombreux, des profils diversifiées,* Note d'Information, 95.41, November, Paris

Minni, C and Vergnies, J-F (1994) La diversité des facteurs de l'insertion professionnelle, *Economie et Statistique,* **277,** pp 45–61

Möbus, M and Sevestre, P (1991) Formation professionnelle et emploi: Un lien plus marqué en Allemagne, *Economie et Statistique,* September, **246,** pp 77–89

MTDSP (1995) L'apprentissage en 1994: une reprise confirmée, un usage de plus en plus diversifiée, *Premières Synthèses,* 3 August, **95** (62), pp 1–8

Münch, J (1991) *Vocational Training in the Federal Republic of Germany,* 3d edn, CEDEFOP, Berlin

Murnane, R, Willett, J and Boudett, KP (1995) Do high school dropouts benefit from obtaining a GED?, *Educational Evaluation and Policy Analysis,* summer, **17** (2), pp 133–48

OECD (1994) *The OECD Jobs Study: Evidence and explanations,* OECD, Paris

OECD (1996) *The OECD Jobs Strategy: Enhancing the Effectiveness of Active Labour Market Policies,* OECD, Paris

O'Higgins, N (1994) YTS, employment and sample selection bias, *Oxford Economic Papers,* **46** (4), pp 605–28

O'Higgins, N (1995) *Why did the Youth Training Scheme Reduce the Wages of Young People? A story of human capital formation, reservation wages and job offers,* discussion paper no 18, Centro di Economia del Lavoro e di Politica Economica, Universita degli Studi di Salerno, Salerno

O'Mahoney, M and Wagner, K (1996) Anglo-German productivity performance, 1960–89, in *International Productivity Differences: Measurement and explanations,* ed K Wagner and B Van Ark, pp 143–94, Elsevier, Amsterdam

Oulton, N (1996) Workforce skills and export competitiveness, in *Acquiring Skills: Market failures, their symptoms and policy responses,* ed A Booth and D Snower, pp 201–30, CUP, Cambridge

Palmidis, H and Schwarze, J (1989) Jugendliche beim Übergang in eine betriebliche Berufsausbildung und in die Erwerbstätigkeit, *Mitteilungen aus der Arbeitsmarkt- und Berufsforschung,* **1/89,** pp 114–24

Pannenberg, M (1996) *Zur Evaluation staatlicher Qualifizierungsmaßnahmen in Ostdeutschland: das Instrument Fortbildung und Umschulung (FuU),* discussion paper no. 38, Institut für Wirtschaftsforschung, Halle

Payne, J (1990a) *Adult Off the Job Skills Training: An evaluation study,* Training Agency (UK Department of Employment) R&D Series no 57, Sheffield

Payne, J (1990b) Effectiveness of adult off-the-job skills training, *Employment Gazette,* March, **98** (3), pp 143–49

Payne, J (1994) Women's training needs: the British policy gap, in *The Market for Training,* ed R McNabb and K Whitfield, Avebury, Aldershot

Payne, J (1995) *Options at 16 and Outcomes at 24: a Comparison of Academic and Vocational Education and Training Routes*, Youth Cohort Report no. 35, Sheffield, Department of Employment

Payne, J, Lissenburgh, S, White, M and Payne, C (1996) *An Evaluation of Employment Training and Employment Action using the Matched Comparison Method*, HMSO, London

Pénard, T and Sollogoub, M (1995) Les politiques françaises d'emploi en faveur des jeunes, *Revue Economique*, May, **46** (3), pp 549–60

Plant, RA and Ryan, RJ (1992) Training evaluation: A procedure for validating an organisation's investment in training, *Journal of European Industrial Training*, **16** (10), pp 22–38

Prais, SJ (1991) Vocational qualifications in Britain and Europe: Theory and practice, *National Institute Economic Review*, May, **136**, pp 86–92

Prais, SJ (1995) *Productivity, Education and Training*, CUP, Cambridge

Psacharopoulos, G (1979) On the weak versus the strong version of the screening hypothesis, *Economics Letters*, **4**, pp 181–85

Psacharopoulos, G (1987) To vocationalize or not to vocationalize: That is the curriculum question, *International Review of Education*, **33** (2), pp 187–211

Psacharopolous, G and Woodhall, M (1985*) Education for Development: An analysis of investment choices*, Oxford University Press, Oxford

Quint, JC, Bos, J and Polit, D (1997) *New Chance: Final report on a comprehensive program for disadvantaged young mothers and their children*, Manpower Demonstration Research Corporation, New York

Quint, JC, Musick, JS and Ladner, JA (1994b) *Lives of Promise, Lives of Pain: Young mothers after New Chance*, Manpower Demonstration Research Corporation, New York

Quint, JC, Polit, D, Bos, H and Cave, G (1994a) *New Chance: Interim findings on a comprehensive program for disadvantaged young mothers and their children*, Manpower Demonstration Research Corporation, New York

Rawlins, VL and Ulman, L (1974) The utilization of college-trained manpower in the United States, in *Higher Education and the Labor Market*, ed M Gordon, pp 195–236, McGraw-Hill, New York

Riley, J (1979).Testing the educational screening hypothesis. *Journal of Political Economy*, **87** (5), part 2, pp S227–S252

Rix, A, Parkinson, R and Gaunt, R (1994) *Investors in People: A qualitative study of employers*, Research Series no 21, UK Department of Employment, Sheffield

Robinson, P (1996) *Rhetoric and Reality: Britain's New Vocational Qualifications*, Centre for Economic Performance, London School of Education, London

Romani, C and Werquin, P (1997) Alternating training and the school-to-work transition in France: Programmes, assessments, prospects, in *School to Work Transition in OECD Countries: A comparative analysis*, ed D Stern and D Wagner, Hampden Press, Creskill, NJ

Rossi, P and Freeman, H (1993) *Evaluation: A systematic approach*, 5th edn, Sage Publications, Newbury Park, CA

Rumberger, R and Daymont, TN (1984) Economic value of academic and vocational training acquired in high school, in *Youth and the Labor Market*, ed M Borus, WE Upjohn Institute, Kalamzoo, MI

Ryan, P (1980) The size and distribution of investments in training for an industrial skill, *British Journal of Industrial Relations*, November **18** (3), pp 334–52

Ryan, P (1984) Job training, employment practices and the large enterprise: The case of costly transferable skills, in *Internal Labor Markets*, ed P. Osterman, MIT Press, Cambridge, MA

Ryan, P (1990) Job training, individual opportunity and low pay, in *Improving Incentives for the Low Paid*, ed A Bowen and K Mayhew, Macmillan, London

Ryan, P (1991a) How much do employers spend on training? An evaluation of the Training in Britain estimates, *Human Resource Management Journal*, summer, **1** (4), pp 55–76

Ryan, P (1991b) Trade union policies towards the Youth Training Scheme in Great Britain: The arguments, in *The Problem of Youth*, ed P Ryan, P Garonna and RC Edwards, Macmillan, London

Ryan, P (1994) Training quality and trainee exploitation, in *Britain's Training Deficit*, ed R Layard, K Mayhew and G Owen, Avebury, Aldershot

Ryan, P (1995) Education et formation professionnelle au Royaume-Uni, *Formation Emploi* (Paris) April, **50**, pp 41–62

Ryan, P (1998a) Is apprenticeship better? A review of the economic evidence, *Journal of Vocational Education and Training*, summer, **50** (2) pp 289–325

Ryan, P (1998b) *The School-to-Work Transition in Advanced Economies: A review essay*, working paper, Faculty of Economics and Politics, University of Cambridge, Cambridge

Ryan, P (1999) The embedding of apprenticeship in industrial relations: British engeering, 1925–65, in Apprenticeship: Towards a new paradigm of learning, ed P Ainley and H Rainbird, Kogan Page, London

Ryan, P and Büchtemann, C (1996) The school to work transition, in *International Handbook of Labor Market Policy and Evaluation*, ed G Schmid *et al.*, Edward Elgar Publishing, Cheltenham

Schmid, G, O'Reilly, J and Schömann, K (1996) *International Handbook of Labor Market Policy and Evaluation*, Edward Elgar Publishing, Cheltenham

Schömann, K, Becker, R and Zühlke, S (1996) Further education and occupational careers in East Germany: A longitudinal study of participation and further education and its impact on employment prospects, paper presented to Second GSOEP Conference, Potsdam, July 1996

Schultz, TP (1995) *Evaluation of Integrated Human Resource Programs. Human resources* development and operations policy, working paper no 47, World Bank, Washington, DC

Schweinhart, L, Barnes, H and Weikart, D (1993) *Significant Benefits: The High-Scope Perry Preschool Study through age 27*, High-Scope Educational Research Foundation, Ypsilanti, MI

Sérandon, A-S (1994) Une évaluation microeconométrique des politiques d'emploi en faveur des jeunes, doctoral dissertation, Université des Sciences Sociales de Toulouse, Toulouse

Simpson, C (1990) Evaluating gross programme outcomes, in *Evaluationg Social Programmes at the State and Local Level*, ed AB Blalock, chapter 3, WE Upjohn Institute, Kalamazoo, MI

Singh, A (1994) Global economic changes, skills, and international comparisons, *International Labour Review*, 133 (2), pp 167–85

Skedinger, P (1995) Employment policies and displacement in the youth labour market, *Swedish Economic Policy Review*, spring, 2 (1), pp 135–71

Sollogoub, M and Ulrich, V (1997) *Apprentissage et Lycée Professionnel: Biais de sélection et insertion sur le marché du travail*, working paper, LAMIA, Université de Paris 1, Paris

Solow, RM (1990) Government and the labour market, in *New Developments in the Labour Market*, ed K Abraham and R McKersie, MIT Press, Cambridge, MA

Spence, M (1974) *Market Signaling*, Harvard University Press, Cambridge, MA

Steedman, H and Wagner, K (1989) Productivity, machinery and skills: clothing manufacture in Britain and Germany, *National Institute Economic Review*, May, 128, pp 40–57

Stern, D, *et al.* (1994) *School-based Enterprise: Productive learning in American high schools*, Jossey-Bass Publishers, San Francisco, CA

Stern, D, Dayton, C, Paik, I, Weisberg, A and Evans, J (1989) Benefits and costs of dropout prevention in a high school programme combining academic and vocational education, *Educational Evaluation and Policy Analysis*, 10 (2), pp 161–70

Stern, D and Ritzen, JMM (eds) (1991) *Market Failure in Training?*, Springer-Verlag, New York

Stevens, M (1996) Transferable training and poaching externalities, in *Acquiring Skills*, ed A Booth and D Snower, chapter 2, CUP, Cambridge

Streeck, W, Hilbert, J, van Kevelaer, K-H, Maier, F and Weber, H (1987) *The Role of the Social Partners in Vocational Training and Further Training in the Federal Republic of Germany*, CEDEFOP, Berlin

Sugden, R and Williams, A (1978) *The Principles of Practical Cost-Benefit Analysis*, Oxford University Press, Oxford

TA (1989) *YTS Progress Report 1987/88*, UK Department of Employment, Sheffield

Tamas, A, Harkman., A and Jansson, F (1995) The effect of vocationally oriented employment training on income and employment, in *Evaluating Labour Market Training: Outcome and effectiveness*, ed I Mikkonen and H Räisänen, pp 105–31, Ministry of Labour, Helsinki

Tan, HW and Batra, G (1995) *Enterprise Training in Developing Countries: Incidence, productivity effects and policy implications*, Private Sector Development Department, World Bank, Washington, DC

Tan, HW, Chapman B, Peterson, C and Booth, A (1992) Youth training in the US, Britain and Australia, *Research in Labour Economics*, 13, pp 63–99

Taylor, ME (1981) *Education and Work in the Federal Republic of Germany*, Anglo-German Foundation, London

Thomas, B, Moxham, J and Jones, JAG (1969) A cost-benefit analysis of industrial training, *British Journal of Industrial Relations*, July, 7 (2), pp 231–64

Trott, C and Baj, J (1996) *Developing a Common Performance Management Framework for a State Workforce Development System: A guidebook for states*, National Governors Association, Washington, DC

Tuijnman, A (ed) (1996) *International Encyclopedia of Adult Education and Training*, Pergamon Press, Oxford

US Department of Labor (1995) *What's Working (and What's Not): A summary of research on the economic impacts of employment and training programmes*, Office of the Chief Economist, US Department of Labor, Washington, DC

US General Accounting Office (1996) *Job Training Partnership Act: Long-term earnings and employment outcomes*, GAO-HEHS-96-40, GAO, Washington, DC

Van den Berghe, W and Tilkon Consultancy. (1996) *Quality Issues and Trends in Vocational Education and Training in Europe*, CEDEFOP (European Centre for the Development of Vocational Training), Thessaloniki

Van der Velden, R and Lodder, B (1995) Alternative routes from vocational education to the labour market, *Educational Research and Evaluation*, 1 (2), pp 109–28

Venau, P and Mouy, P (1995) Des objectifs à la réalité: les bacheliers professionnels industriels, *Formation Emploi* 49, pp 91–103

Walker, G and Vilella-Velez, F (1992) *Anatomy of a Demonstration: The Summer Training and Education Program (STEP) from pilot through replication and postprogram impacts*, Public/Private Ventures, Philadelphia

Weiss, C (1977) *Using Social Research in Public Policy-Making*, Heath, Lexington, MA

Weiss, C (1979) The many meanings of research utilization, *Public Administration Review*, 39 (5), pp 426–31

Weiss, C (1989) Congressional committees as users of analysis, *Journal of Policy Analysis and Management*, 8 (3), pp 411–31

Weiss, C and Bucuvalas, M (1980) *Social Science Research and Decision-Making*, Columbia University Press, New York

Whitfield, K and Bourlakis, C (1991) An empirical analysis of YTS, employment and earnings, *Journal of Economic Studies*, 18 (1), pp 42–56

Wildavsky, A (1966) The political economy of efficiency: Cost-benefit analysis, systems analysis, and program budgeting, *Public Administration Review*, 26, pp 292–310

Wilensky, H (1985) Nothing fails like success: The evaluation-research industry and labor market policy, *Industrial Relations*, winter, 24 (1), pp 1–19

Willis, RJ and Rosen, S (1979) Education and self-selection, *Journal of Political Economy*; 87 (5), pp S7–S36

Wingens, M and Weymann, A (1988) Social science in public discourse, *Knowledge in Society*, **1** (3), pp 80–97

Winkelmann, R (1994) *Training, Earnings and Mobility in Germany*, discussion paper no 982, Centre for Economic Policy Research, London

Winkelmann, R (1996) Employment prospects and skill acquisition of apprentice-ship-trained workers in Germany, *Industrial and Labour Relations Review*, July, **99** (4), pp 658–72

Witte, JC and Kalleberg, AL (1995) Matching training and jobs: the fit between vocational education and employment in the German labour market, *European Sociological Review*, December, **11** (3), pp 293–317

Wolf, A (1995) *Competence-Based Assessment*, Open University Press, Milton Keynes

World Bank (1995) *Priorities and Strategies for Education: A World Bank sector review*, Education and Social Policy Department, World Bank, Washington, DC

Zilbert, E, Hearn, J and Lewis, D (1992) Selection bias and the earnings effects of post-secondary vocational education, *Journal of Vocational Education Research*, **17** (1), pp 11–34ZIMFEP (1991) ZIMFEP school leavers: a tracer study, *Education with Production*, December, **8** (2), pp 75–119

Index

Visit Kogan Page on-line

Comprehensive information on
Kogan Page titles

Features include

- complete catalogue listings,
  including book reviews and
  descriptions

- special monthly promotions

- information on NEW titles and
  BESTSELLING titles

- a secure shopping basket facility
  for on-line ordering

PLUS everything you need to know
about KOGAN PAGE

http://www.kogan-page.co.uk

DATE DUE

HIGHSMITH 45-220